Ordinary Television

Analyzing Popular TV

Frances Bonner

SAGE Publications
London • Thousand Oaks • New Delhi

First published 2003

Apart from any fair dealing for the purposes of research or
private study, or criticism or review, as permitted under
the Copyright, Designs and Patents Act, 1988, this publication
may be reproduced, stored or transmitted in any form,
or by any means, only with the prior permission in writing
of the publishers, or in the case of reprographic reproduction,
in accordance with the terms of licences issued by the
Copyright Licensing Agency. Inquiries concerning
reproduction outside those terms should be sent to the
publishers.

SAGE Publications Ltd
1 Olivers Yard, 55 City Road
London EC1Y 1SP

SAGE Publications Inc
2455 Teller Road
Thousand Oaks, California 91320

SAGE Publications India Pvt Ltd
B-42 Panchsheel Enclave
PO Box 4109
New Dehli 110 017

British Library Cataloguing in Publication data

A catalogue record for this book is available
from the British Library.

ISBN 0 8309 7570 8   ISBN-13 978-0-8039-7570-5
ISBN 0 8309 7571 6 (pbk) ISBN-13 978-0-8039-7571-2 (pbk)

Library of Congress Control Number: 2002104968

Typeset by C&M Digitals (P) Ltd., Chennai, India
Printed in India at Gopsons Papers Ltd, Noida

Contents

To the memory of
Lorraine Miller
1949–1992

Acknowledgements

Many people have helped make this geographically and temporally dispersed study possible and I want to thank them all very much, while absolving them from any blame for what I have done with their assistance, whether that was material, intellectual or emotional, and frequently all three. In the UK, I want to thank my fellow members of the Open University U207 Women's Studies Course Team at whose instance I first started analysing game shows; also John Corner, Jessica Evans, Paul du Gay, Stuart Hall, Julia Hallam, Henrie Lidchi, Alice Marshment, Margaret Marshment and Nickianne Moody. In Australia, I want to thank my colleagues in the Communications and Cultural Studies section of the School of English, Media Studies and Art History at the University of Queensland, but most especially David Marshall, Susan McKay, Alan McKee, Angela Tuohy and Graeme Turner. For their comments on conference papers and articles relating to this work I want to thank Jackie Cook, Stuart Cunningham, Annette Hill, Meaghan Morris and Sue Turnbull. My postgraduate students have also been very useful in drawing programmes to my attention and discussing their implications. I would like to acknowledge, in particular, Rebecca Farley, Kathryn Goldie, Susan Luckman, Andrea Mitchell, Sam Searle, Paul Starr and Gil Woodley. For the last three years, my undergraduate students of Television and Popular Culture have also borne well with my testing out of ideas for this project. For their friendship, as well as their shared observations on television programmes, my gratitude goes to Helen Barnes, Felicity Grace, Rob Jordan, Veronica Kelly, Bronwen Levy, Jan McKemmish, Mark McLelland, Vicki and Ian Pearce, and Barbara Sullivan.

The work on economic discourses and on *Antiques Roadshow* was conducted while I was a Visiting Fellow at the Pavis Centre for Sociological and Social Anthropological Studies at the Open University. I am most grateful for this assistance. An earlier version was published as 'Economic Discourses on Television: The Peculiar Case of *Antiques Roadshow*' as a Pavis Occasional Paper in October 1995. A New Staff Grant from the University of Queensland also assisted greatly in the early stages of formulating this project. A research fellowship in the Centre for Critical and Cultural Studies at the University of Queensland was immensely valuable in getting the project back on track in the second half of 2000.

Finally, for editorial forbearance and much other assistance I want to thank my commissioning editor, Julia Hall and also at Sage, Lauren McAllister.

INTRODUCTION

The critical investigation of television programmes has concentrated overwhelmingly on certain areas of output – news and current affairs, drama of various kinds (including, more recently, soaps) and children's programmes. Some attention has also been paid to sport and, more recently, to talk programmes, while the substantial body of work on documentary film has generated a growing interest in documentary television, but this still leaves a considerable amount of televisual material unexamined. It is the purpose of this book to look at these disregarded programmes – the game shows, the lifestyle programmes, the chat shows and the diverse kinds of advice programmes, as well as the often more serious magazine programmes looking at science or economics, for example – not only to investigate what it is they contribute to the televisual mix, but also to challenge their apparent dismissal.

Although I have long been accustomed to the way books on television neglect the programmes that interest me, I am persistently surprised at how much books claiming to deal generally with television fail to acknowledge even the existence of most, if not all, of the types of television programme considered here. If they are looked at at all, one or, at most, two of the various programme types seem to suffice, although no authors or editors suggest that the chosen type stands in for a missing range of non-fiction television. The sole category to receive much attention at all is talk TV, and this only recently, as a result of feminist scholarship and only in the wake of a level of moral panic about it. After that, it is probably game shows and quizzes which are most likely to be the token type. Two recent collections include a little more, and perhaps are signs that the field in general is being seen as more diverse. Christine Geraghty and David Lusted's *The Television Studies Book* is undoubtedly the most wide-ranging, having separate chapters on talk shows and cooking programmes, plus two on light entertainment. Glen Creeber's *The Television Genres Book* has a section entitled Popular Entertainment (a choice of name which reflects oddly on the previous three sections: Drama, Soap Opera and Comedy) which includes, as well as sport, MTV and advertising, both celebrity and confessional talk shows, quiz shows and daytime television.

Why is so much of the television schedule (even so much of prime-time) ignored? The ratings indicate that audiences are watching, but it is not just academics who concentrate on a limited range of television programming. Popular critics and reviewers also concentrate on a limited number of genres; in their case the overwhelming stress is on various kinds of drama, including situation comedies and, to a lesser extent, soaps, plus documentaries. They are certainly more likely to discuss new lifestyle programmes than academics are to analyse them, but since they are usually acting in the service of promotion, the stress on the new and the expensive is the result of the availability of preview tapes and press kits distributed by the television stations themselves. They do not, then, revisit long-running, non-fictional programmes in the way that they do new series of long-running dramas. In the way that to speak popularly of film is rarely to speak of anything other than features, to speak popularly of television is to speak of drama, including sitcoms, and new instances of other heavily promoted entertainment television.

The promotional path explains the tendencies in popular reviewing, but not the different preferences of the academic. The replacement of entertainment-dominated non-fiction with news and current affairs in the programme types considered can be explained by the serious nature of the information they traditionally convey and their place in formal political debate, but this is an instrumental view of television; fine for someone whose disciplinary background is itself political, for example, but less defensible when it seems to afflict the field of television studies itself. My suspicion is that it is the lightweight, ephemeral character of the forms themselves that is the problem; examining them does nothing to counteract the impressions from the academy in general that television is too trivial to be worth studying. Serious information (or the decline in its prevalence) is worthy of discussion; anything dramatic can call on analogous literary investigations for some kind of precedent, and sport, of course, is nationally and economically important. It is difficult though to convince others of the value of spending extended periods of time looking at game shows and lifestyle programming. It may not just be this kind of awkwardness in the academy and in one's public presentation of one's research field that results in the skewed consideration of television programmes; trying to find a way to approach the material is also diffi-cult. Feminism provided a way to deal with the scholarly disregard for soap operas and talk shows, but one cannot here start from the same position of seeing the cause for neglect in the gender of the assumed viewers. At the heart of the programmes which concern me is their lack of anything special, their very triviality, their ordinariness. They do not even have, by and large, much in the way of narrative interest, though the newer programmes have found ways of enhancing this. Is it perhaps also the case that it is difficult to speak of the ordinary, and easier to speak of the obviously narrative and the obviously publicly informative?

I have chosen to call the critically disregarded programmes 'ordinary television', in brief because there is nothing special about them and because their very everydayness seems to be a partial reason for their not being regarded as sufficiently important to bear sustained investigation. The category itself will be discussed at length in Chapter 2, but its central characteristics include direct address of the audience, the incorporation of ordinary people into the programme and the mundanity of its concerns. Following the fragmentation of the television audience caused by the development of pay-TV, broadcast television, which remains the site where most programmes originate, needed to produce increasing numbers of cheap programmes in order to stay profitable and it turned increasingly to the ordinary to do this. Substantial increases in lifestyle programming and the new category of programming often called 'reality TV', but coming to be known industrially with a little more accuracy as 'unscripted programming', have been the most significant changes. So 'special' have some reality game shows (like *Survivor*) become that it might seem wrong to name them 'ordinary', yet at the core of their claim on reality is their use of 'real' people, the fact that they do employ direct address and, overwhelmingly, that the activities depicted are mundane, even if performed for the surrounding cameras.

To be specific about the range of programmes dealt with, I will include: lifestyle and 'reality'; game shows, whether for prizes or not, and whether using celebrities or ordinary members of the public as contestants; advice programmes dealing with health, holidays and financial matters; chat and talk shows; science and technology magazines; breakfast, morning and tonight shows; and the 'crime-stopper' programmes like *Crimewatch UK* or *Australia's Most Wanted*. The types of programmes I have listed – which would include, from the UK, *The Money Programme* as well as *Blind Date*, and from Australia *Burke's Backyard* and the science programme *Catalyst* – may seem too diverse to be grouped together, yet I will be arguing that they do constitute a field which richly repays mapping.

One characteristic that holds them together is that they all operate as non-fiction. The rather clumsy verb 'operate' is necessary to cover the way in which the content of a science programme has a different claim to being non-fiction than the responses of a contestant in a dating game show. Both assert a reasonably direct relationship with 'real life', both may well be scripted, but only one is likely to attempt truth claims. Non-fictionality is not a pure and absolute state where truth exists and can be tested, but rather, as so often in contemporary scholarship, a muddy area with blurred and permeable boundaries, sustained by an unspoken agreement among those creating and consuming it to act as if the people and the statements they make are different from those in explicit fictions and are effectively 'telling the truth' as they believe it.

OMISSIONS

Some types of programmes that might seem to have good claims on membership of the category have been omitted. All children's programming, whether fictional or not, has been excluded on the basis of its special audience, its particular regulatory protection and the fact that it is extensively covered in specialist literature. Documentaries are excluded because of their 'special' status as privileged representers of the real and their characteristic sobriety, which means that they tend to lack the relationship with mundanity that other members of the grouping have. However, some of the more recent documentary hybrids, like docu-soaps and 'reality' television, are admitted since they do work within the mundane, and, in John Corner's delightful observation on the form, so far from exhibiting sobriety 'in some of its wilder versions, it might be better seen as betraying serious signs of alcohol or drug dependency!' (2000a, n.p.)

The decision to omit religious programming needs particular explanation. As will become apparent in the course of the book, there are several dimensions on which such programming may be seen to be very much a part of the kind of television under investigation. It is, however, premised on a different relationship to truth and belief – one underpinned by revelation and faith – as well as often a very different relationship between presenter and audience. For a substantial proportion of religious programmes, especially those originating in the US, this latter relationship involves appeals for money based in that faith and as an expression of belief. Alternately, religious programmes by public broadcasters, like the ABC's *Compass*, which frequently seems not to require faith of its viewers, opt instead to spend much of the time in high documentary mode, concentrating on religious, or religiously inflected, subjects.

AMBIT OF THE STUDY

The book deals with television in the UK and Australia. The main period of its attention is from 1986 until 2001 with most examples drawn from the latter end of that period to maximize comprehension. Reference will be made to programmes preceding this period in order to trace the development of contemporary televisual forms and practices. Reference will also be made to American television because of its influence on other television systems and because of the direct export of its programmes to both countries considered. It is likely that few readers will be familiar with all the programmes I refer to and I have tried to ensure, wherever possible, that I provide both British and Australian examples. Since I use examples of programmes as indicative rather than of themselves important, I will not normally provide transmission dates. To vary the constant identification of programmes as 'British' or 'Australian' I have tended to identify programmes by the network on which they are screened. Fortunately for a comparative scholar, the channel designations in Australia and the UK do not overlap. Numerical names give Channels 4 and 5 to the UK and Channels 7, 9 and 10 to Australia. In addition, the UK has BBC1, BBC2 and ITV (I have decided not to specify ITV regions, since designation is sufficiently complicated without it) while Australia has the public broadcaster ABC and SBS (the Special Broadcasting Service), also a public broadcaster but one with a multicultural remit and which takes commercials, though it does not screen them during programmes. In this book ABC never means the American Broadcasting Corporation, it always means the Australian Broadcasting Corporation.

There are some difficulties about conducting comparative studies which need to be acknowledged. Were I considering programmes in isolation, it would not be so difficult, but the aim of this book is to talk about a particular kind of programming and to look for regularities and recurrent features across a range of programmes customarily considered separately. The very ordinary everydayness of the category means that its embedding in the national culture exceeds the programme and television itself. One cannot consider national presenting icons like the UK's Carol Vorderman or Australia's Roy and HG without observing their operation beyond television. The transition of catchphrases like 'You are the weakest link, goodbye' into popular parlance (fortunately, in this instance, in both countries) is an important part of the attachment of the programme to its audience. I have tried my best to be (as I am) both British and Australian, but I know that it is not likely to be regarded as achievable by either group. Both countries import and export programmes to and from one another, but these are far more likely to be fictional than non-fictional; ordinary television is more regularly formatted. Anyway, as a number of critics have noted, television programmes do not remain the same when surrounded by material originating elsewhere and watched by audiences with different cultural backgrounds. Watching British programmes in Australia or Australian ones in the UK is not the same experience as watching Australian or

British television on home turf, and this is before one starts to consider differences within the national audiences.

One aspect of Australian programming that became increasingly apparent in the writing of this book was that there are simply fewer Australian examples to draw upon. A smaller population (just over a quarter of the British) means that the amount of money able to be raised by selling advertising or by taxation is significantly less than in the more highly populated country, yet both countries have five free-to-air networks broadcasting virtually 24 hours a day. In almost every type of programming investigated there were more British instances and thus more of a range within each type than was the case for Australia. Some types simply did not exist; there is no Australian equivalent of the programmes which investigate and reconstruct the past, like *Time Team*. It is also characteristic for ordinary television programmes to run for a much shorter time in Australia. *Blind Date*, for example, which started in Australia (as *Perfect Match* before adopting the British title), has been long gone, though it still draws a sizeable audience in the UK. In the absence of a majority of locally made programming, Australian air-time is filled with imported material. Australia has local content regulation requiring 50 per cent of programming to be Australian-made. British programming is customarily over 80 per cent domestically produced.

The programmes considered here from both countries are overwhelmingly those screened on free-to-air broadcast television. Australia's pay-TV system is much less developed than Britain's, but in both instances it is still the free-to-air networks that generate most of the new programmes, draw the largest audiences and set the pace, though for how much longer this will be the case, especially with the changes consequent upon digital broadcasting, is uncertain. While the growth of ordinary television is in large part a consequence of the fragmentation brought about by pay-TV reducing the audiences available for any programme and causing programme-makers and commissioners alike to look for cheaper forms, it is still the free-to-air and the old analogue channels which dominate.

ORGANIZATION OF THE BOOK

The book begins by examining how the body of non-fiction television to be considered here has been discussed to this point. It discusses the question of genre and presents a story of fragmented approaches which, in combination with the critical neglect of the area, make it hard for investigation to move beyond a concentration on particular programmes. It considers the dated industrial term 'light entertainment' as a possible foreshadowing of the grouping being proposed.

In the second chapter the argument for the category 'ordinary television' is outlined and its chief characteristics are explained. As the category is restricted to non-fiction television, the people who appear in the programmes are appearing as themselves rather than as fictional characters and so the following chapter examines the roles they assume as presenters, ancillary on-screen staff, celebrities, experts, contestants and other kinds of non-professional participants.

Chapters 4 and 5 look at the discourses that operate across the range of programmes that constitute ordinary television. Chapter 4 is concerned with those which are pervasive, like consumption, family, health, leisure and sexuality, before focusing on the transformative power of television and, in particular, the case of the makeover. Chapter 5 then looks at those like work, race and education which are absent or disguised.

The final chapter considers the place of ordinary television in a global television market, noting how much more common it is for such programmes to be formatted rather than exported in their original form. In addition to formatted programmes, though, there are some which seem to speak very strongly of the nation, and two examples of this are studied at length – the British *Antiques Roadshow* and the Australian *Burke's Backyard*.

Conventional Ways of Looking at Programmes

There is a range of conventional names to describe television programmes that appear in TV guides, in the various pieces of promotion that form so great a part of daily newspapers and weekly magazines and in the way viewers talk about television. The large 'commonsense' divisions of programmes into news and current affairs, drama (series and serials), sitcoms and soaps, documentaries and sport leave many types recognizable but ungrouped – games and quizzes, various kinds of advice programmes (cooking, home renovation, health) now commonly seen as infotainment, science and technology magazines, talk shows, chat shows and that related, though more mixed, grouping of breakfast shows, morning programmes and tonight shows. Chat and talk shows may not be so clearly differentiated as named categories, but the name of the personality, which is usually that of the show (*Oprah*, *Kilroy*, *Parkinson*), usually acts to displace any need for generic qualifications.

When we come to talk more analytically about television programmes, the categorizations work reasonably well for news, current affairs and the whole panoply of fictional programmes (and, of course, for sport), always accepting the perennial 'blurring of boundaries' which are, depending on the critic, symptomatic of the decline of broadcasting as a whole or part of a refreshing updating of outmoded forms. This may be part of the reason that there is such a healthy amount of work conducted on them. The remaining types are less satisfactorily dealt with, though game shows and, more recently, talk shows have become stable categories which have been reasonably, though not exhaustively, investigated. The term 'science and technology magazines' has no real currency any longer; 'tonight shows', however popularly workable, sounds analytically imprecise; 'infotainment' names different types of programme in different countries; and what is to be done about the growth area of so-called 'reality' shows? It should be possible at least to clarify the generic identification of such common cultural products to a greater extent, but some of the problems arise in the very idea of television genres.

TELEVISION GENRES

At all levels in the discussion of film – industrially, popularly and academically – the idea of genre has proved valuable. Genres are of their very nature changeable, but as implicit contracts between the parties involved they convey information about what it is reasonable to expect at any one time of a generically labelled film text (see Neale, 1990). If one audience member asks of another what the genre of a film just seen is, it may not absolutely always be possible to answer, but usually terms like 'action film', 'sf', 'comedy' or 'arthouse' convey the required information. Critics wanting to write about a specific genre have to be prepared to defend their use of the term 'genre' and their classification of texts, but can still proceed knowing that their work exists in a recognized and respected field.

For television, neither situation is as straightforward. It is much rarer for a question about genre to be asked popularly of television. If not replaced by the very open 'What is it?', the bland 'What kind of programme?' is more likely. The reason for the difference is comparatively clear: someone asking about the genre of a film is likely to be asking only of (fictional) feature films and thus the answers 'An avantgarde piece', or 'An experimental film' are quite unlikely. With television it may be necessary first to place the programme within two generic classifications before being able to provide a usable answer. In as much as it is used at all in television, 'genre' is used to describe two major types, very roughly aligned with form and content. For some types of programme only one name – say news or sport – is necessary for generic classification, but for others – various forms of drama for instance – a two-layered generic description is necessary. Not just series but hospital series; not just game show but dating game show. As critics of genre have long pointed out, regardless of medium, genre is rarely a consistently applied term, and even in the first level of television description genre operates heterogeneously, naming a subject area for sport but a form for series. Away from drama, the second level may not be all that useful, but certainly describing a programme simply as a serial is unsatisfactory (it may be an Australian soap or a classic literary adaptation in six expensive BBC episodes, and the questioning viewer may have an interest in only one such type). Academically, to talk of television and genre is probably only to talk of different kinds of drama series or to signal that a range of programmes is to be discussed, but it is by no means as obvious what the field of study will be, as is the case for film.

Genre is such a slippery term that it is foolish to be concerned about deficiencies in the applicability of generic descriptors, but moves, both popular and academic, have been away from using the term 'genre' to talk of television. 'Programme type' seems far more frequently used, though the most frequent formal place such descriptors appear – programme guides – tend to be stuffier about them than are viewers in conversation or academics in studies. 'Soap' is still seen as too offensive and 'sitcom' as too casual. 'Infotainment' has some currency, but can sound a little derogatory; Australian programme guides prefer to use 'lifestyle programme' if they have to use any identifier for the latter.

Until the appearance of Glen Creeber's collection, *The Television Genres Book*, the main text claiming comprehensiveness in dealing with television genres was Brian G. Rose's collection *TV Genres*, published in 1985. It concentrates on fictional programming with essays on the main recognized genres, like the police show and the sitcom, and deals with news, documentary and commercials, but of the many programme types (surely potential genres) considered here, it devotes space only to game shows, variety (declining even then) and talk. The datedness of the text and the mutability of genres are revealed by how it is no longer possible to use the last category as Rose did – the applicability of 'talk' has narrowed down to the social problem confessional form, of which only *Donahue* engaged Rose's interest, and the other programmes have come to be regarded as 'chat'.

It is too early to say whether Creeber's collection signals the start of a widespread change. The section dealing with genre generally includes Steve Neale noting the problems of defining genres for television and the dominance of highly narrative genres in existing investigations (2001). Graeme Turner observes how the term is absent from industrial usage, while 'format' – a narrower term which refers to something that may be copyrighted – is readily to be found (2001a, 2001b). Almost half of the book is concerned with drama (broken down into drama, soap opera and comedy) and the majority of the rest is concerned with news, children's and documentary programming. There is a change in the approach, though, and this is in the inclusion of a section entitled 'popular entertainment', which has separate essays on quiz shows, talk shows (both confessional and celebrity, which I term 'chat') and daytime TV, as well as sport, advertising and MTV. Toby Miller's introductory essay to the section acknowledges the misleading nature of the grouping's title and also notes the tendency for the programmes to be despised by critics. The rest of this introduction examines the populist debate, especially discussing the issue of the active audience, but calling for its examples as much on sitcoms as on members of the grouping itself (2001). The difficulties of constructing anything other than a 'miscellaneous' grouping remain evident.

All in all, it cannot be claimed that genre is all that fruitful a term for critical work on television, especially for work on programmes apart from the fictional ones, so even though the core elements, especially the implied contract between producers and viewers about what to expect in a text of a given name, will continue to be implicit in what follows, the term will not organize the argument. There is still, however, a problem in naming and in categorizing those programmes that are my concern and which are so inadequately dealt with at present.

While most formal critical work on television pays scant attention, and then only patchily, to members of the grouping I am calling ordinary television, attention is regularly paid in television journalism and reviewing. Most of this is highly ephemeral, but occasionally particular 'name' critics have their musings collected. Even then, most of what is collected displays the same predilections as academic writing, since greatest attention is paid to what is considered important and this accords with the trail of money spent – overwhelmingly on fiction and documentary (reviewers are less interested than academics in news). Ordinary television programmes are most likely to be written about when they first appear, but they are occasionally the subject of articles which reward re-examination.

Raymond Williams' television journalism was conducted from 1968 to 1972 – in other words before Channel 4 began – for the BBC magazine *The Listener*. I want to use this writing to capture something of the ordinary television of that period, even though Williams was most certainly no ordinary television viewer given both his political eminence and his engagement with television scholarship. He wrote a retrospective column on what he had watched each month, so it was not (quite) within the promotional field of reviewing and rarely seems to have involved special advance viewing (less common in this period anyway, given that video was still reel-to-reel). Reading the collection of these, edited by Alan O'Connor (Williams, 1989) (and acknowledging that the selection reflects the editor's tastes), it is notable how much more local semi-documentary there was at that time. Williams persistently talks about programmes with titles like *The Curious Character of Britain*, and it is obvious that these programmes were then significant in showing ordinary people on television, and did so without the set-ups contemporary programmes use to explain local history excursions. A current example is the BBC's *House Detectives*, where experts research house-owners' suspicions about the relationship of their building to historical happenings in the area. The semi-documentary style of the older programmes meant that they usually lacked the informality of contemporary ordinary television, since it usually takes presenters to encourage informality, and the documentary style avoided on-screen intermediaries.

Of particular relevance to my project is Williams' column of 6 April 1972 which begins '[e]very month I mean to write about the small programmes which make up so large a part of decent television' (ibid.: 173). The programmes which he instances are *Gardeners' World, The Craftsmen, Look Stranger, Collectors' World and Going for a Song* (the last of which he uses as an example of a consumerist ideology as opposed to the more respectful concern for work in the preceding). 'Small programmes' and 'decent television' may sound condescending, but should rather be seen as indications of the potential within these types of ordinary television for continual radical programming of the kind that Williams, in his introduction to the collection, notes was 'consciously and deliberately restrained' (xi). Although programmes like this continue to exist, they no longer constitute much of a place to detect in any overt way a connection with a radical cultural tradition, but then the drama and the documentary that Williams wrote about more often and more positively no longer do this either.

CLEAR CATEGORIES

The programmes that will be dealt with in this book fall into a number of accepted categories, with names that operate industrially, popularly and critically. In this section I will indicate what these are, together with indicating the principal examples both from Australia and the UK that I will be using in my argument.

Game shows as a category are now understood to include quizzes, though once the latter term applied to the kind with the more intellectual questions (like the now defunct *Mastermind*). The relegation of 'quiz' can be regarded as a sign of the increased importance of play and fun on television. 'Quiz', with its echoes of school tests, reduces the extent to which answering questions to win prizes is now just a game, on a par with spending 60 seconds in a set of stocks with a couple of dogs licking petfood off one's feet (a challenge set in an episode of the British game show *Don't Try This at Home*).

Game shows are one of the categories of light non-fiction programmes that have been subject to a reasonable amount of critical investigation. Most of the research stresses the role of competition and the nexus of reward and knowledge. John Tulloch has studied this for knowledge quizzes, both intellectual (*Mastermind*) and populist (*Sale of the Century*) (1976: 3), John Fiske has looked at knowledge and at dating games (*Blind Date*) and argued that the latter exhibit a progressive gender politics (1990: 139), a claim I have myself earlier supported only up to a point (Bonner, 1992: 242–6). Garry Whannel says of the public opinion shows (like *Family Fortunes*), that they 'reward normality and penalise deviance' (1990: 105). Mike Wayne, who structures a discussion of contextual analysis around quiz and game shows, notes that as well as shows rewarding specialist knowledge or physical skills, under the dominance of public service broadcasting there were also shows foregrounding camaraderie, like *The Generation Game* (2000: 200). His main concern, however, is with what followed the realization that the genre attracted a comparatively old and poor audience; the first consequence was the decision of ITV not to schedule quiz shows in prime time during the mid- to late 1990s (209); the second was devising forms which would appeal to a wider audience. Lothar Mikos and Hans J. Wulff are concerned to trace the everyday contexts, whether they be crossword puzzles and pen-and-paper games or the product promotions of market-criers from which *Wheel of Fortune* is derived (2000: 104–7) and combine this with a consideration of the televisual situation into which they are introduced.

In addition to the game shows mentioned so far, I will be referring to the recent internationally franchised knowledge quiz hits *Who Wants to be a Millionaire?* and *The Weakest Link*, dating game shows like Channel 4's *Dishes* and the internationally franchised *Streetmate*, as well as shows challenging contestants to perform various stunts, like ITV's *Don't Try This at Home* and its Australian forerunner *Who Dares Wins*.

By far the greatest amount of research into any genre I discuss has been conducted into talk shows, significantly under the influence of feminist studies. Their domination by female presenters, guests, experts and studio audience members makes this unsurprising as does their focus on traditionally feminine matters of social and sexual (im)propriety. Gloria-Jean Masciarotte started the investigations by arguing for the recognition of the place of the denigrated American programmes (especially the early *Oprah Winfrey Show*) as the site of a public feminine authority (1991: 98). Jane Shattuc, looking at the more recent and much more diversified field, is able to distinguish the now far more respectable *Oprah* from the less disciplined *Ricki Lake* (1997: 147–66). Laura Grindstaff calls on her experience of working on some of the shows to explain the industrial imperatives to modulate the extent to which the programmes can be acclaimed as spaces where working-class voices and experience are allowed access to national television (1997). All these are concerned with American shows. For many years talk shows were seen to be an ineluctably American phenomenon and were imported into all other markets, but while there are still no local Australian instances, Britain now makes a number of its own, like *Trisha*, *Kaye* and *That's Esther*, while continuing to import some of the more popular American ones.

Chat shows need to be differentiated from talk ones (though the same term is often used, to considerable confusion) as they are by no means as strongly marked by the feminine and certainly not by the presence of ordinary people and their problems. They are instead the prime site where celebrities are able to promote their most recent cultural products. For many years *Wogan* was the prime British example, though its appearance every weekday meant it did not have the same status as the still running, once-a-week *Parkinson*. The also now defunct Australian example, *Midday*, was, as the name suggests, a daytime version, cut because its elderly audience was deemed insufficiently attractive to advertisers to justify its cost. This type of programme has not been much written about, the exceptions mainly concentrating on the role of the presenting personality, as Andrew Tolson does with his assessment of *Wogan* and *The Dame Edna Experience* (1991).

Science and technology magazines like the British *Tomorrow's World* and the Australian *Beyond 2000* or *Quantum* have attracted a small amount of critical attention primarily concerned with their place in the public understanding of science. They are not often regarded favourably by commentators. Rachel Kerys Murrell has asserted that '*Tomorrow's World* misinforms the viewer as to the real nature of the scientific enterprise' (1987: 101), while Carl Gardner and Robert Young claim that it neglects science in process or subject to disagreement within the scientific community (1981: 174–7). Part of the problem for writers like these is that the tenor of science and technology magazines is so relentlessly upbeat; they are forever announcing new breakthroughs or exciting new widgets that will make life easier or solve hitherto intractable problems. Roger Silverstone has observed how frequently science on television is presented in the form of a detective story with a problem that is unravelled by a hero scientist (1985: 171). For the most part, television science magazines still hold to the master narrative of scientific progress, leaving the more complex, contested world of 'real' science to be acknowledged on television (if at all) in documentaries.

Food programmes are another type of television under consideration here that is widely exported. This is largely because they are, as Niki

Strange has observed, frequently structured, in part, as a tourist excursion where the cook-presenter visits sites particular to the style of dish under consideration (1998: 306–9). Not all programmes are like this, but it is probably the dominant form observable in programmes like those associated with Rick Stein and Keith Floyd as well as the Two Fat Ladies. Nontourist programmes like *The Naked Chef* may combine demonstration with staged familial events for which the cooking is being done. Apart from Strange's article, Phebe Chao has examined the gendered aspects of cooking programmes, as I have myself (Bonner, 1994; Chao, 1998).

Another group of programmes now popularly called 'lifestyle' has had a longer existence as separate, small categories, all of which continue to exist as sub-categories of the new term. House and garden shows (*Gardeners' World, Burke's Backyard, Our House, Better Homes*), advice programmes on subjects such as travel (*Holiday, Getaway, Wish You Were Here ...?*), health (*Good Medicine*) and financial affairs (*Money, Dosh*) have had little attention paid to them in the past or more recently. The exceptions consider recent variations like makeover shows (*Ground Force, Backyard Blitz* and *Changing Rooms*) where Rachel Moseley's article discussing the importance of revelation in appearance makeover shows like *Looking Good* (2000) fills a substantial gap. I have myself written elsewhere about the generic qualities of the overarching category 'lifestyle programmes' (2000).

A reasonably recent category of programme is the clip show, whether composed of bloopers (like ITV's *It'll Be Alright on the Night*), commercials or surveillance film with titles like *World's Worst Drivers*. These are the third of the types of ordinary television that are imported wholesale or for subsequent repackaging. Related to these are those composed of home video like *Australia's Funniest Home Video Show* or the British *You've Been Framed*. John Fiske has discussed *TV Bloopers* (and also *Candid Camera*) as examples of the televisual carnivalesque (1987: 242). Catherine Nicholson, writing of the 1990 Australian programme called, after the host, *Graham Kennedy's Funniest Home Video Show*, notes how from the beginning it worked to remove the idea that viewers made the programme content and to reinsert viewers as audience by emphasizing both the professional studio crew and the presenter (1991: 36–9).

When John Fiske and John Hartley wrote their groundbreaking study *Reading Television*, in 1978, they found it valuable to devote an entire chapter to the category of 'dance'. No-one writing now would do the same. They focused on *Come Dancing*, the sport-inflected ballroom dancing programme, which at that stage had been on British television for 25 years, and on what they called 'spectacular dance', which comprised a substantial part of the large number of variety shows then screening. Both, they argued, managed social tensions arising from class and sexual relations (1978: 133). Since this time, the presence of dance on television has all but disappeared, no-one else has written on the topic and the relevant tensions are handled very differently.

PROBLEM CATEGORIES

There are some types of programme that are common to most broad-casting systems but that do not have satisfactory names, or at least do not have English ones. The most substantial of these are what I feel forced to call 'time of day' shows: breakfast shows, morning pro-grammes, tonight shows and, more occasionally, afternoon programmes. They are all quite recognizable types, even if the afternoon version is infrequent; all are combinations of elements of chat and performance, breakfast ones having more news and tonight shows more humour (though *The Big Breakfast*, screening until March 2002, on Channel 4 may be seen to have challenged this assertion). The modulations and bal-ance of elements reflect the presumed activities of viewers: getting ready to go to work, starting the housework and relaxing after the day's work and the evening meal are over. The pace of a breakfast show is usually the fastest and the weather sections more important; morning shows are more heavily marked by consumerism; both breakfast and morning shows are more informative than tonight shows; the items in a tonight show may be longer, certainly the style is more relaxed and usually the subject matter is more 'adult'. In all of them the presenter or presenters talk to guests, who often include musicians who perform. These differ-ences are all within tolerable limits for considering the programmes as belonging to the same category, but there is no suggestion in any critical work that this is the case. It is rare for critical work to consider these programmes at all, though Hartley has discussed the genesis of daytime television as catering for housewives engaged in domestic labour by teaching them to 'resolv[e] anxiety about their status as housewives with desire for products' (2001: 93)

It is in placing tonight shows in this grouping that I am going most counter to the prevailing practice. The disregard of the category does not apply to them, and they are, not coincidentally, by far the most presti-gious, masculine and expensive. Rose's study of TV genres included the tonight variant within the genre 'talk'. While this may have been acceptable in the US in 1985 when *Donahue* was the only 'talk' show included which would be currently recognizable, it certainly does not seem appropriate now. Rodney A. Buxton has also written of the American tonight show, extending the analysis of the type beyond a concentration on celebrity merchandising into a consideration of the cultural capital the various comedian presenters are able to embody and the contradictions their jokes acknowledge (1991: 413–17). The much richer possibilities of British shows like *So, Graham Norton* or the Australian programmes associated with Andrew Denton and the sports-inflected offerings of the characters Roy and H.G. like *Club Buggery*, *The Dream*, and *The Monday Dump*, have yet to receive their critical due.

One category which has too few members to have been regarded as warranting a separate name is the real-life law and order programmes like *Crimewatch UK* or *Australia's Most Wanted*, which combine interviews, appeals for assistance and re-enactments of crimes to encourage viewers to contribute information to solve otherwise intractable criminal cases. For a small category it has produced a reasonable body of critical writing, most concentrating on the re-enactments or the solicitations for information. Matt Dummett, for example, argues that *Australia's Most Wanted* establishes a relationship with the viewers that positions them as 'amateur sleuths' working with the programme to fill the gaps in what the police know and to solve the crime (1997/8: 40). The grouping is often expanded to include the early reality television programmes concentrating on the emergency services. Annette Hill combines *Crimewatch UK* with such shows as *999* in a discussion of British reality television which I will deal with below in the discussion of recent changes in programming (2000).

LIGHT ENTERTAINMENT

The category closest to my field of ordinary television is the old British one of light entertainment. As an institutional term in British television it named a section of the BBC and was used less formally elsewhere. In either situation, light entertainment referred to professionally and critically disregarded programmes which none the less were very popular with viewers and for which the ties to popular theatrical forms like variety, music hall and vaudeville, even if mediated through radio, were still evident. It included game shows and daytime advice programmes known in the early days as women's programmes, but at its core were variety shows. Fiske and Hartley's chapter on dance, just mentioned, began by asking 'why dance figures so prominently in light entertainment on television' (1978: 127) and explored the answer through a sophisticated consideration of diversion. Formality disappeared from Light Entertainment earlier than it did from other sections of television; regional accents, vulgarity and shameless self-promotion all flourished there first. David Lusted has noted that the pleasures of light entertainment came 'not only from recognising the skills of personalities (from the physical dexterity of the juggler or magician to the verbal constructions of the raconteur) but also the *risks* at stake' (1998: 75) – risks, he further explains, that also apply to the game show. These are both key pleasures of television which continue to apply even more widely than they did when jugglers and magicians were common television sights.

Raymond Williams wrote of Light Entertainment in 1969, looking to see to what extent the category was worthwhile or meretricious. Noting its roots in music hall, he also observed the continuation of a division from that time between the 'tinsel and saccharine' and 'the popular entertainers dealing directly, in song and sketch and monologue, with everyday experience humourously, ironically, sometimes bitterly observed' (1989: 85). Most of the instances of which he approved were sitcoms (like *Steptoe and Son* or *Till Death Us Do Part*), at that stage regarded as part of light entertainment. The disapproved example is one more relevant to the contemporary situation – *Cilla*, at that time a comparatively standard variety show but already including the trade-mark elements of the presenter, including the indisputable 'tinsel and saccharine'. Singled out for particular scorn were the introductory chat with guests and the 'spectacular mateyness [which] brings people in off the street and patronises them, in the most down-to-earth way' (ibid.: 86). Williams' paternalistic socialism is evident throughout his television columns and visible here, but one can feel the justice of his comment and see its applicability, not to all instances where ordinary people appear on screen, but to quite a number. It is possible though that so large has the number of ordinary people on screen become, that rather than anyone reading their treatment any longer as patronizing, it has become natu-ralized into just how being on television is.

Richard Dyer's 1973 study of light entertainment was one of the earliest BFI Television Monographs, published to redress television's being given 'too little serious attention'. He acknowledged the wider ambit of the term but restricted his focus to variety alone. He listed *Cilla* as one of his favourite shows, being much taken with the innovation of incorporating actual viewers into the programme through stunts which started with closed-circuit TV set-ups in shop windows before transfer-ring to the studio. For Dyer the central aspects of entertainment were abundance, energy and community, all of which operated to distract viewers from the drudgery of everyday life (1973: 40). Yet his was not necessarily a celebratory study; the idea of utopia, which Dyer elsewhere finds in the musical, he saw missing from televised entertainment, or at least absent in any way with transformative potential. By excluding all but musical entertainment, Dyer's study was unable to trace the links between the range of programmes which constituted the industrial category of light entertainment, and complicated (though not necessarily improved) its relationship to the everyday.

Despite the persistent presence of Cilla Black, the growth of infotainment programmes and the therapeutic drive of much contemporary television have obscured the continuation of the tradition of light entertainment; but it is still there, still one of the basic forms of popular entertainment. It manages the familiar and structures the repetition and difference which is essential when programmes occur on a daily basis. A format that allows performers to do their well-known turns, to tell the stories that we have heard before, sing again their famous songs and promote their latest products is a highly valuable one. What this description invokes today is the chat show or the tonight show, both of which are direct descendants of the variety show, one of the most common and popular forms of programming in the early decades of television but one which is now quite rare.

As is customary with the public arrival of a new medium, when television began broadcasting its initial content was very much derived from the other media already providing for established audiences. Although live theatre, cinema, magazines and newspapers also contributed, it drew particularly on the closest – radio. Drama, news and current affairs, sport, children's programmes, quizzes and game shows all transferred reasonably readily. Music proved a little more awkward in that, being primarily aural, it provided much more radio content than it could provide for television, but then, at first, television took up so much less time than radio. (In 1936, little more than twelve hours a week were broadcast; when television resumed in 1946, after the wartime break, it occupied only a little more than 28 hours a week, and, of course, there was only one channel). Variety programmes were very successful ways of presenting music, however, for they could combine visual acts with the more substantially aural ones that radio had favoured and thus return variety more thoroughly to its music hall or vaudeville origins. Acrobats, speciality dancers, jugglers and many of the acts that are now regarded as the preserve of buskers found places on television between songs and comic patter. (It was also the place for one of the strangest of radio's great success stories – the ventriloquist. On radio, regular weekly shows were devoted to the lives of ventriloquists and their dummies – ones like those featuring Archie Andrews were enormous public favourites despite what one might think was the necessity of the visual component. Even more strangely, televised ventriloquist shows failed to last very long at all except when they were hybridized with variety programmes, and even so, most ventriloquists were only ever guests.)

Looking at what has happened to variety programmes reveals some of the shifts in television programmes in the 50 or so years in which television has had a significant public presence in the UK and Australia. Variety was music-based and usually studio-set from the beginning, although *Sunday Night at the London Palladium* (ITV 1955–67, 1973–4), one of the highest rating shows of the 1950s and 1960s, was transmitted from the Palladium itself. *The Morecambe and Wise Show* (variously BBC and ITV, 1961–83) and *In Melbourne Tonight* (Channel 9, 1957–90 and intermittently since) were two of the most popular studio-based shows and both had comedians hosting throughout and appearing in short, comic sketches along the way. Singers and musicians would appear together with other comedians, magicians and vaudeville or music-hall acts. There would often be resident dancers as well as a band. An alternative, but not essentially different, version occurred when singers hosted, the change relating principally to the proportions of the types of acts on the show. Named after a comedian, the show would have more comedy and less music, named after a magician – like the British *The Paul Daniels Show* – it would have more magic, but the variety range called on remained the same.

The term 'variety show' has itself completely disappeared. When, now, magicians, for example, do present a programme comprising a number of their acts punctuated by musical performances and interludes of chat with their guests, it is only ever called a special, and there is no place even on a show such as that for the physical acts of jugglers and acrobats. These performers now have no televisual presence. Panel shows which may put one or two singers and a comic monologue between the team games, as in the case of the Australian show *Good News Week*, and chat shows which allow celebrity guests to perform their latest song, carry some of the tradition on, but the name is passé. Rose's examination, conducted when there still were a few American examples, blames its impending death or dissolution into other genres on the growth of MTV, a decline in available talent and the attraction of sitcoms and other media to the comedians who were essential to it (1985: 321–3).

The decline of variety as an observable programme type occurred with the growth of what had been a very slight component of the programmes and a shift to making more overt the main factor in the appearance of artists within the show. There had always been some brief verbal interchanges between the host and certain of the guest artists, but these were of limited duration and served mainly to introduce the title of the item. These, however, expanded into substantial chat segments that would eventually be longer than the item performed. There had also always been a tendency for performers on commercially screened variety shows to be drawn from those appearing on stage or elsewhere locally and for this to be mentioned either in the introductory or closing comments. This combined with the increased time for chat to produce unabashed promotional sessions, and with the decline in (serious and otherwise) discussion programmes unrelated to promotional activities to produce the current situation where very large sections of the schedule are given over to various kinds of promotional chat interspersed with performances only when they are themselves what are being promoted.

The shift need not have been so firmly into promotion; an early and highly successful variation was provided by the BBC's *That's Life*, which was, as Robin Gutch points out, 'a textual hybrid which uniquely combined the conventions of current affairs and variety light entertainment television' (1986: 11). This involved ordinary people on whose behalf it crusaded in consumer investigations, and whose contributions, especially those involving sexual innuendo, it gleefully sought out and incorporated. In an indication of contemporary programme shifts, its presenter, Esther Rantzen, has since moved to an afternoon talk show which retains the echo of her old title, *That's Esther*. The style of *That's Life* continues to some extent in breakfast television where the current affairs inflections seem able to be maintained, but even there promotion dominates.

A further indication that it is the growth of promotion that has altered the variety programme comes from the one area where something of the older form can still be found – the talent show. Since the performers are not celebrities, and so have no separate product to promote, more items can be staged. Comprised of singers and instrumentalists with the very occasional comic, the 'variety' that gives the category its name is provided here by the addition of the competition or, in the case of the most successful recent British version, *Stars in Their Eyes*, competition and the on-screen work of replicating as far as possible the appearance and style of the original performer.

TO INFORM, EDUCATE AND ENTERTAIN

The Reithian concept of public broadcasting which formed the whole British system for decades and which was the model for the public broadcasting system in Australia (even though this was only ever a part of the whole system) insisted that broadcasting had three functions: to inform, educate and entertain. In some of the earlier enunciations of this mission, especially when in a political context, such as over the introduction of television, it was apparent that 'entertain' was very much the least of the three, only really a sweetener for the real activities of education and information. The monopoly held by the BBC until the arrival of the ITV channels in 1955 meant that it was able to hold more firmly to this mission than was ever the case in Australia. It was a very different matter having opposition only from offshore radio broadcasters like the entertainment-focused Radio Luxembourg and competing with a range of entertaining commercial alternatives originating in the same city.

In 1971, one of Raymond Williams' *Listener* columns discussed the concept of 'serious' programming, citing the 'official BBC definition: a programme "whose primary intention is informational, educational or critical"' (1989: 128) and objecting to the utilitarian distinction between fiction and non-fiction that it operated. Entertainment was emphatically outside the serious (although not for Williams whose own listing of serious programmes included both *Monty Python's Flying Circus* and *The Money Programme*), but 'critical' had been added to the triumvirate in its place. In television's own discourse, the most probable place now for the televisually improbable term 'serious' is in current affairs or in medical programming. Certainly it is antipathetic to ordinary television.

The most telling sign of the shifts in television programming that culminate in the need for the term 'ordinary television' is the appearance of the term 'infotainment'. This marks the collapse of the Reithian rubric, to 'inform, educate and entertain', more firmly than any other indicator. Education has become the province of separate programmes tied to actual schooling and hidden in the unpopular hours on public service channels; inform may still be held to apply to news, current affairs and documentary programmes, – though most critics see the need for substantial qualifications here to concede the tabloidization of much news and current affairs, or the decrease in the presence of 'serious' documentaries and their replacement by docu-soaps. Entertainment, however, is triumphantly centre-stage. The function of television now is to entertain, first and foremost, and if information can be provided in an entertaining way so much the better.

INFOTAINMENT

As a change in nomenclature acknowledging the altered field of television programming, 'infotainment' has great power. It registers the hybridizing of information and entertainment and the removal of education as the central move in contemporary television. Unfortunately, the category of programme it describes varies. In the United States and much of northern Europe, it refers to tabloid current affairs programmes while in the UK and Australia it labels programmes that do not have any link to the news but are, rather, lifestyle programmes. This uncertainty is the cause of much frustration for researchers, though programme guides and television viewers negotiate it readily.

The term started to be used in the UK in the late 1980s. An article by Sean Moncrieff in the trade paper *Broadcast*, in 1988, referring to *The Oprah Winfrey Show*, *That's Life* and the Irish programme *The Late, Late Show*, explains the term and what it heralds. At this stage the more formal term 'factual entertainment' was the most powerful synonym and the article wavers between the two with occasional excursions into other phrases like 'real people shows' as the uncertain field is explored. Moncrieff notes of the new category, 'what is new is the belief that the factual entertainment format is one that will save British television from a tidal wave of public indifference' (1988: 19). At this stage there was considerable anxiety about the threat from satellite delivery, although the fragmentation of the audience that has been one of the most influential consequences of the various forms of pay-TV was not clearly registered. In some ways, though, the broadcasters interviewed were quite prescient: 'But with more private lives and less defined programme areas on the box, the result will not just be different programmes but a *completely different sort of television*: the dividing line between what is on the screen and what happens in people's lives will begin to disintegrate' (19, [original emphasis]).

The term had existed prior to this in the US. William Safire mentioned it in his 'On Language' column in 1981, together with 'docudrama' and 'faction' as illustrating 'the trend toward the fuzzing of lines between fact and fiction, truth and fantasy' (1981: 16).

The term did not settle into use rapidly. In 1992, *Broadcast* was still vacillating between the alternatives. Chris Riley noted a lack of agreement about the name, citing 'factual or topical entertainment, infotainment, topical features' as well as himself still using 'people shows'. He points out how the grouping is named more in terms of what it is not, ending up as an area positioned between light entertainment, news and current affairs (18). The naming was obviously lagging behind the developing programmes as the following comment indicates: 'Successful factual programmes are those building tangible two-way contact with their viewers (it starts with the fact sheets). And entertainment shows, too, are becoming less contrived. In "people shows" like *Blind Date* and *You've Been Framed*, contestants and participants are as important as the hosts' (18). Only the 'factual entertainment' example is now one we would recognize as infotainment, though the grouping is one that sees the link that underlies my claim for 'ordinary television'.

Stuart Cunningham and Toby Miller's 1984 study of Australian television used the term in a slightly unfixed way to refer both to tabloid current affairs programmes and lifestyle shows like the ABC's *Holiday* or Channel 9's *Burke's Backyard*, tying them both to the industry catchphrase 'news you can use' and to the shift from conventional news practices to 'consumer journalism' (1994: 51–3).

Peter Dahlgren, writing in this same period, indicates that the northern European use of 'infotainment' had not settled down either, although the tendency to keep it closer to journalism was already there. He discusses a number of shifts bringing entertainment values into journalism, citing tabloid-style news broadcasts, vox-pop talk shows, transnational satellite news, 'so-called reality-based programmes' and 'infotainment magazines'. 'Morning "breakfast shows" are included here, but this format can be found in early and late evening as well. Explicit entertainment segments are mixed with more serious material even including short traditional news segments' (1995: 54–5). He makes clear that what qualifies these programmes for his consideration is their 'serious material', though this term includes their tendency to use items in which politicians engage in rather frivolous pursuits.

In this book, 'infotainment' refers to much the same field as lifestyle programming – the advice shows focused on the home and garden, health and holidays – but also popular science and technology programmes like the BBC's *Dream Lives*. They are programmes where information is made palatable by visual metaphor, stunts and attractive on-screen personnel. Makeover programmes which provide small quantities of advice in between sections of an ongoing narrative of producing a surprise garden, room or appearance transformation for a deserving individual are clear examples.

'REALITY' TELEVISION

The other major change seen in television programmes in the 1990s was the rise to prominence of the category 'reality television' together with a varying conception of what the term describes. Initially it was used to describe what was seen to be an American phenomenon of direct television where footage was taken of what purported to be the everyday activities of people at the 'sharp end' of public service activities – police and emergency response workers. Programmes like the American *Cops* were shot and screened with minimal technical intervention in the way of lighting, editing, commentary or explanation of what was happening. These were copied in many other countries and regarded as more exciting and more 'real', and thus likely to displace the older, more sedate forms of on-the-spot coverage (e.g. ITV's *Jimmy's*, with its carefully edited, thoughtfully composed annual visits to St James Hospital in Leeds, designed in part to reassure prospective patients of the control and competence of health professionals) or the highly crafted views of named documentarists, as well as the briefer segments in current affairs programmes.

Annette Hill, writing of the early 1990s British derivatives of *Cops*, notes the various devices they employed to produce entertaining television. The public broadcast version *999* bridged *Crimewatch UK* and the new form by continuing to incorporate re-enactments and providing advice on life-saving techniques, while using editing and promotional techniques more commonly found in drama programmes (2000: 222–6). The other two shows – ITV's *Blues and Twos* and Sky's *Coppers* – were closer to the American format (as was the Australian *Emergency Rescue*), eschewing re-enactments for a close trailing of emergency personnel and a presentation of events from their point of view. Hill concludes that all three shows are concerned to present the emergency services in the best possible light, counteracting less positive news stories of inadequate funding, endemic racism and corruption (ibid.: 233). They were cheaply made, exciting slices of life and, initially, rated well, but the appeal of being on the spot palled as the drawbacks of incomprehensible dialogue, indistinct, poorly-lit visuals and, at times, inconclusive fragmentary events became more evident.

These programme fragmented into several different kinds of programme. Some of the flavour of the emergency services material was retained by clip shows using various surveillance videos, with titles like *World's Worst Drivers*. Another relative was docu-soaps, where a chosen set of 'real life' people were followed for a period of time as they went about whatever was the focus of the camera's attention – the British *Driving School* was one of the most popular, but *Airport*, *DEA* and Channel 7's *Drama School* were other examples. Combining a documentary style of observation with a soap-opera narrative structure of cliff-hangers, and characters 'cast' as central on the basis of their melodramatic potential, confirmed by voiceover commentary, they took personalization and emotional engagement far beyond what had been acceptable documentary practice, gaining a more popular audience for a lighter form of 'slice of life' programming.

Another derivative of 'reality television' was the more tabloid kind of current affairs with its desire to sensationalize stories and to treat the activities of celebrities as if they were central current affairs content. Its influence could also be seen away from current affairs, cross-bred with clip-shows in programmes like Channel 4's *The Real Holiday Show*, where viewers videotaped their own holidays which were then edited into a show with brief studio segments where the holiday-makers chatted to presenters about the experience just shown on actuality video. 'Real', it appears, can be attached to a wide range of material and may signify only the use of video by the subjects of the investigation. This is not to deny that some of these programmes can provide considerable insight into the lives of ordinary people given the tools to produce their own stories. *Video Nation* was an obvious instance.

The term 'reality television', however, has attached itself most firmly since the late 1990s to a different kind of programme altogether, one for which the name is decidedly inappropriate. These programmes do not assert that they are showing some kind of minimally mediated 'real', as the previous instances, however questionably, certainly did. These programmes, which I shall call 'reality game shows' to differentiate them from their predecessors, involve placing 'real' people in contrived situations, observing what happens and usually reducing the number until only one remains. *Big Brother* and *Survivor* are both widely formatted instances of this; *The Mole* and *Temptation Island* not so widely imitated. Alternatives, like *Popstars* or *Search for a Supermodel*, trace the reduction of a very large number of contenders down to a select group who are then groomed to become professional performers. In all, segments intercut supposedly fly-on-the-wall observation with direct to-camera confessions. 'Reality game shows' signals how they follow most of the characteristics of game shows in having rules, games and winners, and if not actual on-screen presenters, then voiceover ones, while not having their short time-frame and studio location. The term 'endurance shows,' while not having any currency, does describe one of their key features and, through reference to the Japanese programme *Endurance* (awareness of which was internationally circulated in clip shows hosted by Clive James), invokes also the ritual humiliation which seems to attend participants.

John Corner, writing of the newer manifestations of documentary television, notes how shows like *Big Brother* 'mark ... another decisive stage in actuality-based entertainment', and he names this shift one into 'diversion', cautioning against dismissing such work too easily because of the pre-eminence of entertainment in their structure, noting rather that they provide forms 'that are high in exchange value [and] strategically designed for their competitive strength in the market-place' (2000a: n.p.). He notes how performativity on the part of the subjects is now a significant feature as is a changed character of affective investment on the part of viewers, and wonders about the consequences for the credibility of the documentary form (2000a: n.p.). While acknowledging that these programmes do have a documentary derivation (and that their playful approach feeds into other more recognizably documentary forms), it is my view that the set-ups are so fictional that it is better to accept that their game show component is the determining aspect and include them (but less certainly docu-soaps) under my category of ordinary television.

KEEPING THE PROGRAMME TYPES DISTINCT

Television Mythologies, edited by Len Masterman, is a collection of writings on television, politically, though not intellectually, linked to Raymond Williams' television criticism. Published in 1986, and so able to discuss Channel 4 programmes, it was inspired by Roland Barthes' *Mythologies* as, in the words of Len Masterman's introduction, 'a contribution to the long struggle to make the serious consideration of television's ideological role part of the accepted currency of public debate about the medium' (1986: 6). The academics and media professionals who contribute to it write on a range of programmes, but the most distinctive aspect of this collection is the shows they choose to consider. Although they do look at news, commercials and a couple of drama programmes, well over half of the volume's essays deal with 'ordinary' shows. Cary Bazalgette even articulates why this is, in an essay on Su Pollard's presenting of *Disney Time*. She asserts: 'Popular forms are castigated for their conformity and innocuousness, but it could be that their very safety makes a space for changes of a different kind. Rather than the subversive *content* that draws such attention to itself, Pollard offers us the possibility of subversive *readings*' (1986: 33 [original emphasis]). It was the heyday of 'subversive readings' criticism, but the readings in this case were ones triggered rather overtly by the presenter. Even more obviously concerned with subversion within the text is Lusted's essay on television personalities occasioned by the recent deaths of Diana Dors, Tommy Cooper and Eric Morecambe. While noting the place of personalities in the celebration of the cult of the individual, Lusted looks at these three careers to see the social meanings operating counter to the myths of individualism that they embodied for (working-class) sections of the audience (1986).

These were the only attempts to bring the separate essays together. Among the other essays Elizabeth Wilson noted the ambiguity of Russell Grant's turn on *Breakfast Time* among its 'relentless domesticity' and 'façade of familial normality' (1986: 7), Robin Gutch observed the way the populist discourse of *That's Life* individualizes and consumerizes a collective radicalism (1986: 13–14) and Philip Simpson worried away at the conservatism of *One Man and His Dog* but accepted the pleasure it provided him and the other three or four million viewers it attracted, who 'watch it with a relaxed attention' (1986: 20), a telling phrase for inconsequential television viewing. Rosalind Brunt's investigation of the return of *What's My Line?* to ITV in the same month that the miners' strike began, and with unemployment high, identified the programme's focus on incongruous jobs that were rendered classless and entertaining rather then being the site of highly classed labour (1986). Bill Lewis wrote of game shows' discourses of wealth, knowledge and gender relations but ended by noting that they reveal 'the television medium atypically assimilating members of the public into its signifying practices' (1986: 45).

Television Mythologies was published as the changes that were to make ordinary television such a substantial part of the television schedule were already underway. It noted several of the features that were to become further heightened in the course of the 1990s of which 'relentless domesticity', the drive to be entertaining always and everywhere and to incorporate ordinary members of the public into the programmes wherever possible were the most notable. However atypical it was (and is) in its attention to the rarely considered light non-fiction programming, except for the essays by Bazalgette & Lusted it maintained the programmes' separateness from each other, a practice which generally weakens what little work there is on this substantial body of television programmes.

What is Ordinary Television?

Considering the programmes which are the concern of this book only in terms of their genres, as in the previous chapter, makes it difficult to discuss their commonalities and also complicates the way one can discuss some of the changes in television in recent years. In this chapter I will introduce the way in which I believe we can conceptualize these programmes as linked, and in so doing explore the changed televisual world in a way that complements other work on recent developments like that on tabloidization of news and current affairs television (see, for example, Langer, 1998; Turner, 1999) or on changes in the ambit of the term documentary (see Corner, 2000a). One of the key points of the first of these particular debates is that there has been a collapsing of the distinctions between news and current affairs on the one hand and some of the programmes which are dealt with here, particularly infotainment and chat shows.

The key term for my examination is 'ordinary'. I call the programmes that are the concern of this book 'ordinary television' and refer to many of the people who appear on them as 'ordinary people', but this is not to use the term disparagingly. I use 'ordinary' as it has come to be used quite widely within the related fields of sociology, communications studies and cultural studies with the rise in concerns about the quotidian. It usually appears interchangeable with 'everyday', 'familiar', even 'routine', as can be seen in Paddy Scannell's comment about the development of talk on radio and television:

> The voices of radio and television were and are heard in the context of household activities ... [and this] ... powerfully drives the communicative style and manner of broadcasting to approximate to the norms not of public forms of talk, but to those of ordinary, familiar conversation, for this is overwhelmingly the preferred communicative style of interaction between people in the routine contexts of day-to-day life'. (1991: 9)

THE ORDINARY AND THE EVERYDAY

I would like, though, to try, at least at this stage, to avoid any simple equivalence by exploring the terms a little. The one which has greatest critical currency is 'everyday', particularly through the influence of the work of Henri Lefebvre and Michel de Certeau. For Lefebvre, everyday life was composed of all that was not a specialized activity; the everyday thus included work, private and family life, as well as leisure. He does not, though, see it as a neutral term, but one that operates politically. Despite establishing a distinction between 'everyday life' as the contemporary state of affairs under capitalism and the 'everyday', where the utopian possibilities are to be found, Lefebvre does not appear to hold fast to it, and indeed the two terms and states are intimately intertwined, as Alice Kaplan and Kristin Ross point out, using the term 'quotidian' to begin their explanation:

> The quotidian is on the one hand the realm of routine, repetition, reiteration – the space/time where constraints and boredom are produced. Far from being an escape from this realm, segmented leisure time such as the weekend is rather a final cog permitting the smooth functioning of the routine. Even at its most degraded, however, the everyday harbours the possibility of its own transformations; it gives rise, in other words, to desires which cannot be satisfied within a weekly cycle of production/consumption. The Political, like the purloined letter, is hidden in the everyday, exactly where it is most obvious in the contradictions of lived experience, in the most banal and repetitive gestures of everyday life ... It is in the midst of the utterly ordinary, in the space where the dominant relations of production are tirelessly and relentlessly reproduced, that we must look for utopian and political aspirations to crystallize. (1987: 3)

Routine (and repetition), then, is not only a characteristic of the everyday, but, for Lefebvre, a negatively valued one. His project is to transform the everyday, and he calls repetition 'one of the most difficult problems facing us' (1987: 10). Although most subsequent work calling on the everyday disregards Lefebvre's political beliefs about it, the tension between what for him are the transformative and the repressive aspects of the everyday can still be traced in discussions of the everyday and certainly in the investigations of the interrelationships of television and everyday practices. The elements may not be named in this way but the contradictoriness of the everyday is repeatedly remarked upon.

Television itself is not a focus of Lefebvre's work, but his comment that 'cinema and television divert the everyday by at times offering up to it its own spectacle or sometimes the spectacle of the distinctly non-everyday;

violence, death, catastrophe, the lives of king or stars – those who we are led to believe defy everydayness' (ibid.: 11) establishes a division of television content – as providing spectacles of the everyday and the non-everyday – that I will draw on in elucidating my own distinction between ordinary and special television.

For Michel de Certeau, 'ordinary' and 'everyday' interweave at the beginning of *The Practice of Everyday Life*, which is itself dedicated to the 'ordinary man'. It is 'everyday' that is the term he pursues, while 'ordinary' is attached to his consideration of Freud and Wittgenstein. His examination of everyday life focuses on the ways 'users reappropriate the space organized by techniques of sociocultural production' (1984: xiv). He is more hopeful than Lefebvre about the everyday, seeing not the potential for recovering a lost more utopian condition but, in its practices/tactics, the continuation of a striving to resist. Much of his examination of this striving focuses on the reading of texts and the manipulation of space and time, but he also argues that games, stories and legends rehearse the tactics that underpin the possibilities of oppositional activities centred around popular culture (1984: 22–4).

Roger Silverstone calls on these theorists among others to construct the basis of his study of the place of television in managing the anxiety and chaos he sees characterizing social life, (although it is Anthony Giddens' 'ontological security' and D. W. Winnicott's 'transitional object' which are the core terms for his tentative solution). His summation that '[a]t the core of the experience of everyday life is a form of practical rationality that we recognise as common sense and within which the forms and order of our capacity to manage the ordinariness of the everyday are embodied and expressed' (1994: 168) indicates both his concern with matters of agency and an evaluation of routine very different from Lefebvre's. In explaining 'ordinari*ness*' Silverstone first refers to its replacing the phrase 'the taken for granted', then names it 'the more or less secure normality of everyday life, and our capacity to manage it on a daily basis' (ibid.: 166). The term 'normality' here remains unglossed, but Silverstone later assures the reader that the ordinariness of everyday life is not homogenous but varies by virtue of a range of cultural factors (ibid.: 168).

Television programming is not itself straightforwardly part of this ordinariness or everydayness; watching television may well be. Although Silverstone seems to be saying that it is not when he talks of *returning* to the mundane and quotidian after watching television (ibid.: 169), I prefer his earlier statement that television 'is part of the grain of everyday life' (22). In the spirit of this, I see the physical activity of watching television as very much ordinary and everyday; indeed the activities in conjunction with which it is performed – eating, talking, doing housework, playing with pets – are central to the everyday, especially the familial, domestic conception of it. The mental activities engaged in – the making of meaning, fantasizing – may require a return to the mundane, a 'coming down to earth', as the familiar mild disorientation when recalled to social interactions from an intense engagement with a favourite programme may testify. ('What? What did you say?' we may ask a fellow member of the household, somewhat irritably.) A similar distinction (with echoes of Lefebvre) is articulated by Stan Cohen and Laurie Taylor, for whom fantasizing provoked by moments in television programmes is a typical 'escape attempt' from the predictability of everyday life, while the routine watching of the programme is part of the predictability itself (1978: 124–5).

The concerns of this book are not, however, with the relationship between television and its ordinary viewers, important though it is; instead they are with the ways in which the content of television calls on ordinary, everyday concerns and patterns of behaviour, using them, furthermore, not just as topics but as guides to style, appearance and behaviour. It is because my concern is not primarily with 'real' people and how they make use of television in their everyday life, but rather with the use of everyday life by television (including its incorporation of 'real' people into its programmes), that I prefer the term 'ordinary' to 'everyday' in this investigation. What I look at is still a representation of the ordinary, an illusion of normality, but I will eschew as much as possible 'everyday' with its intimations of ethnographic investigation. In doing so I also want to acknowledge Stephen Heath's warning about the way in which a fetishizing of the everyday can lead to a rejection of concerns with value and an uncritical celebration of pleasure:

> Television and its programs (and this approach sees nothing but programs) are projected as value – as to be valued – because of their everydayness and their popularity (which is here the same thing) in a circle in which the mass existence of something is proof of that value and proof of the validity of its acceptance in the name of the everyday. (1990: 286)

Although he does not call on Lefebvre, Heath has a similar belief in the transformative potential lurking within the everyday. His warning is especially pertinent to my concerns, because I do argue that the pervasiveness and even the 'everydayness' of ordinary television programmes renders them worthy of investigation. I have no intention, however, of avoiding questions of value or of the ideological implications of ordinary television, though my principal consideration of them will be postponed until Chapters 4 and 5.

'Ordinary' is called on quite frequently as a descriptive rather than analytic term in John Hartley's *Uses of Television*, the book developed in response to Richard Hoggart's 1958 study *Uses of Literacy*. Hartley refers on more than one occasion to Hoggart's project as producing 'a semio-history of ordinariness' (1999: 16, 27). Hartley himself moves from Hoggart's concern with print to look at television and observes how almost immediately after its introduction in both the UK and the US (and presumably also in Australia) both its domesticity and ordinariness were settled. And how from this point 'television was associated with the company it kept – personal experience, private life, suburbia, consumption, ordinariness, heterosexual family-bonding, hygiene, the "feminization" of family governance' (ibid.: 107). Most of this very useful list of characteristics will recur in my analysis, but the one that most repeatedly appears thereafter for Hartley in conjunction with 'ordinary' and 'television' is 'suburban'. The suburbs are where he sees television embedded, they are the heartland of the ordinary and are inhabited by middle-brow, middle-class people. Working-class people receive surprisingly short shrift. They are mentioned primarily through Hoggart; for Hartley himself they appear invisible, especially in the contemporary world. It is difficult to be certain, precisely who and what constitutes his ordinary suburban world, but it is discursively constructed, not mapped onto a statistically measured society. It may be that the 'middle' referred to is more that in the American term 'middle America', which has recently been adopted into an analogous use as 'middle Australia'. In both countries what it signals is an attachment to the traditional virtues on every one of Hartley's list of the company television has kept and a geographic location, not just suburban but also provincial.

Yet in choosing to talk of class he speaks of a category that has some identifiable location, the parameters of which have been much debated, but which have 'real world' referents. In socio-economic terms, speaking only for Australia (but in doing so speaking for the country which, until recently, was renowned as having the largest self-identified middle class), the size of the middle class has been argued to be about 42 per cent, with an upper class of 14 per cent of the population (Graetz and McAllister, 1994: 203). When it comes to class identity, a little over half name themselves middle class and one third working class (Bennett et al., 1999: 22). What happens to people located outside the middle class in their relationship with Hartley's view of television? Hartley argues that television teaches citizenship, which leads one to wonder whether it also teaches middle-classness and whether this is signalled by Hartley's approving reference to Hoggart's view of television as 'ameliorating manners' (1999: 142). Ordinary television's persistent instruction in better ways to live and better ways to be, as will be investigated later with regard to 'makeover' programmes, could indicate that this may well be so.

Despite the stress I have placed, and will continue to place, on the constructedness of ordinary television and the way that I will define it by the inclusion of ordinary people into its content, actual people, actual audiences even, are not irrelevant. Though there is no necessary correspondence between what is asserted as ordinary in a television programme and what people who view it regard as ordinary, processes may be observed that can be regarded as attempting to bridge the gap. Products espoused by popular presenters like the British Delia Smith and the Australian Don Burke are purchased in such large amounts that retailers need to be alerted in advance to the programmes' content (and the well-known example of Oprah Winfrey's book endorsements furthers the point). Such behaviour is most commonly discussed in terms of aspiration or desire (see Wernick, 1991: ch. 2) and the processes of trying to become someone different, but as I will discuss further in Chapter 4, I regard it more as part of a continual construction of the ordinary. What is presented as constituting the ordinary is not unvarying, and as well as new objects, new presenters may need to be hired to maintain the appearance of relevance to new styles of ordinary behaviour and to keep younger audiences watching. The promotion on British television during the closing years of the 1990s of the 'ladette' presenter, like Zoe Ball or Denise Van Outen, can be regarded in this way.

I have already noted the way in which the word ordinary occurs almost as a synonym for everyday in discussions of television and everyday life, but the term 'ordinary television' itself seems only to have been used previously by one other writer, and then almost in passing. Patricia Holland uses 'ordinary' interchangeably with 'everyday' and 'routine', but also specifically names as ordinary television a grouping of programmes identical to mine, but with the addition of sport, local news and TV specials (2000: 130–42). Her discussion of them, though little more than a brief note, accords well with a number of the points that I will make below. Her description of 'a flow of action on the screen which is light and entertaining, mildly informative and involves lots of chatter, lots of personalities, some music and plenty of laughs' (2000: 131) as well as her insistence that it includes both worthy and meretricious programmes, apply well. It is the inclusion of the extra types of programme which blur what is for me an important distinction between ordinary and special that makes hers a different conception.

KEY ASPECTS OF TELEVISUAL FORM

Analysis of the formal characteristics of television concentrates on two aspects in particular as descriptive of its specificity: liveness and the matter of flow. Neither is without complication and neither is particularly satisfactory in distinguishing television from radio, yet both continue to be used because, despite their problems, they are still analytically fruitful. In comparison to the analyses discussed in Chapter 1, discussion of the programmes here can be more revealing about television itself because such discussion serves no other primary purpose – it is not a way to talk about the political process, identity or aesthetics. Rather, although it is still possible to examine all of these (as I will), the very ordinariness means that television as a medium is more to the fore. Characteristically, then, liveness and flow are especially significant to ordinary television.

As far as television reception is concerned, 'liveness' is always an illusion. Only those present in the studio audience can see a programme actually 'live' in the way that, say, 'live theatre' is live, and what they see is not what the home viewer sees, even if the monitors, rather than the stage area, are watched. Very little television is 'live-to-air' in the sense of being transmitted as it occurs. Even such ostentatiously live programmes as the news are actually comprised of short bursts of live to-camera newsreading interspersed with longer prerecorded segments which may include such obfuscatory material as reporters declaiming 'Here I am speaking to you from the very spot where only ten minutes ago ...'. Yet the importance of liveness to the transmitted material is such that it is reiterated talismanically in scene-setting phrases, of which 'recorded live in front of a studio audience' is one of the most frequent, and fatuous. 'Live' is a good word in the television world and 'prerecorded' is not, despite so much of the promotion of television hingeing on material which is almost invariably prerecorded. It is the costly dramatic form (soaps, sitcoms, series and movies made for TV or for cinema) that provides the core of television's self-promotion, but apart from the very rare extravaganza, liveness here comes through the few sitcoms that have studio audiences or through actors' publicity activities.

Most ordinary television programmes are performed live rather than actually 'live to air', the regular exceptions being those programmes like morning shows or tonight shows which have times of day in their genre name and are usually transmitted live, though with varying quantities of prerecorded inserts. By 'performed live' I mean that the presenters and reporters speak to camera, as if the person spoken to (the home audience members as individuals) was present at the time of the speaking, rather than hearing the recorded words after the passage of days, weeks or even months.

With news programmes and current affairs there is some point to the insistence on time; immediacy is a core point of much of the information conveyed. It is important that, for example, increases in interest rates are reported at the time of their happening, not several days later, or that data on the location and direction of a cyclone is transmitted in time for action to be taken. This is not the case for lifestyle programmes or game shows. Certainly the viewer of gardening shows prefers seasonal related-ness, so advice on what plants to place where does not refer to spring plantings in late summer, but there is still quite a degree of latitude. The fetishizing of liveness is perhaps best seen in that cliché of cooking shows, 'Here's one I prepared earlier'. Viewers are sufficiently literate about production methods that the immediate removal of the finished product from the oven into which an uncooked dish had just been placed could be read as a temporal ellipsis which needed no comment. The prior preparation of several examples of a dish to make for efficient use of studio time does not need to be acknowledged on air – editing is acceptable to cover mishaps after all – but it nearly always is remarked upon. It may be argued that tribute is being paid to the early days of television when the technology was quite primitive and most programmes were indeed live, but it is much easier to read this as part of the running self-referencing to the production of the programme which was once regarded as transgressive television (Turner, 1989) but has long been televisual standard, especially for ordinary television. Showing the cam-era, referring to off-screen crew, risking things going wrong, all these began with actual live-to-air programming, especially tonight shows, and was a sign of their daring, seat-of-the-pants production style seeping into the presentation, but now this is just an aesthetic choice that may signify liveness (and risk) but is no index of it.

Unlike liveness, which is an industrial as well as a critical concept, flow has no formal presence beyond academic circles. It is also more highly contested. Raymond Williams identified and named televisual flow when, alone and bored in his American hotel room, he turned on the television set and started to watch the American system of television broadcasting (1974: 91). The continual presentation of material – pro-grammes, commercials and promotions – was rendered seamless rather than sequential by the interspersing of the shorter within the longer seg-ments, and it was the relentlessness of this and his own powerlessness in face of it that seemed to affect Williams most. Of course, this was in the days before remote control devices and VCRs, and one of the most telling modulations of the concept of flow has been the recognition that people customize their own flows – as they did, though less insistently, before technological developments came to their aid. Among critics of the monolithic aspects of Williams' conception, who none the less do not wish to reject it completely, the most nuanced are John Ellis and Jostein Gripsrud. Gripsrud argues that flow characterizes the US television system (and academic analysis of it) more than any other, but that distinctions between systems are decreasing (1998: 30–1). Even so, he believes that it is still conventional in the US to disregard individual programmes and to consider television as a flow, while this does not pertain in European countries. He retains the idea of flow as part of his argument in favour of public broadcasting and the ability within such a system to require that the 'flow' be diversely composed (ibid.: 31).

In his first discussion of 'flow', John Ellis acknowledged the problems produced by Williams' conception of the individual programme as the 'natural' televisual form, especially the way that it denies much that differentiates television from cinema (1992: 118). His discussion of the related phenomena relied more on the term 'segment' to describe the way televisual material is constituted and repeated not just *in toto*, as advertisements are repeated, but also generically, as programme segments are repeated through being in series or serial form. And it is for this highly televisual manner of operating that Ellis retained the word 'flow', using it to describe how 'Broadcast TV is characterised by a succession of segments, of internally coherent pieces of dramatic, instructional, exhortatory, fictional, or documentary material' (ibid.: 122). Later, Ellis moved to using the term 'discontinuity' and talking of repetition-in-difference to describe the way that television drama implies the continuing activities of its central characters (1999: 68). His argument that contemporary television is marked by obsessive 'working through' is particularly valuable for the type of programmes considered here, although they are not his immediate concern. Ellis sees 'working through' as the process by which an issue is raised – primarily in a news item – and then processed in other types of television from current affairs to drama, in particular through the mechanism of 'chat', by which he means all kinds of discussion (ibid.: 56–7). 'Chat' allows the worrying away in a number of forums at a matter of concern which eventually brings it under a semblance of control. While this is not formally a feature of 'flow', it does contribute to the ways in which television output is held together despite the sheer quantity of material available for viewers to mix and match to their own tastes. A newsworthy item like the availability of IVF for single mothers and lesbians will be discussed as a political concern on current affairs programmes, as a social issue on talk shows, will be the occasion for a joke in a sketch show and will generate a plot-line for a number of different drama series or serials. It may seem for a week or so as if ethical dilemmas about IVF are omnipresent, televisually and in other media.

It is not just as a contributor to this process that time-of-day shows like ITV's *This Morning* (with or without Richard and Judy, but, as discussed in this book, usually with) are relevant to a discussion of flow. These programmes require a set amount of time to be filled every day, four or five times a week, with a variety of light items, interspersed with presenters' continuity chat and interviews. Individual stories may extend throughout the programme – started, then left for a while, then checked back upon. Ads, and promotions of segments from later in the show and of programmes to come are interspersed, as are pointers to stories later in the week or appeals for people interested in appearing on them. While viewers may, of course, change channels in the course of this or leave the room to do some other activity, the programme itself is structured to resemble a slow graze through a variety of possibilities. Viewers are tempted to stay with the flow of undemanding pleasantness, for even if the current segment fails to engage them the promised consequence of an earlier set-up is due any minute. The flow operates on the longer wave of the presenters and the possible dominant story carrying through the various shorter elements.

A different way in which ordinary television 'goes with the flow' is evidenced in the practice noticeable with Australian lifestyle shows which are often screened in pairs, so that 30 minutes of *Better Homes and Gardens* goes straight into *Hot Property*, with the credits and contact details given only at the end of the second show. With these instances, the ads, especially those by the sponsors, are generally domestic and may be hard to distinguish from the programme material. While instances this obvious may only occur a few times a week, it is rare for a piece of ordinary television, especially a 30-minute one, to be scheduled alone. An hour appears to be the smallest acceptable unit of ordinary television. The shift from ordinary television programme to drama or news is not part of a seamless flow, but, except for public broadcasting channels where the flow is always more jarring, the constancy of the ads and trailers smooths the shifts.

Both flow and liveness speak of one of the most salient features of television: its use of, and relation to, time. Mitigating the extent to which it is proper to talk of the flow of television is the way television segments the day into television-friendly units – half hours and hours, or, rather, given the dominance of the commercial system, the television hour (48–52 minutes). The British habit of starting programmes off the hour or half hour except in prime-time seems odd to those from other English-speaking countries, where the near uniformity of temporal organization in 30-minute blocks of programme plus ads plus channel IDs continues to be mapped onto the hour and the half hour, despite the frequency of overruns. Programmes become located with a fixity that may seem supra-temporal, as if it is only 7 pm because *Sale of the Century* starts, or as if it was (until late 1998) midday in Australia because the programme *Midday* occurred then. When, early in 1999, ITV decided to move the *News at Ten*, a national campaign was launched to reassure viewers that it would be possible for life to continue informed and ordered despite the shift. Pay-channel Sky took the opportunity to appeal to viewers unsettled by the change by announcing that it would take over the ten o'clock news slot. (ITV wanted to change the timeslot because of a televisual imperative – the desire not to interrupt the evening movie.)

Although the publicity was pitched at retaining old viewers and attracting new ones, it was obvious from the public discussion that the shift was not a minor matter. Just how serious it was seen to be was revealed a little over a year later when the commercial television regulator, the Independent Television Commission, ordered ITV to reinstate the evening news to the 10 pm slot because the move had broken the public service commitment to provide news services to viewers. Oddly, this was prompted by a drop in ratings for the ITV main broadcast news, rather than any major increase in complaints. Viewers anxious for news services at particular times were catered for not only by the Sky service, but by several 24-hour news channels. ITV itself started one of these at almost the same time as it decided to challenge the ITC decision by calling for a judicial review of the regulator's power to make directions about schedules. The shifts in televisual verities being brought about by the growth of satellite and cable services, including the power of the regular timeslot to order the viewer's diurnal routine, have certainly become notable, even if they have not (yet) rendered the importance of the link between television and time void.

Scheduling is a practice that is concerned to maximize channel revenues by placing programmes in the 'right' spot, and that involves allocating time in terms of the persistent perception of the viewers as grouped in households which include children. The more costly home and garden shows are screened in the early evening with raunchier chat shows coming later and quiz and game shows earlier. Specialized cable channels challenge this but do not eliminate it, as their audiences are usually too small to make figures for individual shows all that significant. As one shifts countries, however, what had seemed natural in scheduling is revealed as shockingly arbitrary. The premier talk shows, so obviously a part of the early afternoon in Australia, occur mid-morning in the UK.

Another aspect of television that is linked to time is repeats. A programme seen once may be rescheduled days, months or even years later. This is primarily the case for dramas or for documentaries; it is rare for ordinary television, except for cooking shows which are easily and commonly repeated. With this exception, in Australia it is unusual for ordinary television ever to be repeated, but in the UK programmes may be repeated within the week – people who had missed, say, *Tomorrow's World* on its first evening showing, could catch up with it in the afternoon a few days later. (The SBS programme *The Movie Show* is one of the few Australian programmes to follow this practice.) These comments and those which follow relate to free-to-air television; pay channels, especially lifestyle ones, happily repeat ordinary television programmes of all kinds. An alternative ordinary television practice, is for particular programmes to be reframed with additional material for much later re-broadcast. Thus *Ground Force Revisited* replays much of an initial garden makeover of a previous year before checking on what has happened since. Chat shows may be partially recycled through the incorporation of 'favourite' segments in anniversary editions or obituary tributes. Apart from the rare *Making of ...* show, replays of game shows seem improbable and it is worth pondering why this may be so. My suspicion is that it is linked to liveness. While the illusion of liveness provides that the outcome is unknown, there is pleasure in watching a contestant win or lose; once the outcome has been decided – which occurs at the moment of reception, not recording – there is no pleasure there to be gained. The viewer who, having learned the answer from an earlier viewing, shouted it out to impress friends, would certainly be held to be cheating if unmasked. It is liveness, so much more a feature of ordinary television than it is of drama or documentary, that ties it more to 'real' time. As a final example of this point, it may well be marketing imperatives that lead actors in newly released films or plays due to open in the local area to appear on chat shows, but the provision of information just when the viewer is choosing for what to buy a ticket contributes both to the profitability of the film or play and the apparent timeliness of the programme.

Of perhaps greater moment in the link of time and television is the way in which Silverstone argues that television has a ritual function (1994: 18–23). Its place in our daily routine is one of the ways in which he believes it contributes to our sense of security (19). This is, in part, what I was referring to earlier with the anxieties over the shifting of *News at Ten*. But as well as its place in the diurnal or weekly 'taken for granted seriality ... of everyday life' (ibid.: 20), television marks older or longer time-frames – for what is so solidly a technological phenomenon, the seasons might seem an unlikely influence, yet they do impact, and on more than just gardening shows. As winter comes, television viewing increases and so the more expensive programmes are screened to offset their greater cost through their anticipated popularity and hence the amount that can be charged for advertising. Silverstone notes the importance of calendar time to televisual practices and notes some national variation, but, struck by hemispheric chauvinism, fails to acknowledge seasonal modulations. Christmas brings festive celebrations that are evident on television throughout the predominantly, or residually, Christian countries, but the reduced viewing occasioned by summer and its attendant holidays in the southern hemisphere means that Australian programme-makers invest less (and screen imported, snow-filled Christmas drama programmes more). Ordinary television, though, with its cheaper production costs and its stress on liveness, and thus the heightened relevance of real world events, moves into celebratory mode regardless of hemisphere – craft instructors show how to make holly wreaths, financial advisers talk of planning holiday spending, game shows break out the reindeer props and chat shows invite Santa Claus.

Stephen Heath's argument about television and time is a little different. So far from being used to help viewers reduce anxiety, television, in Heath's view, is much more antagonistic, consuming time and forcing its pace – 'time needs to be filled and accelerated, as much time *made* as possible' (1990: 278, [original emphasis]). He notes the importance of deadlines to game shows where racing against the clock is commonplace. There would be further evidence were he writing about it today. Improbable as it may seem, lifestyle programmes now operate to deadlines: *Changing Rooms*, *Ground Force* and the like require their makeovers to be accomplished in two days flat and make much of the difficulties the self-imposed time limit creates; British cooking competitions, from the light-hearted *Ready, Steady, Cook* to the life-or-death seriousness of *Masterchef*, demand tight timekeeping and feature countdowns. Narratology has long been aware of the usefulness of deadlines for delivering tight stories and intensifying reader engagement, but this is not Heath's explanation for what he calls the 'panic around time' (ibid.: 278). Instead, he sees it as part of an insistent production of 'forgetfulness, not memory, flow, not history' (279). The relevance of deadlines to flow is certainly high; as time ticks away the viewer is sped onward through the programme, but, to my mind, any panic occasioned is the channel executive's, brought about by the possible loss of the viewer to another channel. Quickening urgency and the knowledge that an outcome will be delivered if only the viewer stays, is a panic over time, but the time is that of the viewer's attention.

The late 1990s development of reality game shows like *Big Brother*, *House from Hell* or *Survivor* imported the longer time-frames and 'cliff-hangers' of serial drama into the reality game show, derived in part, as noted earlier, from the kind of reality TV that focused on the work of emergency services, shows that Corner has called dramas of 'bodily risk and bodily threat' (2000b: 687) and that themselves relied on constant races against the clock. Reality game shows also customarily use deadlines, but the one that really counts is at the end of the series. Like the deadlines within the individual programme, the purpose is to retain viewers across the run of the series and maximize ratings. The production of these programmes may be seen as responses to the proliferation of programme choices offered to viewers and the decline of the power of loyalty and ritual behaviour to determine which choice is made. Australian survey data from 2001 revealed that only 36 per cent of programmes tuned into are watched in their entirety (Dale, 2001: 32). Game shows are still scheduled at the same time every weekday and lifestyle ones offered every Tuesday at 8 pm for those who appreciate such regularity, but younger viewers, in particular, need more reason than habit to return to, or stay with, a show.

One can read the double passage of television time as one in which the individual programmes within the daily schedule of free-to-air broadcasting operate one kind of seriality, one kind of flow, sometimes speeding up with a deadline, sometimes slowing down for a rhapsodic travelogue sequence, against the weekly plod of the schedule where Wednesday brings an abundance of lifestyle programming before Thursday returns viewers to drama. The regularity which they both provide supports Silverstone's feeling that television can function formally to enhance personal security. Obviously, this does not describe the experience of the obsessive surfer, with extensive pay services connected, whose security is more likely to be enhanced by a multiplicity of choice than by a high level of predictability. Problems, however, arise for both categories of viewer when the regularity of what is offered is upset. The most extreme version of this comes with a catastrophe that can take over the schedule.

Patricia Mellencamp takes this into account in her consideration of the relationship of television to anxiety, where her position is very different from Silverstone's. For her, 'anxiety is television's affect'; the routine and the repetition do not so much order chaos as await its eruption. 'TV time of regularity and repetition, continuity and "normalcy", contains the potential of interruption, the thrill of live coverage of death events' (1992: 80). Yet she is aware of the contradictoriness of the simultaneity of continuity and the potential for eruption; most of the time television is concerned with regularities not catastrophes, and most catastrophe coverage is contained within news programmes which operate much more, as Silverstone suggests, to show chaos contained. In the way that the gossip (or even the comedy) that Mellencamp later examines may begin as a catastrophic eruption but be neutralized through repetition, so the catastrophes she examines, through their continual recapitulation eventually exhaust the viewer's capacity to remain interested. From being glued to the set for the first day of the Gulf War, viewers happily allowed themselves to be satisfied by intermittent news updates only days later in a shift that demonstrates the power of Ellis' conception of 'working-through'. Catastrophe and the threat of death is not the only kind of interruption to which regular programming is subject; there is a range of special event television which, while it includes disasters, also involves celebrations in the shape of award nights or charity specials and sports spectaculars.

As I have already intimated, I regard ordinary television as constituted in opposition to special television, whether that is seen as a TV special or, in Dayan and Katz's term, a media event (1992). Whether it is Olympic Games, Red Nose Day telethon or celebrity funeral, or even the disaster marathons that Tamar Liebes discusses (1998), at the core of the special programme is that it is out of the ordinary. It is as much a characteristic of special television that it disrupts regular scheduling, as it is of ordinary television that it constitutes it.

Stanley Cavell's discussion of the unexceptional character of events in the histories of ordinary people illuminates the distinction; it is not that there is an absence of events in the lives of ordinary people (or, one might add, ordinary television), rather that the regularity of these events is of a different order from the exceptional events that are held to comprise a more traditionally constituted form of history. Cavell decides it is most illuminating to refer to the alternative as *uneventful* and notes how it is 'an interpretation of the everyday' (1996: 258). The parallel with the uneventful concerns of ordinary television and the eruption of special event coverage is not complete, since there are many other types of programming (drama, news and sport in particular) which fall between these extremes, but I want to retain the idea of the uneventful as a valuable synonym for the ordinary. It clarifies the programme exclusions I have effected to note how many – news and sport especially – are marked by being considered 'events' and, at least in certain ways, exceptional. It needs to be stressed that it is the televisual aspect which is uneventful. For the individual who does win one million dollars on a game show it is undeniably an important event and decidedly out of the ordinary. For those engaged in watching this happen, however exciting they may find it for an hour or a day, it is still uneventful and parallels Cavell's comment that the oddity of referring to the birth of a child as 'a blessed event' lies in its being considered an 'event' (ibid.: 256).

More precisely than just through absence, through not being special or an event, ordinariness is located in three aspects of television: in the mundanity of its concerns, in the style of presentation and in the people included within the programme. Ordinary television requires the similarities between the worlds of the programme and the viewer to be stressed, and all three aspects contribute to this. This is very much in contrast to news and current affairs or drama, where the depicted worlds are more distant – unknown and dangerous, glamorous or, at least, far more exciting (in Lefebvre's terms 'denying everydayness') – and the distinction between the viewer and the televised material is maintained.

MUNDANITY

To discuss the three areas in which television programmes exhibit their ordinariness, I begin with the mundanity of their concerns. Infotainment programmes concentrate on the domestic – home, garden, food, clothing, with occasional excursions into leisure through looking at holidays, some of which are not completely unachievable. Domestic concerns are also called on to render more ordinary what might seem 'escapes' from the mundane. Cooking programmes are a televisual staple, but especially in the UK the ambit of food programmes has broadened. The preparation and presentation of a dish is often no longer the end point of the programme; it may well be that it is used to emphasize the ordinariness of a different situation. Thus ITV's *Dishes* inserted cooking into a dating programme (as the basis on which the choice of who to date was made). The sex, romance and living habits which were the topics explored over the food preparation were rendered even more mundane than usual by the setting. Channel 4's *Late Lunch with Mel & Sue* instituted as routine an occasional aspect of many daytime programmes and other chat shows – the preparation of a dish by a celebrity. Being able to cook and being willing to share (the sight of) this with the audience, here signifies the ordinary side of the celebrity.

It is characteristic of coverage of stars or celebrities that the questions asked by interviewers move them towards us as much as they move them away (Turner et al., 2000). Celebrities' presence on chat shows is usually motivated by the desire to promote the latest product, be it book, CD or film, but in the chat with the presenter which makes this less stark, attention usually shifts to the ordinary aspects of the celebrity's life – family, likes and dislikes – in conjunction with experiences of a life so different from our own. The majority of celebrity houses visited in the celebrity panel show *Through the Keyhole*, and the objects on which the camera focuses (mugs, books, posters, bicycles) exemplify their closeness to us rather than their distance. When they appear on game shows, a variation of this applies, since frequently their mere presence on something so ordinary as a game show, doing the kind of things we could do ourselves, signals their ordinariness.

Although the number of food programmes and cooking segments in the general morning or afternoon shows has grown, especially in the UK, in the last few years, the major growth area for ordinary television has been in the number of programmes based on the fabric of the home and/or garden. The ostensible aim of most of these programmes is the visual improvement of the area, but this does not negate the way that the focus of investigation is on mundane domestic arrangements. Pet-based shows which (perhaps unsurprisingly) are screened to a much greater extent in the UK than elsewhere are part of this concentration on the domestic mundane through their concern with domestic animals, but their narrative focus is rarely on the ordinary – the pets are ill, in distress or neglected, as titles like *Animal Hospital* or *Pet Rescue* make obvious. It is rather the segments on pets within other infotainment shows – like the 'road tests' of pet suitability in Channel 9's *Burke's Backyard* – that present pets as just another element of domestic life.

Away from the obvious domesticity of most infotainment programmes, the social problem-based, confessional talk shows are conventionally regarded as of their essence bizarre, but the centrality of personal relationships to the issues they explore means that no matter the extremities of the day's particular relationship problem, the terms of the discussion – sex, family and the limited conception of ethical behaviour that is usually drawn upon – keeps the more ordinary part of the extra-ordinary displayed in the centre of the screen. Solving the problem or berating its exhibitor most often involves validating ordinary 'normal' behaviour. Furthermore, the extent to which both popular and academic criticism of talk shows stresses the social (usually sexual) problems in their discussion of content overlooks the way most talk shows spend time each week on much more mundane matters through their recourse to segments where the 'problem' is people who wear clothing inappropriate to their size or age, and the 'solution' is calling on 'image consultants' to make them over and produce a less 'extreme' appearance. Even greater mundanity is possible: *Oprah* has featured an item on orthopaedically correct bedding, which tried to persuade audience members to part with their old, but beloved, pillows; the no-longer-running BBC show *Vanessa*, in a celebration of medical personnel, has had two doctors compete at making hospital corners on a bed.

The terms by which reality game shows are discussed similarly lead one to conceive of them as distant from the mundane, yet the premise of many of them begins squarely in the mundane itself. *Big Brother* immures its contestants in a house and tests their abilities at dealing with boredom and the foibles of their housemates more than it exhibits their abilities to perform the tasks set each week. Many others, like *Flatmates* or *House from Hell*, similarly focus on people's abilities to cohabit. Although *Survivor* or *Treasure Island*, or others based on isolating people in unfamiliar surroundings, start far from the mundane, they rapidly come down to mundane matters of performing a range of daily maintenance tasks and negotiating relationships with one's fellows. The call on 'reality', while on the one hand referring to the non-fictional aspect of the programmes' design (supporting their industrial name 'unscripted television'), also signals the way in which, for the majority of formats, the basic set-up involves taking an ordinary situation and twisting it in some way.

More traditional game shows are much more clearly dominated by mundane concerns. I have elsewhere discussed how contestants are required in the introductory chat to place themselves in terms of what they do, where they live and often also in terms of their family situation (Bonner, 1992: 240). In the further chat which interrupts the question-and-answer segments, those contestants who have not been eliminated are asked for more information, and it is the family details that are most often elaborated upon. When contestants on the current quiz success *Who Wants to be a Millionaire?* phone a friend for assistance, the host asks them for details about the person called, identifying the connection through family or sporting club. Game show questions, too, especially now that *Mastermind* is gone, are likely to focus on ordinary concerns like popular music, common expressions and recent news events. *Who Wants to be a Millionaire?* is a fine example here, too, since although the degree of difficulty of the questions increases as the amounts at stake grow, the majority of the questions asked in the course of the show are the easier ones and they rarely stray into anything more esoteric than very popular national history.

PRESENTATION

The second aspect in which ordinariness is evident is in terms of presen-

filmed (in the studio, on location or a mix of both), the presence or absence of a studio audience and the figure of the presenter. Most ordinary television is studio-based; apart from holiday shows, the principal exception is the home or garden shows, and these now focus overwhelmingly on the properties of ordinary people. Studio sets frequently mimic sections of living-rooms, of varying domestic detail but never very far upmarket. Sets of shows made for particular times of the day modulate as some assumed diurnal pattern is traced, but since the room mimicked is usually that in which the main household television set is believed to be located, this is effected not so much by a shift in what pieces of furniture are evident, as it is in terms of formality – breakfast shows are presented from more casual sofas than those used later in the day. The bed which featured in Channel 4's *The Big Breakfast*, which signalled its difference from shows aimed at older viewers, was merely a more extreme example of this practice. But not all ordinary television is amenable to such illusions of domesticity. A casually dressed studio audience is often the nearest a game show's set comes to being domesticated, since unlike breakfast shows, for example, quizzes do not have domestic referents, but rather occur in pubs or in school halls, echoes of both of which locations can often be noted in desks, display boards or fruit-machine-style props.

Presenters need to convey at least an appearance of ordinariness. Exceptional intelligence or insight must be disguised or disavowed, as must high social status. These may still be found in the more traditional forms of documentary, but only when they can be disguised as eccentricity are small amounts admissible on ordinary television (as Patrick Moore's intelligence was in *The Sky at Night* on the BBC, or as class has been, for example, in Lucinda Lambton's various appearances, or in the *Two Fat Ladies* series). Appearance is more problematic, since gender plays so large a role. A much wider range of types of males are acceptable, though the very good-looking are rarely used; for women (and cooking programmes do provide a number of exceptions here) the range is much smaller and good looks are no disqualification at all. In this, the social demands on women to make themselves attractive at all costs (to their health, their free time, their bank balance) continue and flow seamlessly into the many instances of personal makeovers which pervade ordinary television and are usually performed on the faces and bodies of women. Presenters' clothes, too, must relate in some ways to viewers', and like the sets, they become a little more formal as the day progresses. With few exceptions, presenters' clothes can only be a little bit smarter or more formal than those that viewers might be assumed to be wearing if they were in public and of that age and shape. The referent in this instance, though, is not the clothes that the viewer might be assumed to

this regard, the separation by which those on television are in public while those watching are in private is undisguised. With very rare exceptions – *Fantasy Football League* comes to mind – presenters need to look sharp.

The reason for all this 'almost' closeness is that presenters are intermediaries between audience and guests and they need to be able to bridge the gap when the guests are other than ordinary, either through being celebrities or through being exceptional in other ways. In chat shows they may have to do this, as Philip Bell and Theo van Leeuwen indicate, simultaneously with indicating that they, too, are privy to the lifeworld of the rich and famous (1994: 196). Thus Michael Parkinson can refer to one celebrity having said another is 'the sexiest man alive', and carry the authority of being on first-name terms with the original speaker, but he can only draw publicly on comments made on the show, in the site shared with viewers. His information needs to appear to come, as ours does, through the media, and, like us, he wants to hear the other side. To maintain this ability of the presenter to ask on our behalf, many entertainment industry-focused shows use a special gossip reporter, like John Michael Howson, to provide insider information, leaving the presenters free to be photographed for other media outlets and to consort with celebrities at premieres and charity extravaganzas, but at the same time to remain an outsider needing information when presenting their own shows.

This same flexible positioning can apply also to the material under consideration. Tony Robinson, the presenter of the popular British archaeology programme *Time Team*, provides a good example here, carrying a public resonance of 'pastness' through his role in the comedy series *Blackadder*, but eternally naive about archaeology and history, despite his initially being suggested as presenter by regular expert and consultant Professor Mick Alston who had met him on an archaeological study weekend. Operating with the same core group of experts across many series, Robinson's lack of knowledge remains comparatively constant, but when presenters deal with different guests on each programme, the extent of their apparent knowledgeability may vary as they seek instruction to encourage one guest to talk more, or, (at times on the very same topic) when a different guest has moved too rapidly over the material for the assumed audience, they may themselves provide information.

Almost certainly, the most highly desired aspect of ordinary television programmes is that they are comparatively cheap to produce. Largely studio-based and, requiring little if anything in the way of post-production and with most of the props and guests able to be supplied by eager promoters, their main cost may well be the presenter's contract. Popular presenters can command significant amounts even when they are not guaranteeing exclusivity, for not only do they attract large followings directly, they can also be used in very thoroughgoing publicity. Even the size of the contract may be itself a promotable item; the shift of Australian comic sports presenting duo Roy and HG from the ABC to the commercial Seven Network was accompanied by speculative articles about how much it had cost. Very popular presenters, like Oprah Winfrey, set up their own production companies with themselves as the principal asset.

Presenters are frequently found as celebrity guests on programmes of a very different genre from their own, either for straightforward promotion or to help manage some bad publicity. This latter can be done apparently indirectly by appearing to be a good sport while presenting their point of view on whatever the issue is to the sympathetic ear of a fellow. ITV's Trisha appeared in this way on *Late Lunch with Mel & Sue* during the controversy over fake guests on British talk shows, though Australian footballing celebrity Sam Newman put his side of a paternity story, not through an ostensibly 'neutral' show but on *The Footy Show*, where he is a regular guest. Presenter mobility is more significant, though, when presenters move across different genres, leaving game shows to present infotainment ones, or doing both at the same time. In such instances the category of ordinary television may be seen to be coherent at an industrial level. This also applies in the morning or afternoon time-of-day shows which frequently contain segments of several different types of ordinary television: infotainment, chat, counselling, variety. Here, it is not so much a matter of presenters crossing the genres, as it is reporters used in these segments continuing to report on the same area later in the day in the stand-alone, prime-time versions, thus acting to tie the worlds of ordinary television together.

One of the key aspects of presentation, indeed for some one of the key characteristics of television as a whole, is the importance of the aural component, especially talk. When we have an opportunity to see archival footage of non-fiction programming from the early days of television, it is likely to be the presenters and their speech that seem most 'quaint', and quite risibly out of date. Words are more distinctly enunciated and the insistence on the distinction between those appearing on the screen and those watching it is much more noticeable. The presenters' formality, and their accents, even more than their costuming and their decorum, make them seem wrong for the medium as it is now. This applies across English-speaking television, even if it is most evident in the disappearance of the Received Pronunciation (RP) British-inflected Australian English spoken on the ABC and, to a lesser extent, on all Australian television until the late 1960s, and in the more recent prevalence of Estuary English or a regional dialect on British television.

So much of television content is structured around talk, from the Address to the Nation down, that it is no surprise that a considerable range of terms is necessary to delineate the range: interview, debate, discussion, vox-pop, chat – but it is the last that most pervades ordinary television, even when what is being conducted would formally be called an interview or a discussion. Ellis' (1999) use of 'chat' to cover all interpersonal interchanges does not apply here. There is a superficiality to the exploration of topics on ordinary television, since both intellectual depth and intense emotion (other than pleasure at whatever transformation television has just brought about) are rare.

What both Ellis and I am referring to here is in part what Norman Fairclough calls 'conversationalization', a move to a more conversational, more everyday language on television (1995: 9). His main concern is with news and related public discourse and he concentrates more on public broadcasting, but the conversationalization he finds evident in those aspects of the media which address the viewer as citizen is noticeable also in the already conversational genres like the quiz or the chat show. Formality is now highly inappropriate for most of the time on non-fiction television and acts as a particular generic marker, saying 'not ordinary television'.

To return to Holland's discussion of ordinary television, she notes that 'the small-scale, domestic medium with its incessant words and images seems more like another group of people in the corner of the room than any sort of demanding cultural [or, even more, political] experience' (2000: 131). It is indeed the point of ordinary television that it is undemanding and just like another group of not particularly special people in the room, and it is this that makes those programmes that are none the less able to maintain an educative role (and, once again, I think *Time Team* provides a good example) so rare and so valuable. (I will explore this further in Chapter 5.)

It is useful to consider the conversational style that permeates ordinary television through the term Paddy Scannell uses for what he calls 'the most fundamental aspect of broadcasting's communicative ethos' – sociability (1996: 23). Sociable interactions, as Scannell, following Simmel, describes them, are unforced, the participants are at ease with one another, and the talk is for talk's sake (22–4). Obviously, it does not describe all of the interactions taking place on ordinary television, but it frames most of them. The questions in a game show are far more purposive, but the interchanges that surround them are sociable, as are the exchanges on a chat show. Some of the difficulties that fuel the intermittent moral panics over talk shows are caused by the absence of sociability from many of the interchanges. Scannell's discussion of sociability as a characteristic of broadcast talk, draws mainly on BBC radio of the pre-television era. He claims that it is marked by equality between the participants because distinction of social status and the like are set aside (22), yet the examples he gives are consistently concerned with homo-genous groups or situations when the interviewer is the only bearer of difference. Although he fails to register this, it should not be seen to negate his point.

Corner talks of 'nosy' or 'snoopy' sociability in his brief discussion of docu-soaps and reality game shows (2000b: 687), and the modulation is valuable, although for him it names the relationship between viewer and programme. *Big Brother* is constructed most clearly around a 'nosy sociability', producers assuming viewers are interested in everything that is going on, for why else would there be so many cameras in so many places, not to mention the 24-hour internet coverage? That such interest is, at heart, sociable is evidenced in the very ordinariness of most of the discussions about the programme and especially in the impression of closeness to the contestants that is built up during the series.

Ordinariness on television is enhanced by a tendency to construct comparatively homogenous groups, – or at least to segregate those whose accents or behaviour signal class too clearly. *House Detectives* and *Masterchef*, with their overwhelmingly middle-class participants, provide a view of a different ordinary world from that in which the British version of *Animal Hospital* or the old darts-based game show *Bull's Eye* occur, but the terms on which the discussions are enacted are the same – sociability means that any conflict or disagreement must be glossed over and preferably resolved with a joke. The only break from this that is pos-sible occurs when the expert gives instruction, and this is as likely to occur in the middle-class as in the working-class-populated programmes. For the most part, though, class is rendered as invisible as possible. With few exceptions, everyone is treated as if their situation and opportunities resembled everyone else's. In this way Hartley's conception of television as suburban, middle-brow and middle class may well have point. People are identified more by their placement in families than by their employment, and distinctive cultural activities are treated more as hobbies. Their politi-cal or religious beliefs are as taboo as they would once have been at middle-class dinner parties. Sociability allows no place for differences that really matter and sociability is a primary value for ordinary television.

This is also significant in the way in which viewers are addressed – in terms of an assumed individuality based on domestic interests and their involvement in the programme itself. Robert Stam introduced the concept of the 'fictive "we"' to discuss the production of an illusion of community on television news (1983: 39), but it is far more evident in ordinary television. The presenter who announces 'We'll be back in three' speaks primarily for the programme and the personnel associated with it. But 'we' can be much more presumptive, including the audience in a quite emphatic way. When Don Burke tells us that 'we' will next see a particular garden or plant, as long as we stay with the programme, that is exactly what we see. It is 'we' who are told that we will immediately see how the date generated by *Dishes* goes, though the to-camera report of the people involved is addressed to the presenter. The reason for this distinction is that 'real' ordinary people on television cannot make claims for knowledge of the programme and its audience and cannot actually address their compatriots at home (except for the 'hi mom' which signals ignorance of, or disregard for, proper televisual behaviour). They must use the intermediary of the presenter. 'We' is fictive indeed. Hierarchies are not really done away with; ordinary people are certainly subordinate to those with regular televisual presence.

THE PEOPLE INVOLVED

Ordinary people do not have to be present on screen for a programme to be ordinary television – the preceding characteristics are enough – but it is still far more likely for ordinary people to be present, at least in the audience, where they can be shown enjoying themselves, whether or not they are called on to enter more fully into the programme. They are free set-dressing, free talent, eager to appear. Indeed, when the cult Australian political panel show *Good News Week*, the format of which is loosely based on the British *Have I Got News for You*, went on tour, audiences paid to see it recorded. Game show contestants are far more often ordinary people than celebrities and the ordinariness of those whose homes or gardens are made over is a requisite. It is probably now more ordinary to have been on screen (in a studio audience at least) than not. In one sampled episode of *Dishes*, two of the three young men cooking to win the date had prior experience of being television talent – but then dating game shows prefer, even require, the extrovert who is able to be at ease in the studio. An early contestant on the British *Who Wants to be a Millionaire?* announced his desire to have appeared on television before his thirtieth birthday which was due the following week. It was advanced and received as a very modest wish.

The media industry uses the term 'talent' not, as might be surmised, to refer to the professionals appearing on camera (though it can be used for anyone other than regular performers), but to the amateur appearing with them. What is here termed an ordinary person is there termed talent and the term indicates, since not everyone is good talent, that ordinariness is not enough. The 'talent' may be a professional in her or his own field, appearing as an expert; a person with a good memory, fast reflexes and calm nerves who will not go to pieces on a quiz show; or a bubbly eccentric who can enthuse about the virtues of alternative health therapies on a lifestyle programme. But, regardless of this, their prime ability is to project a personality on television; without it they have neither talent nor presence. This reminder that some are more usefully ordinary than others should put a dampener on any temptation to perceive ordinary television as necessarily a democratizing force.

The development of the docu-soap was one in which documentary television was made more ordinary. The people followed were special only in as much as they were being filmed going about their ordinary business for television. The sites in which docu-soaps are filmed may be special (an airport, a cruise ship, a zoo) but the people are not. Andrew Bethell, managing director of Double Exposure, a British company producing a range of factual television, has spoken of the desirability of setting docu-soaps in places that make 'a direct connection with what the majority of the potential audience have experienced', citing one about a large shopping centre as well as, arguably, the most successful example, *Airport* (1999: 14). Here it is not just the people focused upon who are like those viewing, but those passing by as well.

Ordinary television plays a very important role in the fulfilment of what Stam calls television's 'inbuilt need to flatter the audience' (1983: 27). Stam writes of the importance of television's being 'watched out of desire ... in the hope that it will please' (ibid.: 39). Concerning itself with ordinary matters, asserting the centrality of the domestic and the familial operates to do this, as does placing people who spend most of their time relating to television as viewers up there on the screen. Ordinary television with its incessant solicitations for participation does not say 'This is what you can dream about, this you should aspire to', as much as 'Come on, why aren't you here already?'

CONSUMPTION

The genre that is arguably at the centre of the category ordinary television and, as I argued in the previous chapter, also signals most strongly the demise of the 'educate, inform and entertain' rubric is infotainment, revealing in its hybridized name not only the combination of the latter two words of the phrase but also the eradication of the first. Jeremy Tunstall argued in 1993 for the usefulness of the term 'edinfotainment' to maintain the presence of education, but the 'deliberately awkward' term (Tunstall's own comment, 1993: 80) achieved no currency. Even within his own chapter on the category, Tunstall used the term 'mixed programme' far more often. John Dovey has commented on the '[t]idal waves of entertainment [that] have flooded into discursive zones previously reserved for education, information and enlightenment' (2000: 7). Enlightenment has rarely been discussed as a basic function of television, but education certainly was, though it is no longer a televisual activity apart from those specifically designated distance-education programmes which have not so far been displaced onto the internet.

Robert Allen's argument about television operating a gift economy is a valuable way to explore the recent rise in infotainment and the way it relates to other genres included in ordinary television. He focuses on free-to-air commercial channels, explaining the relationship between viewers and the compound of channel and the advertisers who make the operation possible, as founded on the 'gift' of the programme to the viewer who responds by attending to the advertisement. Ideally, this response is actualized with the purchase of the product (1992: 119–20). With the wide dispersal of remotes and VCRs and the consequent breakdown of such an economy as impolite gift recipients zap away from, or zip through, their side of the implied relationship, channels can respond to maintain the economy only by synchronizing their commercial breaks and, indeed, their general scheduling, or by incorporating products into the programmes themselves. Ordinary television, with its many inclusive practices, is ideally placed for this latter activity. Throughout the day and for significant sections of early evening prime-time, ordinary television returns the gift economy to large sections of broadcast television, while some cable channels, usually with a variant of 'lifestyle' in their names, base their entire content on it.

This is taken even further in Australia with the development of masthead programmes which are infotainment television produced in conjunction with glossy magazines and provided to channels under a form of barter system, whereby channels are provided with the programmes without charge and, in their turn, provide free advertising for the magazine, making a profit from the sale of 'spare' advertising during the programme's running time. The practice has been growing in popularity in Australia since the mid-1990s; *FCTV* was the televisual version of *Family Circle*, while *Better Homes and Gardens*, like *Good Medicine*, names both the magazine and the television show. There are magazines linked to television programmes in the UK – *The Clothes Show Magazine* was an example – but they do not (as yet) seem to have the same barter relationship that masthead ones do.

While the system is differently constituted for public broadcasting funded primarily by licence- or tax-payers, it is not easy to see all that much difference in programme content. There are several reasons for this, and all relate to changes in the operation of broadcasting systems internationally. For the English-speaking world, only in the UK has there been any period when public broadcasting set the terms of operation. Public television now must commission much of its programming from independent production houses whose ethos is attuned to the more profitable commercial sphere. Furthermore, foreign sales have become highly important to public broadcasters expected to provide more of their budget from their own activities. While this is most evident in the production of drama programmes timed to accommodate the 'commercial hour' (that is to allow for advertisements), it is relevant to ordinary television too. The result is that it is difficult to tell from internal evidence whether a programme has been made to be screened on public or commercial channels. Even the extent to which product information is available on-screen during infotainment programmes is an unreliable indicator; more details are given on BBC's *Ground Force* than on ITV's *Carol Vorderman's Better Homes*. Nor is there a necessary variation for less populist public broadcasting programmes; arts review programmes provide an upmarket equivalent of the kind of cultural consumption advocated in chat shows.

It is not only infotainment programmes which re-insert the gift economy into television content, game shows have long shifted product promotion into the programme itself. The restraint imposed in the UK for many years by restrictions on the size of prizes was eased, as were many others, following the waves of deregulation, thus ensuring that unforseen consequences for advertising of the technological changes of the VCR and the remote control were able to be countered by regulatory and legislative changes to maintain the really important components of the television system, the promotion of products and services. In the analysis of the international success achieved by *Who Wants to be a Millionaire?*, little attention has been paid to the innovation of a quiz show which does not display material objects as prizes; but this, in its own way, is the most radical aspect of the programme.

While not (quite) all ordinary television is involved overtly in product promotion, to infotainment and game shows – the more consumer-oriented of my category – must be added chat shows which concentrate on conversations with product promoters (including celebrities) and reality game shows where product placement is substantial. To say that ordinary television is concerned with the construction of consumers, though, is to state the obvious. Perhaps it is still possible to be too blatantly consumerist. While segments of morning shows suggest gifts at Christmas time or near St Valentine's Day, and the Shopping Channel makes no pretence of its raison d'être, the 1997 Australian programme *What on Earth*, called a shopping advice show, was decidedly short-lived. Its producer justified it, by analogy with cooking or gardening advice programmes, as necessary because parents were too busy to pass on such basic domestic knowledge to their children. Viewers paid it no attention.

CELEBRATING THE MEDIUM ITSELF

Certain types of ordinary television are not so heavily marked by consumerism and one very telling alternative involves the celebration of the televisual medium itself. There is a variety of ways in which this celebration is conducted: game shows based on archival footage like the ABC's *Flashback* or the BBC's *Today's the Day*; light television history programmes with titles that are variants on 'Where are they now?'; hagiographic, behind-the-scenes specials on current television performers; and other variously composed clip-shows. The reason for such a wealth of programmes based overwhelmingly on old or foreign television may be because watching television is so much an ordinary part of the lifeworld, or it may be no more than the ready, and cheap, availability of the raw material. These compilation shows can be seen quite straightforwardly to celebrate the medium, but clip-shows and video diaries should also be seen as doing a similar thing.

Clip-shows were one of the growth areas of the 90s; a potent sign of cheap television, they recycle already existing video and have as their principal cost the payment of a presenter to direct a preferred response. The tone of the clip-show presenter is most commonly a little tired and very cynical. It assumes a shared response from viewers, thereby disarming criticism of the opportunism of repackaging through a display of insider status. The presenter can set up a fictive and knowledgeable 'we' who are far more sophisticated than the strange foreigners whose television programmes or advertisements we are encouraged to deride. The clips are generally of three kinds: one recycles surveillance video of ordinary people (*World's Worst Drivers*); another recycles professional television product (whether in the game shows and light history programmes noted above or compilations of more contemporary material, from commercials to aggressive wildlife film); and the last encourages ordinary people to become producers of video comedy (various countries' funniest home videos). This last indicates another way in which ordinary television can bring viewer and medium together, through production.

Although for *Australia's Funniest Home Video* it is done deep in denial, this programme, like the Australian documentary film-making competition *Race Around the World* and those programmes which give more ordinary members of the public camcorders to produce diverse kinds of content, whether that be for Channel 4's *The Real Holiday Show* or the video diary proper (the ABC's *Home Truths* or BBC's *Video Nation*), rest on a truly different way of incorporating the ordinary person into the programme – through admitting their technological proficiency. Not that one can homogenize such programmes to too great an extent. The *Home Truths* family who filmed their attempts to set up a toy shop in provincial Victoria, as well as Olivia Rousset winning the first *Race Around the World* (before moving immediately into professional production), are both instances of 'us' becoming one of 'them', neither fictive nor 'we'. 'Real' members of the viewing public, given the tools of production, in addition to the permission to appear on screen with the professionals, are capable of producing a more formal, as well as a quite casual, product. In doing so, they show the extent of the control over the ordinary person on TV, especially when they are set against those whose amateur video is screened only if it reveals the mishaps or humiliations of being ordinary, and even then with its humour 'claimed' by the professional doing the voiceover, as is the case with *Australia's Funniest Home Videos*. Those producing the visuals on this programme are seen only on the final episode of the year, where, if they have received a prize, they are allowed to thank the sponsor. The game show contestant or the vox-pop chatting to an interviewer in the street has more freedom than this. *Race* and video diary programmes, on the other hand, are important in showing ordinary people transfigured by holding the technology as well as being the talent, but we must remember that a careful selection process has preceded their being given such access. In the majority of cases access is limited and control over self-presentation restricted, both through professional retention of editing and encouragement to behave 'badly' to be more entertaining.

Even though cynicism dominates the tone of programmes celebrating the medium, those that are made fully within the profession can exhibit other tones. Surely the most respectful is the much formatted *This Is Your Life*, a programme which, since it requires cinematic or televisual footage, is given to celebrating the careers of television personalities. This, like the promotional *Making of ...* show (more common for films but also evident for television), and blooper and foreign television clip-shows, ostentatiously brings viewer and medium closer together by demystifying production and tying down television history. They represent a television world in which the past was invariably naive and the foreign, bizarre. But *This Is Your Life* takes both itself and the ordinary very seriously indeed. It stresses the ordinary domesticity of the person focused upon, as their old teachers, co-workers and relatives appear and reminisce. Over-determined as ordinary by its tracing of common life events which, as the person 'honoured' is invariably some sort of celebrity, are designed to show the 'authentic' person *behind* the celebrity, this programme is never cynical and it even has something of a formal mode of address with a referent outside the televisual world. The pompous reading of the life history from the totemic red book is offset by the familiarity of the greetings of family and friends and also by its echo of the delivery style of the untrained master of ceremonies at the many celebratory functions that punctuate the ordinary non-televisual life – farewells, school and sporting club awards night etc. In a typically circular fashion, the format has been taken back into the everyday life-world and organizations like these at times now structure events to mimic *This Is Your Life* more precisely.

FORMATTING

Unlike drama (in the UK and Australia at least), ordinary television is rarely imported; it is far more common for local versions to be developed from a licensed format. This is especially the case with game shows which are the programme type most commonly considered to be made to a format. It is rarer for magazine-style shows, especially of the info-tainment type, to be developed to a franchised format, since the structure of the programme – a sequence of segments, usually of varying length – is common across many programmes on varying topics, and individual distinctiveness is likely to be found only in the personality of the presenter. Albert Moran has noted the extremely weak legal basis on which formatting operates (1998: 15–17). Only when some kind of through narrative is evident (as with the interior decorating makeover programme *Changing Rooms*) is there sufficient distinctiveness for it to be worth the while of the producers to buy the format. As Moran notes, this is done both to protect the new producers from the possibility of legal action and, if it is available, to gain access to the production materials and even the consultancy services associated with the original (1998: 19–23). Using a proven outline, customized to local conditions and calling on local personnel, reduces the risk of failure (as well as lawsuits for passing off or breach of copyright).

Acting as a significant bar to importation or to cross-border transmission when different linguistic communities are receivers is the fact that most ordinary television is speech-based. As David Morley and Kevin Robins note (following Ien Ang and Liebes and Katz, all working on *Dallas*), successful exported programmes in these situations should not be speech-based; if they are, they need to be polysemic or multi-accentual (1995: 64). This helps to explain why the ordinary, both speech-based and comparatively singular, is ill-suited to importation but well-placed for formatting. Only the most impoverished television systems import game shows and examining this can extend our understanding of the factors involved in formatting. Why might it be that watching unknown people from your own country answer general knowledge questions posed by a televisually familiar host seems reasonable, while the idea of watching unknown people from a totally different country engaged in answering the same questions asked by a foreign host lacks appeal? Unless the foreign ordinary person is competing directly against the local, there seems no point in watching people from, say, Lyons, who might as well be from Romford or Wollongong. They do not function half as well as our surrogates; they reduce the ordinariness, and more importantly, the connection it is possible to feel with the programmes. Ordinariness implies connection, and while that may no longer also imply the local it certainly still implies the national, on broadcast television at least. On the differently organized pay channels this can differ, as geographic or genre streaming allows imported ordinary shows to be screened for much smaller audiences, as is the case on UKTV in Australia or on lifestyle channels in most countries.

There are two kinds of ordinary programmes that are commonly broadcast in their imported form. The first is the cooking programme, where either the link with tourism or the claim to 'authenticity' based on locale or host increases the value of the 'foreign' product; for example *The Medici Kitchen* which, despite its American origins, was screened in Australia with its Italian host and locale both part of the promotion, or the British *Two Fat Ladies*, which sold widely, more on the presenters' personalities than the tourism content, though the latter did no harm. The other kind of ordinary television to be imported is confessional talk shows from the US. Although British television is now recording a significant number of these, more are imported from the States, especially since these provide more extreme instances of (mis-)behaviour. Australia has so far been unable to produce its own talk shows and screens only imported American ones. Both types of imported programme require a viewing relationship in the importing country based on difference, as the people on-screen are constructed through accent and anecdote as other than the people watching. In this they are quite different from the majority of ordinary television.

In the clip-shows, like *Tarrant on TV*, but associated far more in both the UK and Australia with Clive James, segments of other people's television, frequently other people's ordinary television, are presented precisely for their otherness, for their not being familiar, although anchored by a presenter and a nationalist rhetoric rooted firmly in anglophone culture. They are predicated on 'our' being ordinary and 'our' television being normal, while 'they' (whoever they are) are peculiar. A kind of willed ignorance operates to disavow the possibility of any other nation de-contextualizing and recycling footage of British people sitting in bathtubs of baked beans or custard (for charity, of course) or Australians betting on cockroach races, to the accompaniment of a snide commentary on the national characteristics being exhibited. Yet the worldwide trade in clips (including out-takes and home video) probably approaches that in formats. Many countries buttress their norm of what is ordinary television by deriding the television of foreigners. This is one way in which ordinary television can operate to construct an everyday version of the national against the putative flood of global television.

CONCLUDING CHARACTERISTICS

I want to conclude this first look at ordinary television by returning to the non-professionals upon whose presence and compliance so much of the content is based, and to suggest the existence of what could be conceived as a collusive community, which operates to insert television further into the ordinary everyday. Ordinary television needs ordinary people to agree to collude to produce the appearance of being ordinary. The most obvious examples are those who offer up their friends and relatives to be 'surprised' on the many shows that have this as a starting point, from *Don't Try This at Home* in the UK or *Love Rules* in Australia, to the house or garden makeover shows. To these must be added those who offer themselves up as cases for treatment or as contestants, those who are persuaded to take part by friends (a favourite alibi for dating game shows) and those who become members of studio audiences, whether or not they are chosen for individual attention by the hosts. If one also adds those who phone in, fax or email such shows as use these devices, not to mention those who vote on reality game shows, there results a very sizeable group of people who aid the production of the ordinary on television. The number is slightly reduced by those people who regularly turn up as studio audience members and others who appear more than once on game shows, (though the ones with sizeable prizes try to weed out 'professional' contestants), but even so, it is a substantial number that is directly implicated.

In 1999, a scandal centred on the BBC programme *Vanessa*, exposed a lack of 'authenticity' of talk show guests and ones who appeared repeatedly in different guises. The level of apparent public outrage and the defensive reactions of the television channels (for the scandal soon spread beyond the BBC) indicated how important it was for ordinary people on television to really be 'ordinary'. It also revealed the existence of agencies for those wanting to display their peccadilloes on television, as well as the desperate life of researchers searching for talent to assuage the omnivorous medium. Helen Swords, an assistant producer on *The Big Breakfast*, speaking to Patricia Holland, mentioned how her demonstrated ability at finding 'ordinary people' to appear on television made her a desirable employee (2000: 135).

The omnivorousness of television is well known: programmes are needed 24 hours a day and pay-TV brings more and more channels seeking audiences, but ordinary television also seeks more and more people for its content as well as its home audience. The number of ordinary people required even just by first-release broadcast television is worth contemplating. The British quiz show *Fifteen-to-One* required 75 people a week as contestants, but this is an extreme example and will not be used in the following attempt at an (under-)estimation of the needs of British television. Few game shows operate on less than three contestants per programme and most channels have at least three game shows every weekday. Talk shows vary from two to twelve ordinary participants; the average is probably six, and there are at least five different British-produced such programmes every weekday. Lifestyle and infotainment programmes involving members of the public range widely, but it is safe to say that they call on a minimum of two people, usually a couple, and it would be a rare day that saw a channel have fewer than five such shows. To all this should be added the roughly 20 British television programmes each weekday across the five channels that require studio audiences – and few of these audiences seem smaller than 60. Admittedly, it is common for two editions of a weekly show to be shot back-to-back 're-using' the same studio audience, but even so, this (extremely) rough measure indicates that British television each week (not including the weekend, which operates by different principles) needs 6560 people to volunteer their services in order to make programmes happen. With adjustments for people reappearing and 'off-season' weeks, that still means something like a quarter of a million ordinary people each year turn up 'on the box', and over 20,000 of those have a speaking role.

And this is not just a matter of the desperation of 'filler' programmes; approximately one third of the top-rating UK programmes are ordinary ones (though with the exception of *Who Wants to be a Millionaire?*, the very top-rating programmes are dramas). In Australia, with many fewer locally produced prime-time dramas, ordinary television rates even higher. As a characteristic of television, which is especially prominent in the ordinary variants, to omnivorousness should be added the incestuousness of television (though this is shared with other media forms). Nothing really interests television as much as television itself. The self-referentiality that I talked about for clip-shows is evidence of this too. The final one of these characteristics is a related one – television's self-importance, evident in the way in which appearance on television is offered as itself a prize worth having; think of the numbers of people each episode of *Who Wants to be a Millionaire?* 'wastes' by not calling to the competition desk, either because they did not answer the given question correctly or because they were not fast enough in doing so. All they go away with is the knowledge that they did get named on the screen. Yet it is also ordinary television that is most likely to offer itself as sufficiently important to be able to intercede for the ordinary person – and to be right in its self-estimation. It can reconcile a mother with her estranged child on a talk show, Cilla can find lost relatives, a daytime show consumer investigation segment can harass a delinquent landlord to the point where he finally makes promised repairs. All that is needed is that the individuals concerned give up their private status and become television content. This is not interactive television and it certainly is not access television, but it is a form of television that involves viewers, that calls on ordinary people themselves in its production of a televisual version of the everyday – admittedly one that is more glitzy, more exciting and more special – but still one that is anchored in the mundane.

In the previous chapter I discussed the category of Light Entertainment. Precisely what was included within it, apart from its formal use to describe a division of the BBC, was never completely clear, though variety shows were definitely central. Ordinary television takes over much of the content and virtually all of the connotations of light entertainment; it is popular and it certainly is not prestigious. One could argue that it is unimportant – real television, serious television, television worth writing about is drama or news or current affairs or documentary or special events or even sport. I've chosen to argue otherwise. Not unimportant and, given its cheapness in a time of decreasing television profit margins, and not likely to disappear, ordinary television lets us see just what is regarded publicly as ordinary. Although this will be investigated more fully in Chapters 4 and 5, it is already obvious that the televisual ordinary centres on home and family, holidays and relationships and, of course, mediated entertainment.

The People Involved

In an instruction manual on television performance for would-be news and information personnel (presenters, reporters and subjects), William Hawes observes:

> If your appearance is consistent with your conception of your personal and professional life, then you are indeed fortunate. For many others this consistency is not so obvious and needs some adjustments. You are basically seeking a dominant image that the public will admire and remember. Your image may not, alas, express the true depth and dimension of your soul, but your image is what you are for television purposes. (1991: 12)

The description of information Hawes uses is sufficiently broad that it includes many if not most types of ordinary television. While rather sanctimonious, the point he makes is an important one; what the viewers see is the presenting persona not the person. All the regularly appearing television people that will be discussed here have achieved what Hawes calls the dominant image and though it may modulate over the years, it is very, very rare for its essentials to change and for the person to remain employed. Newly revealed characteristics are interpreted in ways consistent with previously established frames. Cilla Black was a wholesome, down-to-earth, young female singer when she started, and the wholesomeness and the down-to-earth qualities have been called upon throughout her subsequent presenting career, being especially useful when producers in the 1980s were looking for someone who would not look too sleazy while hosting the British version of the Australian dating show *Perfect Match*, retitled *Blind Date* for its British version (and later retitled the same in Australia).

It seems likely that the disconsonance to which Hawes alludes exists quite frequently, but it is relevant only in the chat and gossip that surrounds well-known figures (thus Cilla is talked about as really being far more 'posh' than she appears in her shows). The value, just in terms of self-protection, of having a persona distinct in some ways from one's actual self is revealed by the case of Gilbert Harding. Andy Medhurst has written about how Harding was, probably inadvertently, 'the first paradigmatic television personality' (2000: 264) in the UK. Harding rose to fame in the early 1950s when there was only one television channel and no real conception of what a television personality might be. Although he had been a radio presenter and started presenting television, it was as a panellist on the quiz show *What's My Line?* that he achieved notoriety for his rudeness which came to be seen as his lovable trademark (ibid.: 251). Much of Medhurst's discussion of this is how the rudeness, which was read by adoring viewers as an act, was not something scripted or staged, but part of the actual Harding: 'He wasn't after all enacting a fictional role, but trading on an aspect (however heightened) of his own personal attributes' (264). As he followed what was to become the regular path of a television personality, promoting his programme and his self in off-screen appearances, he carried the rudeness with him, as he would have been obliged to do, even had it not been in his nature. Because it was so early in the development of television, he was significant in the actual creation of the television personality, but he was unprepared for the phenomenon and was made unhappy by having to repeat in interview after interview that his television behaviour was 'not affectation, but simply the way he was made' (ibid.: 252). Now presenters and other television personalities are much more knowing.

When Richard Dyer wrote about light entertainment of the early 1970s, he could still talk about how few performers were products of television itself and how many of the most proficient had radio backgrounds, but, even so, regular television practices had been established. The term 'presenter' does not appear to have been available at that time, since Dyer speaks of 'announcers', 'linkmen' and 'performers', instancing Bob Monkhouse, Hughie Green and Rolf Harris. Speaking of those who had successfully worked out how to address a mass audience configured as individuals or families, he identifies the successful tone as 'a kind of pally, blokeish ... cheerfulness ... a cross between a verbal elbow nudging and a cosy, cooing interest for the mass individual addressed' (1973: 18). Although 'cooing' sounds a wrong note, this continues to describe the mode of address of a large number of those who appear regularly on television in roles which allow them to address viewers directly.

In the founding discussion of the television personality, John Langer differentiated the personality from the cinematic star on a number of dimensions: stars were 'larger than life' while personalities were 'part of life'; a distance is maintained between star and audience while personalities insist on intimacy and immediacy; contact with stars is sporadic and uncertain, with personalities regular and predictable; stars play parts, personalities play themselves; stars are idealized and revered while personalities are experienced as familiar (1981: 355). The bases for the differentiation are evident in the list itself. Television is domestically received, regularly scheduled and repetitive. While Langer noted changes that had occurred in the extent of idealization (and other aspects of distance) of the star – and this has only increased in the period since he was writing – the distinction still pertains. He also notes: 'Television personalities also become anchoring points within the internal world that each programme uniquely establishes in and for itself' (ibid.: 357). We see television personalities so often and their persona is so consistent and coherent that we feel we know them, and in knowing them our entry into the programme they are associated with is made easier and more predictable and our likelihood of remaining for whatever it is that makes them appeal to us – their signature distinctiveness – enhanced.

While there has been little change in the basic characteristics of the television personality, the term itself has faded. 'Celebrity' is now far more common as the word to describe those people whose names and faces are widely recognized beyond their immediate circle and whose activities are of sufficient public interest for stories about them to attract readers and viewers to mass-media outlets. Langer himself moves to using the term in his more recent work (1996, 1998). 'Celebrity' lacks the distinctiveness of 'television personality', since it can be applied to people in many more fields, but in as much as television is still the central communications medium, most celebrities appear there sooner or later, if not as regular performers, then as chat show guests.

In what follows, though, I shall be using 'celebrity' to refer only to one of a number of different roles for on-screen presence in ordinary television. Although many of the people considered are celebrities as well as presenters, for example, they remain presenters on their own shows and only become celebrities when they appear on other people's programmes; the roles and responsibilities are distinct.

The presenters

Presenters are the people who are there to greet us at the beginning of a programme, to smooth us through transitions during it and to bid farewell to us at the end. They provide an important reason for watching a programme, or for refusing to do so. Viewers develop allegiances to particular presenters and follow them from show to show or welcome them back after periods of absence. One of the oldest types of programme ephemera sent by broadcasters to fans writing in to the programme was photographs of the presenters. Although not quite all ordinary television programmes have presenters, the majority do, and so important are they to the form that their names may be part or, at times, all of the title (*Rex Hunt's Fishing Adventures; Carol Vorderman's Better Homes; So, Graham Norton*; though this is most especially the case with talk shows like *That's Esther, Trisha* and, of course, *Oprah*). This gives extra point to the description of most infotainment programmes as 'presenter-led'. When channels cancel or fail to renew programmes hosted by presenters with a large popular following, they may retain them on contract to prevent them taking audiences to other channels. Kerri-Anne Kennerley was moved to unspecified 'special projects' after the cancellation of her Channel 9 programme *Midday*. Tim Ferguson was similarly retained after the failure of the Australian version of *Don't Forget Your Toothbrush*. It seems a variant on the business practice of 'gardening leave'. Both presenters were later found on Channel 10.

There are now probably as many women as men presenting ordinary television programmes, but this is not spread evenly across the types of show. Women are rare as game show presenters, especially for quiz shows. In Australia there had never been a successful instance and in the UK, despite occasional forays by Angela Rippon or Sarah Kennedy, women had rarely broken through from the frivolous games, especially dating ones, where they are perhaps more prevalent than men, to controlling the more serious business of asking factual questions about bodies of intellectual knowledge. Although *Who Wants to be a Millionaire?* is now screened in over 40 formatted versions, only Canada, of the ones I have been able to check, has a female presenter. *The Weakest Link* has changed matters here. So central to the format has Anne Robinson become, that she provides the template on which other countries' presenters are groomed (except for the US version which bought Robinson herself along with the format). Other shows attempting to capitalize on the popularity of 'nasty' presenters and selfish contestants seem to regard women as the obvious people to place in this presenter role. *Greed*, which had a short run in Australia in 2000, used Kerri-Anne Kennerley, and Carol Vorderman has been named as the person to host one of the new ITV shows. In both cases it involves some transformation of the presenting persona, and *Greed's* failure may be seen as, in part, due to Kennerley's problems in adapting. It seems as if the traditional conception of women as bitches is sufficiently resonant to displace the greater traditional link of masculinity and knowledge. The greatest challenge to masculine domination of game show presenting, though, is surely Sue Barker's sucess in presenting *A Question of Sport*.

Traditional gendering can also be seen in the greater tendency for men to host gardening programmes and women advice shows based inside the home. The BBC daytime room makeover programme *Big Strong Girls* is an exception, but it is premised on the oddity of female 'handymen', and uses a male presenter to set this off. The inside/outside, public/private dichotomy probably also explains the dominance of women on talk shows dealing with personal problems and men on chat shows, especially the more prestigious evening ones, dealing with celebrities and the public world.

Presenters speak on behalf of the programmes as a whole; they are embodiments of the programme's ethos and are permitted to speak as the authority which determines its shape and direction. They do not often do this in the first person singular, preferring the plural, 'We sent Anne to investigate this new holiday experience' or 'Phone us to have your say'. Stam's 'fictive we' includes the production team and the on-air person-nel in these instances, but it is spoken by the presenter in almost all instances. Formal power over the programme's composition is the domain of the programme's producer, but such a person is hidden from viewers, and the apparent power is with the presenter (and given the dis-parity in salaries, actual power may at times reside there too). Don Burke, presenter of the long-running Australian gardening show *Burke's Backyard*, ensures tight control by being Executive Producer and head of the producing company of the programme.

All on-screen presenters and most other employed personnel address viewers directly both in their speech and in their look to camera. The direct address aims to establish and maintain an intimacy between pro-gramme and audience, through familiarly binding 'you at home' into the programme in a number of ways. It may be through informing the viewer how to perform some task, through the revealing of snippets of personal information, or through inviting participation vicariously by, for exam-ple, encouraging the answering of game show questions. Andrew Tolson notes of direct address that it operates in a hierarchy above indirect address (1985: 19). This gives more apparent power to those allowed it compared to the less important people who must talk to those who can speak directly to 'the people back home'. Of those on screen, only the presenter can properly talk directly to viewers to bind them in.

The presenters of television programmes are thus intermediaries between the viewers and the programme as an entity as well as its con-tent; although, of course, they are themselves also programme content.

Even more, they are intermediaries between the ordinary life-world of the viewers and the customarily less ordinary world of their guests who, if not celebrities or political figures, are marked out from the ordinary by their presence on the stage rather than in the studio audience or by the televisuality of the product they are promoting. The presenter may at times be a more noted celebrity than the guest, but this is not the desirable state of affairs. To achieve the necessary closeness to the audience through which televisual popularity is mediated and which, I believe, is more necessary for daytime than evening chat shows, the presenter needs to make a performance of being ordinary, and this can be done in a couple of ways. A major one is by recounting personal data in a way designed to reduce the distinction between viewer and presenter. When Kerri-Anne Kennerley talked about her husband it was of his domestic preferences, not his (considerable) wealth, but her most personal exchanges were about her beloved dogs. When one of them died while she was still presenting the most popular locally made daytime show in Australia, it led to an outpouring of maudlin sympathy from her viewers, culminating in one of them sending her a painting she had made of the dog.

When Rosanne Barr started a chat-cum-talk show on US television after many years of having been an extremely high-profile celebrity, the stress on this aspect of the presenter was considerable. She was helped by having been television-based and her principle sitcom role being located in the working class; but even so, the stories circulating about her wealth, about problems in her personal and professional life and, above all, knowledge of the circles in which she moved, made the persistent assertion of her intermediary position appear a difficult task. The protocols of ordinary television helped make this not as awkward as it may have seemed. In one of the first programmes, when she was still establishing her role, the comedian Lily Tomlin was the first guest. Rosanne began the interview by reminiscing about her first encounter with Tomlin as a shy fan, placing herself immediately outside the world of celebrity and at one with ordinary viewers. There was some jostling as Tomlin, too, tried to be just 'plain folks', and engaged in devices to undercut her celebrity, but the formal aspects of the role of presenter ensured that it was Rosanne, the presenter, who would win.

Of talk shows proper, Jane Shattuc has noticed the way in which Oprah Winfrey, for example, confesses moments of the personal to bring her closer to her audience (1997: 95). Their weight problems are her weight problems, their addictions remind her of hers (and she reminds us). This does not quite work for chat shows which operate on a lighter note, even in the daytime when the ordinary personal (rather than the celebrity personal) holds more sway. Denise Drysdale is arguably the female performer with the longest career on Australian television, starting as a teenage go-go dancer, moving on to become a comedienne and singer, winning two Gold Logies (the highest award in Australia for a television personality) in the 1970s during the earlier years of her professional partnership with Ernie Sigley, before both suffered the decline in popularity that moved them from evening to daytime TV. Finally, in 1998, for the very first time, Denise became the host of her own show, when she moved, after 35 years with Channel 9, to the Seven Network. Despite what must be a remarkable professional competence, since that kind of longevity is not achieved without it, the hallmark of her persona is being an ordinary working-class woman who is a bit 'daffy'. Denise, drawing on her basic skills as comedienne rather than presenter, does her ordinariness in her patter and in the mundanity of her references to her family. Interviewing Jackie Collins during a shopping spree in Melbourne's Casino complex, she played (again) the wide-eyed working-class innocent let loose among the outrageously expensive designer items, awed at the spending power and consumer knowledgeability of the celebrity.

This example also reveals the other way in which she and a number of other celebrities perform ordinariness through a display of apparent incompetence (Melanie Giedroyc and Sue Perkins are younger British presenters who do variants of this). Performance in this mode, like an assumed ignorance of the world, operates as another device to diminish distance, making her (Denise or Mel or Sue) more like us (the viewers) and less like them – the actual celebrities who do not become clumsy or self-conscious (unless they, too, want to endear themselves to the audience during their moments of being 'real', as opposed to being 'stars'). Denise regularly appears to blunder through interviews, and it can seem that only the fact that her guests are promoting some film or other product could maintain their compliance. Again and again things fail to work smoothly and the absence of retakes, rehearsal or even competent use of the teleprompter seem glaring. It is true that the elevation of the qualities of liveness effectively sanctions, if not requires, a roughness around the edges, and most hosts of live programmes vaunt their ability to transcend glitches of various kinds (and you cannot vaunt if you never display), but this appears a presentation mode restricted to women. Such men as engage in it do so in a fictional persona – as was the case with the Australian shows featuring Norman Gunston, the alter ego of actor Garry McDonald.

Husband and wife presenting partnerships provide additional opportunities for the ordinary personal to be included in the programme, since instead of tales about 'my husband' or 'my wife' being part of the verbal display, the spouse is displayed visually and the verbal component can show some of the minutae of *being* a couple. The Australian programme *Better Homes and Gardens* capitalized for a number of years on having a husband and wife presenting team and its 'studio' location supposedly within their own home. Banter between Noni Hazelhurst and John Jarrett in the moments before throwing to the next segment purported to be ordinary domestic chat about collecting the children or being late for other tasks. This suited a weekly house and garden advice show perfectly, extending the domestic aspects beyond the customary appearance of domesticity into something with actual claims on the 'real'. When the marriage broke up, though, it was a serious problem for the programme, but it has now settled down into the continuing domestic situation of the single mother with a helpful (male) neighbour.

For Richard Maddeley and Judy Finnigan, the couple who long hosted ITV's *This Morning*, and who have now moved to Channel 4, presenting offers a slightly different situation. The domesticity of a regular morning show would appear well suited to conjugal chat between presenters and, at times, it is, but this was less often engaged in. It may be that the daily character of the programme, and its greater length, would render regular 'intimate moments' excessive. Running gags, like Richard's 'millennium cupboard' and Judy's exasperation with it, none the less operated to produce a space in which viewers could feel 'let in' on a relationship which is presented as being just like theirs.

For some programmes, especially those that are able to arrange contra deals with advertisers or sponsors, the cost of a 'name' presenter is the greatest production expenditure. The expenditure is justified not so much because of the internal cohesion produced through the presenter's continuity nor even through any direct drawing of faithful viewers, but because of the presenters' role in promotion. A recognized name attracts viewers, most certainly, but part of the contract between production company or channel and the presenter involves tacit or explicit agreements to be available for promotion purposes, like attending openings, awarding prizes and giving press interviews. Certain presenters can become network faces. When Kerri-Anne Kennerley was still presenting *Midday* for Channel 9, the network's publicist praised her understanding of publicity and co-operation with its demands with the words 'she's from the old school, she's a company woman, she knows the value of publicity, you know she's not gonna say "Hey give me some money", she's been in the game too long, ... [she's] professional' (Heidi Virtue, Channel 9 publicist, quoted in Turner et al., 2000: 143). This type of use of a presenter requires that they do in fact work with just one network – and in Australia this is almost always the case. In the UK, Noel Edmonds has operated similarly for the BBC (and Johnny Vaughan looks as if he will take over this role), while Cilla Black does the same for ITV, but there are exceptions, though few are as widely shared among channels as Carol Vorderman. Vorderman works on the BBC, ITV and Channel 4. She promotes her individual programmes, but her wider promotional work is either explicit advertising, like her endorsements of Komon schools or for the government, as the face of its campaign to raise standards in maths (Woolf, 1999: 5). None the less, a Channel 4 executive was quoted, when her contract was last renewed, as saying 'Carol is an enormously valuable asset to the channel' (BBC Online News 4/12/98).

Some presenters achieve a special status which leads to their being iconic at a national level. They can serve as a touchstone by which other people are judged. In 1998 when *Changing Rooms* was shifted from BBC2 to BBC1 because of its popularity, the presenter, Carol Smillie, was said to be 'taking up Anthea Turner's girl-next-door role'. The typically greater longevity of male presenters' careers means that there is less turnover of occupants of a particular style – Bruce Forsyth has been occupying the 'Brucie' role for nigh on 40 years. John Ellis discusses this iconicity as being a notable characteristic of national television before the 1980s in what he terms the 'age of scarcity' when television 'gave each nation its own private life' (2000: 47). Yet despite the plenitude provided by pay-TV, the processes of celebrity ensure that certain television performers retain this power to be 'nation's favourites', or at least widely, if not universally, recognized within the nation, though unknown outside. Ignorance of such figures can prove socially problematic as it marks one as different, either a 'foreigner' or 'stuck up'. The latter term marks the popular disdain for those who claim the distinction of not being ordinary.

When the virtual newscaster Ananova was first being promoted before the launch of the service, she was described as looking like a cross between Kylie Minogue, Posh Spice and Carol Vorderman. In the UK such an announcement would have been puzzling only in terms of what features of each would be chosen; in Australia, however, it was incomprehensible. Who was this Carol Vorderman person and why was she being hybridized with two famous people? Vorderman is a perfect example of the national icon with no recognition factor beyond the nation and its expatriates. At the core of Vorderman's fame is her 18-year presence on Channel 4's *Countdown*, the high-rating afternoon quiz show, as the resident mental arithmetic whiz. When her contract was renewed for £5 million over five years, in 1998, she was described in a way she had not been previously, as co-presenter. Early in her career she had been the presenter of the BBC science and technology programme *Tomorrow's World*, though this had ended when the BBC decided that the washing-powder ads she was doing on ITV constituted a conflict of interest. It has taken her some time to transcend the handicap of mathematical freak-ishness which worked well for science-related shows (like *Testing, Testing* and *Gadgets*), but reduced the extent to which she could be regarded as an unexceptional, ordinary person. It was probably only with *Carol Vorderman's Better Homes* that she finally shed the dominance of the science and maths specialist presenter persona. The 'twist' of this house makeover show is that it is a competition between two couples to improve the market value of their home by suggesting some additions and using the team's work to produce it. As the presenter of it, Vorderman has adopted what has become a common feature of British female presenters – running about on camera in the manner once the preserve of Anneka Rice – with the aim, one assumes, of conveying excitement and intensifying the tone of the programme. As is typical of makeover shows, this tone is one of a desperate rush to meet the self-imposed deadline.

When presenters move across subject realms, as Vorderman has, what they perform can be regarded as a lateral harmonization of areas; the quiz show, the science programme and the house makeover are brought closer together through being refracted through the single persona of the intelligent woman who is also attractive, and in, every other way (except her celebrity and its attendant wealth), ordinary. Having achieved this harmonization in the minds of the viewers and channel executives, she integrated her science and house makeover experience in 1999 by presenting *Dream House* on the BBC, the subject of which was domestic uses of new technology. Vorderman and her team did new technology makeovers on ordinary people's houses, the team faced challenges set by Vorderman in constructing the 'Dream House' and various members of the public with technologically exceptional houses were visited. In May 2000, Vorderman was one of two celebrities chosen to appear competing for charity on *Who Wants to be a Millionaire?*, further integrating her public persona, before reasserting her ability to range over programme types by presenting *Star Lives*, a celebrity profile series, for ITV in 2001.

A similar, though so far less extensive, lateral harmonization, and one equally valuable in attracting viewers, was performed in the selection of the host of the Australian version of *Who Wants to be a Millionaire?* The choice was Eddie McGuire, previously know as the presenter of *The Footy Show*, a blokey, knockabout sports panel show, immediately announcing that the quiz show was envisaged as having more appeal to male viewers than previous such shows might have been thought to have in Australia.

Lateral harmonization not only performs a synchronic linkage across current programmes, it also operates diachronically, tying past programmes in to current readings. In this way it answers Karen Lury's call for researchers to take account of the accumulation of personal and generational memory in our assessments of particular individuals' performances (1995/6: 115). While I began this chapter with a comment about the consistency of the key aspects of Cilla Black's persona from her days as a young pop singer, this continuity is available only to the older members of her audience; for the younger viewers of *Blind Date*, she has only ever been 'mumsie'. Presenters who have done stints on either the British or the Australian version of *Play School* carry a very particular quality into their subsequent work and are able to elicit affectionate audience responses based on childhood memories long after. When Trish Goddard returned to the UK to present *Trisha*, after years in Australia, none of her Australian work in a range of ordinary television programmes could be called on to tie her new programme into the schedule or to place her performance in viewers' memories. Much, however, was made of her having been an Australian *Play School* presenter, since even if the particular performance had not been seen, its flavour could be accessed.

It is customary for ordinary television presenters not to have a profile that extends beyond the country in which they live, because of the way in which ordinary television is sold as a format, not exported as it is. Only for those types of programmes which have international sales – cooking shows (Floyd's various), a few celebrity interview programmes (like Michael Parkinson's) and American talk shows – is it possible for a presenter to build up an international profile. Special one-offs like the Eurovision Song Contest may, over time, give someone like Terry Wogan a degree of international presence, but generally it is rare for a national presenter to have cross-border recognition. Occasionally, though, a presenter will work in more than one country. Cilla Black and Denise van Outen both have presence in Australia through doing shows based here. Pay-TV, which does screen imported ordinary television programmes, alters this, but the small viewing numbers mean that it fails to register all that much. Although the British version of *Ground Force* screens in Australia on cable, while the Australian version is on free-to-air, only the local personalities have any renown. Charlie Dimmock, the labourer who became so prominent that she now has her own shows in Britain, has no celebrity status in Australia.

The extremes of presenting styles can perhaps be noted by contrasting game show presenters with those of cooking programmes. Game shows are particularly tightly controlled. The presenter needs to introduce the assistant, the contestants and the prizes, explain the rules, ask the questions, give the answers and produce a winner, and do so usually in 24 minutes, often five times a week (though perhaps recorded on a single afternoon). The repetition of catchphrases, details of sponsors, rules and prizes means that little time is left for any individuality, yet game show presenters, who are frequently ex-comedians, none the less produce very loyal viewers. Their skills in delivering one-liners and off-the-cuff repartee pay dividends.

In her study of the game shows of 50 nations, Anne Cooper-Chen notes how varied the protocols of game show presentation are internationally, although nationally they may be quite tight. American hosts are overwhelmingly white men, and while they speak, their assistants do not (1994: 159). She claims that this holds generally true also for Australasia, North America and (her categories) northern and western Europe (though the non-speaking female assistant has been much less common for at least the last two decades). Where women do present in western countries they seem strongly associated with dating game shows, except in the US where they are not even evident on these (ibid.: 161). The homogeneity of English-speaking programmes she attributes to formatting (165). In contrast, the most common pattern on Asian game shows is for a male/female pair to co-host and to have a multiplicity of assistants (162). In the period since her study there have been a few shifts – assistants speak a little more on US shows, and her comment about the necessity for female hosts to be youthful, while males can be white-haired, needs some modulation. There are still patriarchs among presenters, but a sign of change may be detected in the decision of John Burgess, a middle-aged, male Australian game show host, to have a face-lift and to be so open about it that he was shown having it on *Good Medicine*, a medical advice show.

Cooking show presenters, on the other hand, are given a much freer rein and are perhaps a little more likely to be female than male. Great and pervasive flamboyance, rather than a quick pause for a one-liner, is characteristic, and while once it may have been more available for men than for women (see Bonner, 1994), in the wake of the *Two Fat Ladies* and the various shows featuring Dorinda Hafner, this no longer holds true. Idiosyncrasies are cultivated and paraded by the presenter and cherished (or loathed) by viewers. Jamie Oliver, of *The Naked Chef*, spread the use of the term 'pukka' far beyond either of its initial linguistic ranges and was repeatedly shown sliding down the balustrade of his London flat (it even featured as part of the set of his 2001 stage show). The integration of his ordinary life into the programme through the use of his flat as the location, his regular suppliers and his cooking for friends and various members of his family, was an extension of an existing practice of combining ordinary life and the programme, characteristic of programmes with a domestic focus. Even though Delia Smith never strays from her immediate concern with the display of dish production, surrounding material informs us that her demonstration kitchen is in her own home. The *Two Fat Ladies* visited old haunts with personal connections as well as new ones, to cook for selected groups.

Not all cooking shows operate within a repertoire marked by the ordinary. The presenters differ from those of many other types of programme by being professionals in a highly skilled area before they become television entertainers and educators. They are thus outside the ordinary before the programme begins and may choose to enter that domain, through the domesticity of their concerns (food and nurturing people), or to remain outside it, by demonstrating dishes destined for restaurant tables or by guiding viewers through exotic domains. Niki Strange discusses this latter aspect under the term 'Tour-Educative', to stress the significant amount of attention paid to tourist sights and activities in programmes like *Madhur Jaffrey's Flavours of India* (1998: 306). Dorinda Hafner's *Taste of Africa* had considerably less cooking instruction in it than Jaffrey's, but her presenting persona is a particularly rich one and much of this and her subsequent *Taste* programmes concentrate on Hafner's encounters with other extroverts as they chat about food.

Andrew Tolson has talked of the 'anecdotal effect' of television where the constant telling of brief incidental stories, either in chats between presenter and guest or just by the presenter, or even in the very format of a programme, has become a dominant form of televisual rhetoric (1985: 25–7). He is concerned primarily with the British chat show *Wogan* and with *This Is Your Life*, but the recounting of previously told stories or the restaging of them can be found in presenters' monologues and dialogues pervasively, cooking presenter Keith Floyd providing an extreme example. In a later article, Tolson returned to *Wogan* and similar programmes in order to trace consequences of the rise to dominance of anecdotal rhetoric. He is concerned with shifts and modulations in the popular public sphere (long centred on television), which include an increasingly ironic stance, and the development of what he terms a 'synthetic personality' (1991: 198). At its most extreme, in the chat show *The Dame Edna Experience*, presented by Barry Humphries in his Edna Everage alter ego, Tolson finds it also evident elsewhere and characterizes its importance in the matter of the loss of the corner-stone of the popular public sphere, 'the so-called real person who *speaks from experience*' (ibid.: 198, [original emphasis]). *The Kumars at No 42* demonstrates the continued usefulness of synthetic personalities for chat shows.

This is a very important point for a consideration of ordinary television. Although he acknowledges a fragmented audience, only some of whom attend to the kind of programmes he discusses, in Tolson's view the audience more generally is led to question the sincerity of personalities in a way that resonates throughout television and beyond (1991: 197–9). Because ordinary television is much more diverse than the chat and talk shows Tolson discusses, the majority of presenters, while certainly adopting presenting personae, do not operate through a synthetic personality. Sincerity, while it is extremely difficult to describe, is something that can be projected more successfully by some than by others (Don Burke, for example, does it very well) and it remains an important quality for many types of presenters. Certainly, it is for those giving gardening advice or help on caring for pets, and would seem an irrelevance on dating shows and an encumbrance on tonight shows.

For those types of programmes, where, arguably, the majority of presenters adopt a persona with little interest in sincerity, preferring instead irony, campness or excessive bonhomie, it may well be that the burden of sincerity, or at least of some kind of empathetic 'realness', is switched to the ordinary people appearing with them. This is not to say that ordinary people are unable to be equally synthetic or camp, but that these are performance modes inappropriate to most quiz contestants or makeover clients. Tolson notes the possibility of a generational specificity in the appeal of synthetic personalities (1991: 198) and this seems to have continued. The Australian presenting duo Roy and HG (of *Club Buggery* and *The Dream*) are a current example, as is another Australian, Elle McFeast (*Live and Sweaty* and several subsequent specials), and both examples appeal more to a younger audience. While they operate from a fully fictional identity (like Edna Everage), this is by no means essential to the phenomenon; Denise van Outen (in ITV's *Something for the Weekend*) does the same type of performance and has an appeal similar, under her own name, to that which, earlier, Julian Clary had. Although the ordinary people who appear with them all 'play up' to the outrageousness of the presenters, their ordinariness is required to offset the presenter's antics and repartee.

Reporters and other regular personnel

Presenters are supported on air by a variety of ancillary personnel (and, of course, a very sizeable crew behind the scenes). The main roles to be considered are reporters, tradesmen for the makeover shows, regular musicians for such variety shows as remain and 'hostesses' for game shows. I am retaining the term 'hostesses' primarily for rhetorical effect; it has no longer any industrial, and indeed little popular, currency. 'Experts' are difficult to categorize since some are regular and some appear, like celebrities, intermittently. (These intermittent presences will be considered in the next section.) Some experts prove so popular with viewers that they become regulars. They may even be institutionalized. In September 2000, ITV's *This Morning* ran, on its 'Looking Good', segment, a succession of ten hairdressers showing recent trends, and after all ten had been given exposure, viewers were invited to vote for their favourite to become the regular hair expert for the series. This same process, which is effectively an audition of potential talent, is used less formally for many of the on-air roles.

The principal additional people are those termed reporters, though they are very rarely journalists. Mike Budd, Steve Craig and Clay Steinman, writing of television news, refer to correspondents as 'extensions of the anchor' (1999: 126), and this relationship can be discerned here, too. Reporters extend the presenters' range. They are sent out (apparently) at the presenter's bidding to do the various tasks that comprise the show – road-testing cars, showing how to make compost, displaying holiday accommodation – and while they may show us their findings directly, the hierarchy of the show is never in doubt and they return their temporary authority to the presenter before leaving. The whole extensive on-air team of *This Morning* – reporters, specialist health advisers, fashion experts, cooks and all – is referred to in publicity material as 'The Family'. There is no doubt that the 'parents' of this family, the ones that held the whole thing together during their tenancy, were the presenting duo Richard and Judy. Lifestyle programmes are regularly given to referring to their on-screen personnel by group names which avoids the problem of identifying subordination and stressing the hierarchy involved. 'Team' seems the most favoured term.

Gender can complicate the display of relationships between the people on screen when apparent power operates contrary to what traditionally may be expected. As noted above, both men and women present and the same applies with support personnel; both men and women are reporters, though diversity in the other roles is more limited. None the less the power shown is not always that where women are subordinate to men, although this has taken some time to clarify. One of the earliest instances of males subordinate to a female presenter was on Esther Rantzen's enormously popular programme *That's Life*. This populist magazine programme started in 1973, before the great growth of ordinary television, and regularly provided a great diversity of items about the 'real lives' of ordinary, (predominantly) working-class people (Gutch, 1986: 10). Esther's male reporters seemed at the time strangely infantilized, dressed in bright jumpers and performing antics to amuse their presenter and the viewers. In retrospect they were harbingers of current on-screen manners, with the casual yet almost hyperactive approach now very widespread.

Kerri-Anne Kennerley's interactions with her on-screen musical director on *Midday* provided a valuable example of a disguised representation of female power. The main framework of these showed her as a slightly flirtatious daughter constantly seeking her 'father's' approval. At various times in each show, she announced her intentions to him and he 'let her' sing or dance, or he grumpily approved certain other kinds of actions, but his power was illusory; she told us what would be in the show and that was what was there; she spoke to the studio audience and to the viewers, while he spoke only to her; she did the interviews and the guests spoke to her but not to him. The function of these segments was both to disavow and assert her power as the name talent. This is no longer an act that is commonly found, but it was in a programme targeted at older viewers and it was a situation where she took over a programme from a long-running male host.

The musical director served the role of interlocutor, a frequent device in those descendants of variety shows that retain a band in the studio to play for guest singers, like the ABC's now defunct *Roy & HG's Club Buggery*. The blokey banter (since all musical directors I've noticed have been male) ensures a friendly, casual tone on such programmes, but is much more difficult for female hosts to engage in.

Game shows, as *Who Wants ...* and *The Weakest Link* demonstrate so clearly, do not really need more than one regular person on screen. Magnus Magnusson ran *Mastermind* unassisted for years. These examples, though, are of quiz shows that lack arrays of glittering prizes. Material prizes require display and it is the process of this display which leads to the presence of people other than the presenter and the contestants. Both men and women may act in these roles, but when there is only one assistant it is almost always a woman, though Julian Clary's first regular television appearance was as the assistant to a male host on a quiz show. This seems to have been judged not the best use of his 'cheeky' persona, for that show did not have a second season, but he did get his own show, *Sticky Moments*, very quickly afterwards.

In the early days of television, there was no doubt that just as the male presenters were hosts, so the women regularly with them on set were hostesses, with all that implied of supporting the men and being attentive, both in the mode of the wife and, less overtly, the bar companion.

Chosen for their physical appearance, they acted as living set decorations, displaying prizes or escorting contestants from place to place or manipulating props. Initially, they did not speak; in Australia they even belonged to a different union (Models and Mannequins Guild) from presenters (Actors' Equity) and an arrangement between the two unions forbade speech to any but actors. These unions have since merged into the Media Arts Alliance and the formality of the distinctions has disappeared. The function of hostesses was, and substantially still is, to be displayed by the host for the audience to look at; they are objects to be consumed visually. Their absence from the most 'serious' knowledge quizzes, and from the even more 'male' sports quizzes, may appear odd given that these are the types of game show to have greater proportions of male viewers. Are they then provided for the female audience? This is not as improbable as it might seem since not only do they themselves display attractive clothing on what most would regard as attractive bodies, but they act to facilitate displays of masculinity from the host. Most commonly, in the UK especially, they accompany the older ex-comedian hosts, providing an initial trigger for their sexual repartee, before it is transferred to the contestants. The camp presentation style that characterizes a significant number of British presenters, most notably Bruce Forsyth, is rendered toothless by the interchange with a pretty girl. One should note, though, that any variant on the trademark line 'Give us a twirl', by Bruce or others, is justified now in terms solely of the display of the dress, not the legs.

As the 'hostesses' began speaking and the term became rarer, being replaced by 'assistant' or even occasionally 'co-presenter', so the fiction of equivalence between what was required for the roles in terms of sexual attractiveness developed, helped just a little by allowing popular assistants to continue after they were known to be married or despite the occasional sign of the disappearance of youth. The complexity of such a situation for mass-market texts, like high-rating game shows, was revealed during the late 1990s in Australia with a scandal over Channel 9 *Sale of the Century* assistant Nikki Buckley's first pregnancy. Not much of the scandal was over her continuing to work while pregnant, though some of it was couched in these terms, especially as she worked so far into the pregnancy. What the scandal was actually about was sexiness and the extent to which a shift in attitudes to the maternal body had spread throughout the varying demographic groups watching the programme.

Buckley exposed the pretence that assistants were no longer sexy set dressing by both continuing in the job while pregnant (i.e. not really available in fantasy for the male gaze in the same way) and by continuing to dress as she had before (i.e. in a way that most would regard as 'sexy').

The revealing sexiness of her clothing, unremarked upon before she was pregnant, became a major topic of both media-based and private popular conversation. While certain kinds of ordinary television are able to promote an attitude to sex that bears some resemblance to what actually prevails among those who are sexually active (though most often in straightforwardly sex-based game shows targeted at teenagers and young adults, like Channel 4's *Something for the Weekend* or Channel 9's *Love Rules*), the majority of the programming is quite conservative, as was *Sale ...*, with its substantial audience among the elderly.

The non-pregnant Buckley had a particularly wholesome persona, regularly appeared in promotional articles described as a 'nice woman' and had such a good figure that her clothing style was uncontentious, but a continuation of this while pregnant exposed some of the contradictions of the show. In some ways it was obvious that the female co-presenter was still there as sexy set dressing, but the ideal of the family vaunted by the programme, in common with other game shows, was usually very separate from it. Nikki did the sexiness and the ordinary contestants did the family (and if contestants happened to be pregnant they shrouded themselves decently). Sexiness and the maternal body were normally kept separate, not brought together by a public figure who was so frequently in the nation's living-rooms. The scandal started away from the channel on talk-back radio, natural home to conservative demagoguery, moved into newspapers and then involved the television network. It made possible a wonderful piece of programme promotion, a great self-righteous display of progressive social goodness by the network (once it had checked its numbers) as they defended Buckley's right to continue to work and dress 'as she pleased'. She continued to present during her second pregnancy, similarly dressed, but confessed in magazine articles that it was more difficult since the pregnancy itself was not as trouble-free as the first. She has not returned to the programme since the birth of her second child, although she continues to work on air in a lifestyle programme on pay-TV. The example demonstrates a problem with assumptions of what is shared and ordinary and with how unspoken practices can erupt and display their meanings and contradictions. This will be explored further in the next chapter.

The continuing sexualizing of female bodies on television, which intensifies when they occupy subordinate roles, can also be seen in the reception of Charlie Dimmock from BBC's *Ground Force*. She is now identified by the programme as a water-garden specialist, but initially was seen most often as a female labourer. Despite her gardening skills and experience, the aspect of this assistant to presenter Alan Titchmarsh that was most remarked upon was her choice not to wear a bra while working on screen. The programme itself ignored the issue, which circulated as trivial gossip on radio and in the press, acting to encourage viewers to tune in. Although the decision to give Charlie her own programme was announced early in 1999, *Charlie's Wildlife Gardens* was not ready to air until autumn 2000, and it was 2001 before she was able to escape the garden frame for the 'challenge' format of *Cheer for Charlie*. Becoming a presenter involves the assumption of apparent power over the programme itself, and while the sexualized female body can exhibit power in spaces that are already marked 'sexual' (like *Something for the Weekend*), it needs more negotiation when on other kinds of programmes it moves from subordinate to dominant. Charlie has now made this transition quite effectively, though her own shows are generally short, six-episode series rather than the much more continuous *Ground Force* in which she continues to be a supporting player. (Male bodies, too, are readily sexualized for televisual purposes, but the equivalent Australian example is actually of a presenter. The host chosen for *Backyard Blitz*, a Channel 9 programme which operated as something of a spoiler for the Australian version of *Ground Force*, was Jamie Durie, promoted both as a horticulturalist and as an ex-member of the male strip group Manpower. He does not all that often take his shirt off while working on the show. Channel 7 fought back against this move by having as its *Ground Force* presenter the son of Australian film star Jack Thompson.)

Because ordinary television programmes run in series which, if successful, get extended, regular personnel become well known to the audience, especially since even minor on-screen presences can be used in promotion of the programme and its associated spin-offs like magazines and books. In keeping with this practice of lifestyle programming to produce various kinds of branded merchandise associated with the show, all three regular members of the UK *Ground Force* team (the one so far unnamed being Tommy Walsh) also have books giving advice on gardening. The friendly personal tone adopted on the programme and in print, in conjunction with the giving of advice about matters which, ostensibly, relate to the viewer's domestic situation, operates to give greater prominence to the more junior on-screen personnel. This means that the distinction between regularly appearing personnel and visiting experts is eroded as both types become individualized members of the 'team'. Regulars can become *de facto* experts, as Charlie would appear to be about water gardens, and experts can join the 'family', as the successful hairdresser on *This Morning* did. While the assistants may be given greater authority and the term 'assistant' be displaced by 'team member', there remains no question on air that one person (and for *Ground Force* that is Titchmarsh) is the senior member, indeed *the* presenter.

Celebrities and experts

So far the people under discussion have been those appearing regularly on the programmes, week after week, sometimes going on holiday, but not (if presenters) without promising to return. Other people marked out from the ordinary as 'special' in some way appear less regularly. These may either be celebrities or experts, though it is the character of television to produce celebrity for those who appear more than a couple of times, so experts often morph into (minor) celebrities.

Celebrities are people with a high recognition index. Their activities, both public and private, are of considerable public interest. They attract viewers to programmes they appear on as well as to other media they appear in. Their presence on ordinary television programmes is central both to the constitution of a number of types of such programmes, especially chat shows, and to the management and promotion of their own careers. While their presence is staged as a 'natural', even social, event (they are 'guests', they are thanked for stopping by), they are contradictory commodities whose production and management is controlled by a complex industry.

> Celebrities are brand names as well as cultural icons or identities; they operate as marketing tools as well as sites where the agency of the audience is clearly evident; and they represent the achievement of individualism – the triumph of the human and the familiar – as well as its commodification and commercialisation. (Turner et al., 2000: 13)

Although the presence of a celebrity on a chat show (and indeed on most media sites) is a sign that they are operating as marketing tools, promoting the most recent product, this is rarely given prominence. Instead the focus is on the 'achievements of individualism', stories of how they made it and how it has not changed the person they really are. The idea that their presence on a television programme is work is given little if any prominence. Bell and van Leeuwen observe how the questions asked of celebrities on chat shows persistently try to link any fictional work (their film, book or song) to actual experiences in their real lives in order to reduce the gap between performance and person (1994: 194–5). Biographical foundations are constantly sought which function to shift the focus from the work and its artifice to the 'real' and its naturalness. In so doing, any idea that the production and revelation of the 'real person' is also work is further distanced.

As noted earlier, celebrity has come to displace the term 'television personality', but this occurs only when it involves a movement of the personality away from whatever their 'home' on television is. A presenter remains a presenter on his or her own show but becomes a celebrity when guesting on another, or when promoting their show in a magazine article about their new house or baby. Whether a person's celebrity arises from television appearances or achievements in other fields, there are a number of roles celebrities can fulfil on ordinary television. They can appear on chat or talk shows, they can open up their houses or gardens for investigation on a range of programmes – primarily lifestyle ones but also game shows and the daytime magazine style ones – and they can appear as themselves as contestants on various game shows.

The chat show is the most obvious place to find celebrities on television; the majority of chat shows talk to few people who are anything else. Indeed, the status of a chat show seems intimately linked to the stature of the celebrities it can attract. *Parkinson*, with its cosy interchanges between presenter and, at most, three very high-profile guests, is probably at the apex and able to be sold internationally on the basis of the guests' prominence, even if it occasionally includes celebrities with strictly national followings (Carol Vorderman and Paul Merton have both been guests bemusing to Australian viewers). Chat shows offer celebrities opportunities to promote their latest product – film, book, song, even favourite charity – and to maintain their own public profile between products. In return for the opportunity, celebrities must be willing to talk about other matters, overwhelmingly their personal lives, disguising the promotional work as an apparent chat between friends. This trade, effectively of privacy for free advertising time, is completely naturalized. As Bell and van Leeuwen say, 'they must obliquely, through "chat", show their non-celebrity humanity' (1994: 190). We watch chat shows to see what celebrity X has been up to lately, to hear them talk of working with celebrity Y or to listen yet again to them telling familiar anecdotes. It is not that there is necessarily a naivety about the process, rather a feeling that it is a good trade. As viewers we get all those data about all those interesting people we love, or love to hate. The functions that celebrities serve in the contemporary world in the formation of social identity, as exemplars or warnings, as providing in their very life stories entertainment as sensational or as moving as any overtly fictional text, can all be performed by appearances on chat shows, though usually this is complemented by many other appearances on radio, in newspapers and magazines (see Turner et al., 2000 for more on this).

Game shows are another place the celebrity on the promotion trail can appear, or where a fading celebrity can establish a new career. Perhaps the heyday of celebrity game shows was the late 1970s and the 1980s, when versions of *Blankety Blank* were widely franchised and highly popular. In these programmes there were both regular and occasional celebrity panellists of varying levels of celebrity, including such substantial figures, in the British version, as Spike Milligan and Beryl Reid. There still is a wide range of celebrity game shows, including *A Question of Sport*, which started in 1970 and can count among its list of major guest sporting celebrities HRH Princess Anne. In the main, though, celebrity game shows operate with minor celebrities as their regular guests and the panels are filled out by visiting celebrities whose introduction by the host provides a place for the promotion of whatever their current 'real work' is. The most common contemporary form of celebrity game show is the celebrity special of a prime-time show which normally uses only ordinary contestants. This accords better with the work schedules of celebrities and, since they usually play for charities, enables them to promote themselves in a very positive light. At times the regularly appearing celebrity, whose function is often to be a team captain, becomes a more significant celebrity because of the regular television exposure, and the television work becomes one of their main activities.

The range of games celebrities may be asked to play can relate to their field of renown, as when musicians are on musical quizzes, or have little relevance to it. The appeal of a programme may range too, with more sober shows like ITV's *Through the Keyhole*, which asks celebrities to guess the celebrity occupier of a particular home, appealing to a mixed audience, and more comically nonsensical ones, like BBC2's *Shooting Stars*, targeted at younger viewers. Though celebrity game shows are far more popular in the UK than in Australia, there have been Australian versions of the comic ones, most notably *Good News Week*, which started off as a version of BBC2's *Have I Got News for You* but, especially after its move from the ABC to Channel 10, became much more varied. This is one example of a programme that certainly enhanced the celebrity status of its resident team captains Mikey Robbins and Julie McCrossin.

Celebrities on game shows are not recent phenomena. The example already discussed of Gilbert Harding is of a game show panellist of very minor renown (certainly not a celebrity) at the beginning of his engagement on *What's My Line?* who achieved major celebrity status as a result of the programme. This happened to many other people on the game shows of the early days of television and has continued to be the case. Regular celebrity panellists who develop a strong public following and become identified with a particular programme are of great value to it since they enter a reciprocal promotional relationship: promoting the programme while doing their other activities and their other activities while on the programme. They become walking billboards. This is no doubt one of the reasons that the three permanent members of *Have I Got News for You* each reportedly receive an annual £4500 clothes allowance.

The remaining significant programme type on which celebrities appear is lifestyle programming where the investigation of the personal life of the celebrity moves from confession to exposure as their house or garden is visited (and in some instances, like *Burke's Backyard* or the episode of *Ground Force* which visited Nelson Mandela, given a makeover). Here there is usually an attempt on the part of the celebrity to appear more ordinary and less special or wealthy. The houses inspected on *Through the Keyhole* always belong to celebrities yet rarely seem particularly extravagant. Objects highlighted tend to be, on the whole, relatively mundane. When Don Burke visits dramatic and extensive gardens they are either tourist spots or belong to professional landscape gardeners; celebrity gardeners offer up much smaller, simpler patches of earth to Burke's remediating gaze. But these are just accoutrements to the celebrity persona; there are more intimate aspects that can be exposed. In mid-2000 the British talk show host Trisha hosted a programme called *Celebrity Heartbreak* where celebrities, like soccer player George Best, talked about their highly publicized relationship problems. This presents a particularly strong case for there being virtually no part of a celebrity's life which is inaccessible to the television camera's gaze.

Unlike celebrities, experts are present on ordinary television because of their specialized knowledge. The distinction between expert and celebrity may be very much a shifting area, but at core, celebrities need to be willing to move outside their areas of expertise and hold up aspects of their private lives to the public gaze, while an expert need do neither. Private matters may be revealed over time but, unless this is in the course of the expert transforming into a celebrity, will be of little moment.

The less celebrity-driven daytime chat shows have many experts, regular and occasional, as do talk shows. Magazine-style lifestyle pro- grammes call on expert advisers, and makeover shows may draw on a pool of expert interior designers (as does *Changing Rooms*) or use new experts each week (the real estate valuers in *Carol Vorderman's Better Homes*). Financial programmes, from the popular, like Channel 9's *Money* or Channel 4's stocks and shares game show *Show Me the Money*, to the more sober, like Channel 9's *Business Sunday*, regularly feature visiting analysts. History and archaeology programmes like *Time Team* or *Meet the Ancestors* have experts helping them both with advice and more materially in their reconstructions.

The experts on *Antiques Roadshow* play a far more substantial role in the programme than is the case for most others. The presenter introduces the town or city from which the outside broadcast comes and closes the show with a round-up of its highlights, but for the rest of the time the screen is filled with ordinary people, the objects they have brought along and the experts who are identifying and valuing them. The pool the experts are drawn from is comparatively small (most work for the major auction houses) and almost all of them have achieved regular status, though by maintaining their singularity of focus and lack of a publicly available private life they remain experts rather than celebrities. What they say cannot credibly be challenged, and when an owner says that he thought his possession was of a different period or by a different crafts-person, he is gently shown why the expert is right. That such a challenge is made at all is unusual in televisual terms; far more frequently experts are unable to be challenged by ordinary people, only by other experts or, very occasionally, by an interviewer, and both of these occurrences are far more characteristic of current affairs than ordinary television.

There are certain programmes, though, where experts are not so highly rated. The very highly paid British talk show presenter Robert Kilroy-Silk is particularly dismissive of them. Livingstone and Lunt report a number of occasions when *Kilroy* encourages those who reject expert advice and quote an interview with Kilroy himself where he is explicit about not liking experts and preferring the opinions of 'real people' who have experienced whatever it is that is under discussion (1994: 98). Livingstone and Lunt believe that discussion programmes like this, which regularly oppose expert and lay opinion (especially in a climate where it is the lay opinion that is valorized), have established a different relationship between expertise and a laity validated in populist terms. The result is that they distinguish between expert and ordinary people in terms of their social roles, with experts accorded on-screen labels revealing institutional affiliation, better miking and, for the British programmes, front-row seating (ibid.: 100). This is not a genre that, as yet, has a significant local presence in Australia; similar American pro-grammes allow the possibility of the same kind of dispute, but undercut its success by placing the experts with the subjects on stage, facing the studio audience who stand for ordinary people.

The opposition between expert and lay is treated somewhat differently by Graham Murdock, reporting on his own lengthy experience as an expert in a range of television programmes. Murdock notes an exchange underpinning the appearance of experts which is remarkably similar to that engaged in by celebrities: 'Being interviewed and providing on-the-record comments ... is a contractual arrangement whereby research find-ings or scholarly expertise is exchanged for public visibility' (1994: 109). He notes a preference on the part of television producers for the factually supported, positivist, scientific form of evidence, much at odds with his own approach to sociological understandings where the 'claims to a hearing rest ... on the coherence, authority and explanatory power of their arguments' (ibid.: 113). While much of his discussion is concerned with current affairs or documentary programmes in which the expert's views can be edited or modulated by accompanying visuals, he also notes the recent growth of programmes of greater relevance here, where the opposition of discourses of experience and those of expertise are accorded greater equality (121). The personal example he gives (which sounds very much like an episode of *Kilroy*) was one in which the presenter elicited his views, then asked for contributions from the studio audience labelling them 'experts in television' also, on the basis of the amount of it they had watched.

Experts on talk shows have a distinctive role in that the structure of the shows supports their authority more; their advice is usually taken after the testimony of the people whose behaviour is under scrutiny and their interrogation by presenter and the studio audience. It is thus open to challenge only by the presenter who retains the last word. Shattuc speaks at length about American shows' choice of experts, whose primary identification on-screen owes not so much to institutional affiliation as to their being the author of a related self-help book or course. Overwhelmingly, this is the place for the female expert, especially psychologists and therapists, though the person Shattuc nominates as the 'prototypical therapist' is Gilda Carle, whose qualifications are in organizational behaviour and whose professional work is in communication (1997: 126).

ORDINARY PEOPLE

Participants

The most numerous of the categories of people who get named when appearing on ordinary television is that of participants, usually contestants or 'examples'. They only appear on about half of the total number of ordinary television programmes, but they are a clear sign of the 'ordinariness' of the shows on which they appear. The term 'examples' has neither popular nor industrial currency. Industrially, they are, as was noted in the previous chapter, 'talent', whether they are taking part in a game show, taking a sick animal to a television vet or videoing their holiday for *The Real Holiday Show*. What the term notes here is the situation where an infotainment show takes an ordinary person as an example of the issue under consideration, be that a financial problem or the solution to a common household query. 'Examples' function to personalize the issue as one involving people just like them.

It is worthwhile contrasting them with those who are scrutinized by documentaries to observe the difference. Participants in documentaries hardly ever engage with on-screen intermediaries who stand between themselves and the viewers; they may very occasionally acknowledge the off-screen camera operator or director, but if they are framed for reception it is after the event and by a voiceover. The sociability that is able to be evinced in the interchanges between presenter and contestant, for example, make the ordinary television programme paradoxically more 'natural' than the documentary. Customarily, documentary formats operate on the illusion that the filming is not happening. While viewers know that they are not really being given transparent access to the real, the pose that this is the case continues. In contrast, on ordinary television the whole panoply of the production of an entertainment for a body of viewers (and often for a studio audience as well) is acknowledged and much of it is on display. The behaviour of presenter and participant has no direct counterpart in the world away from television (the preparation, the possibility of editing and the delayed transmission which makes it possible for those participating to view their own performance are among those factors rendering it very different), but the encounter follows a familiar form. It is very unusual for a person to appear on a programme he has not watched; the programme teaches its participants what is expected of them before they arrive in the studio where they are instructed again by production staff. One of the simplest ways in which viewers learn appropriate behaviour is through noticing the amount of screen time given to particular responses. Some shows favour brief, heart-warming anecdotes; others like something a little racy. British dating show contestants know that time is allowed for the display of performance skills, to such an extent that the introductory sequence can resemble an abbreviated talent show.

Programmes need to have a regular source of ordinary participants and shows frequently conclude with announcements of how viewers can cross the divide and get on the show. *Who Wants to be a Millionaire?*, among others, filters would-be contestants through a phone quiz (advertised during the programme), and since the calls are charged at a premium rate this becomes a revenue stream. Programme websites can also be used to attract participants. *This Morning*, for example, posted the following announcement in October 2000: 'We're looking for slimmers to start our new diet. So if you want to lose two dress sizes by Christmas and are free to join us every Monday for ten weeks, then send us a photo and all your details.' The amount of time being requested here would rule out a substantial number of potential participants. Journalistic articles on dating game shows regularly include statements about how workmates dared a participant to go on the show or even filled in the application on his or her behalf. Getting on the show, then, is embedded either in the experience of watching it or in the kind of sociable interaction that the programme attempts to enact. The participant is already, to some extent, there.

That there is an eagerness to appear on television is nowhere more evident than in the numbers volunteering to participate in high-rating programmes. For the second series of the American endurance show *Survivor*, 49,000 applied to be part of it. The 50 shortlisted were extensively tested, physically and psychologically, to ensure that they were able to handle what they would encounter. Sixteen people were eventually chosen to appear (Idato, 2000: 2).

The major site for ordinary people to represent themselves on television is on game shows which have a voracious appetite for contestants. The term 'represent themselves' covers the situation discussed above when ordinary women and men are being represented neither by actors nor through documentaries or news programmes where they are framed as in some manner exceptional or exemplary, and where they are expected to ignore the televisual apparatus. Game shows are one of the principal places on television where we can see ordinary people showing, unreflexively, what 'being a woman' or 'being a man', or indeed 'being an ordinary person' on television means. To talk of this as a situation in which the person is in control of their representation is to go too far, but the opportunity for ordinary people to produce a television persona within the constraints of the programme's format is available. This is not to deny that the unfamiliarity and the pressure of the situation has led many people into performances they regret.

Contestants on all but a few shows are immediately identified by name, occupation and home town. Their appearance allows viewers to add gender and usually some idea of ethnicity and age. On prime-time programmes this is generally followed by a short chat with the host during which the most probable question to be asked is about family. This is not the case on those programmes which start with a large number of contestants, like *Fifteen-to-One* or *Who Wants to be a Millionaire?* In the latter, the majority of people do not even speak, they are identified by on-screen labels, type in their answer and then, unless they are the fastest correct respondent, disappear from view. *Who Wants ...* has a cannon-fodder view of contestants, though once the person is chosen for the hot seat the normal exchange begins.

The ordinary people who bring their varied objects in to be identified and valued by the experts on *Antiques Roadshow* demonstrate very clearly that they have learned by watching the show the type of behaviour expected. This programme has been running for over 20 years on BBC1 on Sunday evenings. It operates not just to a strict format – for example, if a particularly valuable object has been found it will be used to produce a climax at the show's conclusion – but also has recurrent narratives played out in each encounter between the ordinary person and the expert. The ordinary person must always be surprised at how much their object is worth, and keep silent about any recent valuations they have received. They must appear ignorant of the value of their table, painting or ornament and they know that the stories elicited about its acquisition to frame discussion are given more time if there is a family story of its passage through several generations, rather than if it is a recent purchase.

The owners move, as other ordinary people do, from 'lack' to gratitude. They arrive at the filming of the programme with an object about which they ostensibly have only 'family' knowledge, and, thanks to the programme, they have this knowledge augmented by expert information and advice about care, insurance and potential market value. It is similar to the movement of the successful game show contestant, arriving with nothing and leaving with prizes, or the recipient of a house, garden or wardrobe makeover entering with a mess and leaving with a bounty both material (the new garden) and intangible (the knowledge about how to achieve similar outcomes on their own). The appropriate response to the programme's beneficence is gratitude. *Antiques Roadshow* participants thank the valuers even when their hopes have been dashed and their object is revealed as a fake. For many years, losing contestants on the Yorkshire TV game show *3–2–1* happily accepted a ceramic model of a cartoon dustbin. Part of the enjoyment for viewers of home or garden makeover shows is in watching the face of the surprised owners as they try to do the 'proper' thing and show joy at the transformation. Viewers' attempts to guess if the reaction is an honest one fuel subsequent programmes, like *Changing Rooms Revisited* where past recipients reveal their 'real' reactions, although in most such cases the presenter is able to present some aspect about which gratitude is still felt.

Even in the reality game shows, ordinary people go through most of these phases. They are identified in the same terms, even though it is rare for these contestants to be married or to have children. Because, for some of the contestants at least, their day-to-day behaviour will be the focus of attention for a number of weeks, there is space for a gradual revelation of the chosen persona. This only occasionally happens and most people remain more or less as they have been initially presented. As the programmes became more common, contestants learned that here extreme behaviour is more valued; a tantrum gets more play than the quiet acceptance of a situation. If sexual activity is on the agenda (*The Villa*), it starts as soon as possible. The expression of gratitude is less apparent both because the contestants are often chosen because they have abrasive personalities and because relief at escape may overwhelm it, but gratitude is relevant and does get shown. Only one person wins, but the gift of exposure is given to many and this is, after all, what television gives most freely.

That television exposure itself is a valued gift can be seen most clearly on those shows which visit a viewer's home 'unexpectedly'. Even when the point of the visit is to expose some failure of housekeeping protocols or to commit mayhem (as *Noel's House Party* did), those visited grin and go along with what happens, honoured by the attention. When friends or colleagues arrange for an unaware individual to be whisked away by a programme presenter to take part in ITV's *Don't Try This at Home* or Channel 9's *Love Rules* it is always met with compliance, and usually excitement. Of course, should someone refuse to take part, the show could go no further. This must surely happen, but such refusal is not often acknowledged on air and the picture of the relationship between ordinary people and the television programme remains one where television asks and a grateful populace says 'yes'. A degree of credibility is maintained by the (very) occasional vox-pop refusal, which serves also to show what a 'good sport' those who agree to whatever stunt has been set up are. Channel 7's *Surprise Chef* does start by showing presenter Aristos Papadroulakis having difficulty persuading people to allow him to cook for them, but it is unusual in this.

The public row over the ethical nature of a set-up involving Australian current affairs presenter Jill Singer for a prospective item on celebrity candid camera show *Surprise, Surprise* included Singer's comments on knowing that the programme required her to sign a waiver before the segment could go to air. She commented that only because she worked in television did she know of the power of this device to veto screening, but the debate implied that only those who already had television exposure would want to exercise such a right (Dodd, 2001: 8). A television professional's dignity might well be damaged, but ordinary people could be expected to enjoy the experience.

The studio audience

The final and most populous group of people involved with ordinary television is the studio audience. They could also be regarded as the most ordinary in that they are more diverse than those chosen as participants since they do not need to be articulate or particularly attractive. The studio audience acts as surrogates for home viewers and also cues them to the appropriate response, adds to the impression of liveness and provides feedback in the studio on the progress of a show. Increasingly, people in the audience are allowed to speak on camera, but there are still programmes, like the majority of game shows, where it never happens and where those anxious to communicate through television are reduced to holding up posters.

Getting a studio audience can be a substantial undertaking even if no members of it need do more than watch the show and clap when directed to do so. While very popular programmes can be choosy about who to accept, others solicit passers-by. Jane Shattuc describes the differences between various US talk shows' studio audience recruitment. For *Oprah* and *Donahue*, popular and restrained programmes, viewers wrote in asking for tickets and were allocated a restricted number each month in advance (1997: 73). *Sally Jessy Raphael* and *Geraldo*, however, examples of the newer unrestrained shows, had a more haphazard approach: 'they often had to resort to pulling in pedestrians to fill up seats, including workers on lunch breaks, lucid street people and unsuspecting tourists' (74). They also sat plain-clothed security personnel among the audience.

Signs on pavements near television studios regular advertise tapings which can be attended and researchers canvas various social and sporting groups to send along their members. Being part of a studio audience for any kind of show can become something of a day out, costing little more than a bus fare. Because much taping takes place during the working day, audiences are often disproportionately composed of retired people.

Having a studio audience is advantageous in a number of ways: it can provide actual people to interact with; it provides a focus for those more intimately involved with a show to perform at; and it enables the home audience to have some surrogate on which to model their own behaviour. Sarah Kozloff says of the latter that 'the viewer isolated at home can now get the sense that he or she is experiencing the narrative communally, and his or her reactions are likely to be augmented by the example of the studio audiences' (1992: 80). A studio audience is, however, almost always a larger group of people physically present together than is the case for the home viewer. The audience for the eviction night

Big Brother shows were more similar to sporting or concert crowds than the more normal studio audience; not only more numerous than for other studio-recorded programmes, but also far more noisy, ebullient and uncontrolled than would be desirable in the average living-room. Yet they still functioned in the way that the programme producers desired a studio audience to do, still showed how a committed fan of the show would react.

To ensure that the studio audience cues the one at home to enjoy the programme, all shows using live audiences also use warm-up people to prepare the audience in the studio for having a good time from the moment the presenter arrives. The studio audience is brought to a peak of excitement that needs to be both visual and aural, so that the home viewer is persuaded about the worth of a programme. Many people are reasonably regular studio audience members. John Deeks, a very experienced Australian warm-up man, who is also the main provider of voiceovers for the Seven Network, has noted that 'only about 30% have not been to [a television taping] before' (quoted in Meade, 1999: 19).

There are now many opportunities for studio audience members to step out from the crowd and to speak. Some may be plants – people placed in the audience but already chosen as interested parties willing to speak on an issue. Others may have been screened in discussion with the warm-up person or the presenter during ad breaks. Yet others may have been nominated as participants without their knowledge by the friends sitting with them in the audience. The audience for game shows like *The Price is Right*, where contestants emerge squealing from the audience to 'come on down', is vetted as it files in and only the most ebullient are called upon. In the course of the show, apparently spontaneous solicitations from the stage bring some of the nominated people into the camera's eye. People left standing at the beginning of *So, Graham Norton* are asked embarrassing questions; those behaving oddly in the front row of *Baddiel and Skinner, Unplanned* may have found themselves on stage for the duration of the show; while others have had their lunch-boxes as well as their opinions scrutinized during *Late Lunch with Mel & Sue*. Interactions with the audience extend much further than these examples, but the extent to which they name programmes aimed at a younger audience is meaningful.

The kind of programme that assumes a studio audience sufficiently quick-witted to behave naturally when confronted by a (hyperactive) presenter is not often targeted at older audiences, though talk shows provide an alternative. Livingstone and Lunt record comments of people who became members of the studio audience for *Kilroy* or ITV's *The Time, The Place*, both comparatively serious audience discussion programmes; some saw themselves continuing a long series of different acts of political engagement and anxious to get their point across; for others 'Participating was a bit of a joke: "they just said it was a laugh, a chance to get on TV, and because you got a bit of food and wine afterwards, they just went along for that aspect of it"' (1994: 117).

Active viewers

In using the term 'active' here I am not following the 1980s tradition associated with John Fiske to talk of viewers making their own, supposedly subversive, readings of televisual texts. Instead, what I intend is to talk of those viewers who become actively involved in the operation of a programme. At the end of the previous chapter, I referred to the collusive community of viewers who made production possible. The focus there was on those who actualized their involvement by appearing as contestants or members of the studio audience. Now I want to turn to those others whose active participation is not a visual one. These are the people who write, phone, email or fax messages to programmes for use on air, as well as those who vote in reality game shows. The involvement is attenuated by the lack of physical presence, though arguably they have a greater impact than those studio audiences who are heard but not seen. The message-senders are, like writers of letters to the editor, vetted and chosen from a range to suit what the programme wants to say at that time, but as with letter writers, there is no reason to assume that their messages are fabrications – so many viewers send messages to choose from, it would be wasteful to employ someone to create them from scratch when all they would need would be a little editing.

Those viewers who vote on reality game shows not only help fund the programmes' production, they operate to make it less predictable and to take a small amount of the guesswork out of producers' attempts to cater for audience desires. While they are not necessarily representative of the audience as a whole, and the number of votes by no means indicates the number of people voting, it can be argued they represent those who are most committed to the show. The show may seem to 'belong' to them more than television programmes customarily are able to. The range of shows incorporating voting viewers into their format is wider than reality game shows – *DIY SOS*, the BBC renovation show, calls on viewers to vote for one of three households who would like their incomplete or botched renovations fixed up in forthcoming shows. The triviality of the activity and the extent of their involvement, not to mention the ambit of their power to determine the direction of the show, is hardly what was being envisaged by those writing of the democratic potential of interactive television, but they are interacting and having their desires noted. Shows in which audience members are able to vote, as compared to those where they are not, are able to build more vociferous loyalties and to gain more extensive promotion in other media. It is also probable that targeted advertising in these shows is able to be sold at higher rates – slots in *Big Brother* certainly were.

An additional way in which viewers may become active is encouraged by the programmes but occurs elsewhere – in chat rooms set up on dedicated websites associated with the programme. It is now quite common for lifestyle programmes (as well as the current affairs and other more political programmes which first started the practice) to conclude with a voiceover or on-screen announcement that one of the guests will be available in the chat room to talk to viewers on-line. The programme here acts as an intermediary in setting up the possibility for direct exchange between viewers and those who have been featured in programmes, but instead of all possibilities of such exchange being filtered through the presenters, as is the case with letters, calls and emails, because interaction occurs in the slightly more private on-line space, the presence of the programme is reduced to a frame and regular personnel disappear.

The distinctions between the various people who take part in the ordinary television programmes are subject to various levels of erosion. Audience members become participants and experts mutate into celebrities. Presenters may even become themselves celebrities, but only on shows other than their own, while assistants of various kinds may get promoted to presenting their own programmes. On some of the magazine shows, reporters may move into the presenting chair or the presenter may go reporting, but otherwise the presenter is the most stable of the roles. Despite the hope of many participants, it is rare for ordinary people to be able to use their appearance on a programme to move into the field professionally; it is possible, from explicitly designed talent shows, but few go from, say, game show competitor to well-known person, though those few that do, like Australian Barry Jones or Fred Housego, the London cab driver who eventually had his own programme on heritage curiosities, encourage others to see it as a route to fame. Such fame may be brief, but it can still be influential. The huge number of applications for *Survivor* mentioned above were responding not just to the programme itself but also to the celebrity status of Richard Hatch, the first survivor. He was touring Australia for promotional activities (including an appearance on *Celebrity Who Wants to be a Millionaire?*)

at about the same time that the second series was being shot, in Queensland (Idato, 2000: 2) and it looked at that time as if he had found a new career. The majority of contestants on the first British series of *Big Brother* went on to try their hands at television presenting or reporting, but few if any were able to sustain it; a minority of the Australian *Big Brother* contestants were given more than guest spots in the media, and one extended his spot on *Neighbours* to a more extensive role.

The ordinariness of the programmes is in keeping with the personae projected by those appearing on them. It is rare even for the celebrities appearing to retain all that much of the air of being special. Occasionally, a film star will appear on a chat show and retain the aura of being different. Joan Collins makes no pretence of herself being ordinary, though she is often found in its surrounds. For the most part, though, the people who appear on ordinary television seem just like those who watch it, just a little better looking, a little more articulate, a little luckier. It is being on television that makes the difference, and given how voracious the medium is, surely we can all achieve that.

Pervasive Discourses

When one looks across the considerable range of programmes that constitute ordinary television, there is not the discursive diversity that such an ostensibly disparate body of work might be imagined as generating. A relatively small number of discourses and discursive positions recur. The main variation is age-based, with those types, like reality game shows in particular, that appeal to younger viewers having different positions from the more traditional programmes like game shows and lifestyle ones. Quite a small group of preoccupations cover the entire range, though few programmes draw on the full set. Consumption, family, health, sexuality and leisure are at the core. They are both articulated to one another and tightly articulated to the self and thus amenable to the overarching discourse which is about the power of television in the transformation of the self.

Televisual discourse is insistently about television itself. Ordinary or not, through station IDs and programme promotions, television trumpets the gift of entertainment it brings its viewers. Ordinary television, through its inclusion of viewers into programmes and constant solicitations for more people to become programme content, offers the added gift of actually appearing on television. There seems no space to argue that such appearance is anything other than highly desirable. To say that one does not wish to appear on television is to mark oneself as 'stuck up' or, more probably, lying. Being on television is a validation of worth as friends and acquaintances comment admiringly and family members tape the show. Even being a member of a studio audience is good – it brings one closer to the programme; one has some 'insider knowledge' (another gift from the television gods); one knows what it is 'really like' on set. And all this is before any object or money is won or any keepsake proffered.

Ordinary television goes further, though, in that it explicitly presents itself as setting out to help people. Many of the shows give advice, helping viewers with their day-to-day problems with gardening, cooking or relationships. Far more directly than the drama programmes which may be drawn on in the processes of identity formation, ordinary television establishes a role for itself as addressing our everydayness, showing us ourselves (or our surrogates) and indicating ways we can improve. By focusing attention on some aspects rather than others, it informs us of what it thinks is important, what we share with others. It establishes a picture of the ordinary, the everyday, the normal. Battles over televisual representation are not just trivial 'me-too-ism', they have real point, since exclusion from this picture is an assertion of marginality, of being – for these purposes at least – beyond help.

CONSUMPTION

As was noted earlier, when the development of the VCR and the remote control gave power to viewers to avoid ads, consumption, always a presence on advertising-funded television, had to move more strongly into the programmes themselves. This is not to suggest that this was completely new, rather it was an intensification of an already existing practice. Even when there were tight restrictions on how much could be won on British game shows, contestants competed for prizes. From the very beginning of television, new products, especially household ones, were discussed in information programmes aimed at housewives. Presenters of cooking programmes advocated new commodities or, as rationing slowly retreated in Britain in the years after the Second World War, told a nation no longer familiar with foodstuffs like bananas how to use them. Product tie-ins started far earlier than commonly believed. *Muffin the Mule*, a BBC children's programme, broadcast from 1946 to 1950, involved the production and sale of Muffin toys and transfers to decorate nursery furniture.

Consumption is one of the most pervasive of televisual discourses. Of all the types of programmes being considered, arguably only reality game shows and docu-soaps fail to feature it prominently. From game shows giving prizes through all the various house and garden programmes hawking wonderful 'new ideas' for spending money domestically, to science and technology programmes promoting new gadgets, ordinary television advocates consuming goods and services. The development of infomercials, even if they are screened in the early hours of the morning, and of pay-TV shopping channels, take this to extremes for they no longer have programmes into which products may be placed or advertisements dropped; instead they are all product, all consumption. They are, however, quarantined from other types of television, emphatically marked out as different. Very briefly, in 1997 Channel 10 aired *What on Earth?*, called by its producer a 'shopping advice programme', which attempted to produce a programme solely devoted to the promotion of products without any other content to disguise the nakedness of its intent. It was not a success and was dropped after six episodes. During late 2000 in the UK another attempt at a shopping advice programme also began a six-week run, albeit at 1 am. ITV's *That Prezzie Show* stayed with the comic and the gimmicky, featuring singing robot lobsters, little chairs for mobile phones to sit on and that old stand-by, chocolate body paint. Viewers tested the gifts and experts in the studio discussed them. It reappeared in 2001, so perhaps the inclusion of ordinary viewers made it more appealing. Yet in the categorization given on programme listings, where most of the programmes I am considering appear as 'entertainment', 'quiz' or 'magazine', this show is actually listed as 'consumer', alerting viewers to its distinctive lack of disguise and similarity to infomercials.

Despite the assertion of *What on Earth?*'s producer that in today's hectic and atomized world people need guidance about shopping, it is hard to think of any other area where people in the contemporary world are now more persistently informed. This is not to say they are better equipped to make informed decisions about consumption. Generally what is provided is information about availability. It is reasonably rare, even when lifestyle programmes test several different makes of a product with the aim of recommending the best (itself no longer a standard approach), for them to broadcast adverse findings. *Burke's Backyard* occasionally still follows this practice; it dismissed several types of programmable watering systems as unacceptable during October 2000. A programme on consumption with a thoroughgoing critical component continues to have a place, though not, it would appear, in Australia. In 1996 the ABC's *The Investigators*, the only Australian programme operating on behalf of consumers in seeking to rectify their wrongs, ceased operating after 12 successful years and consumer investigations became only an occasional item on the more sensationalist of current affairs programmes. A short-lived attempt to produce a replacement on a commercial network ceased when Channel 9 pulled an Australian version of *Watchdog* after two short series in 2001. The British situation is a little better; Rachel Moseley mentions there being a consumer competence component in the 1999 BBC2 daytime show *Shopping Town*, where it is hybridized with docu-soap (2000: 301). In prime-time, the BBC's

Watchdog continues to fulfil the consumer affairs protection function and on BBC2 the weekday early afternoon programme *Working Lunch* does some consumer stories. It is notable that all these are on the public broadcaster. The idea that consumption is not just a continual flow of pleasure where objects or services fulfil desires and solve problems is otherwise not seriously contested.

It is worth considering motoring programmes for an example here. *Top Gear* has had a long run on the BBC, although, oddly, there was no motoring show screening in Australia during the 1990s between the end of the long-running ABC show *Torque* and the beginning of 2001 when *Dimensions on the Move*, a lighter lifestyle-inflected programme started, also on the ABC. At the heart of these programmes is the road test of a new model car, but there are also smaller items on related matters which may be car accessories or advice on driving in foreign countries. Given the centrality of the continual parade of new models and the way that the evaluation of them is customarily in terms of performance and then their suitability for particular types of drivers and particular situations, there is no equivocation that the purpose of the programme is to advise on the purchase of cars and other motor vehicles. Yet a car is a major purchase, and for the overwhelming majority of viewers one they make no more than every five years, and then not necessarily of a new vehicle. The address to the viewer assumes that consumption is the point, but the actual consumption is hardly ever of the displayed, discussed and lauded object. Whether the viewer watches for some kind of fantasy investment or for the acquisition of knowledge about the product which can then be socially traded like sports statistics, the viewing does not lead in any direct way to a decision to consume.

The same is true of the newest subject matters for ordinary television – real estate shows which discuss the process of buying and selling properties, follow individual buyers and vendors and give advice on preparing properties for auction. The Australian ones started with *Hot Property*, hosted by the actor Michael Caton, fresh from his appearance as the father of a family fighting to save their home from redevelopment in the film *The Castle*. He continued to present its follow-up, *Hot Auctions*. The Channel 9 alternative, *Location, Location*, is similar to the British ITV show which adds an extra '*Location*' to its name. *A Place in the Sun*, the Channel 4 programme on purchasing property in foreign countries (primarily southern European ones), which is broadcast four times a week, must surely be only of fantasy value for the overwhelming majority of its viewers. Houses of any kind, let alone holiday ones, are even less frequently bought than cars, yet the programmes rate very well. The combination of vicarious consumption and socially useable information (so that one can pass on advice to friends contemplating real estate transactions) is, presumably, the attraction.

The desire for knowledge, which I am suggesting is a motivation for watching motoring and real estate programmes by those with no intention of purchasing such expensive items, can be regarded as a form of epistemophilia. It can apply much more widely to all manner of factual television programmes. Using the term 'epistephilia', Bill Nichols discusses it as a pleasure relevant to documentary realism leading to a 'distinctive form of social engagement' (1991: 178) marked by distance and reasoned analysis. John Corner, establishing a typology of the range of pleasures offered by television, cites the pleasures of knowledge as one of his seven categories. He notes the problems such a concept brings, since television is regarded favourably for its role as a popularizer of knowledge, yet is simultaneously subject to disdain for trivialization and the blurring of distinctions between different orders of knowledge. The latter is particularly evident in the jumble of memorized facts required for quiz show success (1999: 96–7). Lynne Joyrich's discussion of the pleasures Elvis fans take in their knowledge of the performer demonstrates a less serious way in which the concept can be used to refer to what she terms a 'knowledge without anxiety' (1993: 87). Joyrich notes the way fans adopt a partial approach concentrating on aspects of the detail of Elvis' life and disregarding the totality and its implications. Calling on Freud's discussion of epistemophilia as being generated by curiosity about reproduction and sexual difference, but rejecting the anxiety such a desire for knowledge produces in the child, Joyrich claims that in renouncing any desire for closure and stability, the Elvis fan 'is empowered to revel in the pleasure of speculation without subjecting herself to the frustration provoked by an actual lack' (ibid.: 86). Something of this same enjoyment of knowledge of details may be operating here, but the sheer pleasure in acquiring information, its ability to give some sense, however illusory, of control over the subject matter is only part of the appeal of information programmes like these. I think that there is also a form of (low-level) social utility to information so acquired and that it is a way in which the sociability displayed on television in the provision of such advice is spread more widely, still with a televisual referent.

While motoring and real estate programmes cannot operate on the assumption that their viewers will buy the touted product, house and garden shows, and many others, like cooking and money advice ones, do anticipate and prepare for viewers' emulation. And with cause. Equipment hire companies report increased demands for any tool promoted in the previous week's home-improvement programmes. The scheduling of gardening programmes in both the UK and Australia for

Friday evening is based on the assumption that people can visit garden centres on Saturday morning, buy suggested plants and plant them over the weekend. The availability of fact sheets assumes that the advice and the products advocated will be taken up by a significant number of viewers. The BBC's *DIY SOS* is one of many programmes producing fact sheets (also available on-line) which, while rather cryptic about processes, provide good contact details for suppliers. As the fact sheet for a Victorian bedroom says: 'Returning to traditional techniques, Chris plastered the walls using lime plaster and horse hair from the Cornish Lime Company (tel: 01208 79779). It's a technique no longer used in modern houses so seek technical advice.' Channel 9's *Our House* is similarly general. The fact sheet for a bathroom renovation reads more like a summary of the programme than a guide to using the advice given.

> Next step is a meeting between Shirl and Natasha to design a DIY vanity. Shirl takes the appropriate measurements and notes on Natasha's desired look, then he's off to the workshop. The end result is a sophisticated, streamlined vanity with loads of storage space. Natasha has chosen to finish the vanity with Formica colours including New England Elm and Caramel (trim).

The useable 'facts' in both instances relate to products and service providers not techniques. While this emphasis on consumption benefits providers of goods and services, the stress on speed and scant attention to technique can mislead inexperienced viewers about the ease of some of the renovations discussed. A front-page story in the *Sydney Morning Herald* at the beginning of 2001 quoted both Australian and British safety experts' concerns about the significant increase in household injuries since house and garden shows became popular in the mid-1990s (Nixon, 2001: 1).

It is, however, a very different story when it comes to gardening fact sheets, for there the information provided may be considerable. The starkest contrast is available with the sheets for *Burke's Backyard*. The details available for a painting and decorating project entitled 'Colour House' glossed over technique and provided names and telephone numbers of suppliers, but the information on plants was detailed and extensive and recipes using the fruits of one's gardening labour were given in full. This indicates that the programmes understand that it is the smaller purchases, like plants and foodstuffs, that are more likely to be taken up by viewers, though, even so, only a small proportion of the total viewing audience can actually be out buying the new variety of *impatiens* or other bedding plant or object recommended. Every viewer, though, must be addressed as if he or she were a member of that special proportion, while not being alienated if only watching to daydream of possibilities.

Considering all this leads to a need to be cautious about precisely what is being claimed about the televisual discourse of consumption. Shopping channels provide examples of absolutely direct selling, of broadcasting designed to sell particular objects to viewers *right now*. Other channels operate indirectly, most commonly under the guise of helping viewers with problems, problems which, not coincidentally, most often have product solutions, though that product may itself be a book of advice, as is frequently the case on talk shows. The power of products, and services and information about them, to solve problems and bring happiness is the most pervasive message. Although individual programmes promote specific products (and may need to ensure that sufficient stock is available before going to air), the discourse that surrounds them is a generalized one about, at its simplest, 'more good stuff'. There is no immediate requirement for the 'stuff' to be expensive. A constant refrain in the Australian version of *Ground Force* is about the desirability of cheap plastic plant pots which can be painted to look more expensive. The important message is one about not being complacent. One can never have enough 'stuff', and television's role is to alert viewers to the existence of more products and services for their utility in the endless project of the self.

At the beginning of the 1990s, Paul du Gay and I wrote about the television drama programme *thirtysomething* and its portrayal of its characters as exemplary representatives of the service class, their project of self and the tutelary role they played for others of that class and those of subordinate classes in instructing them in ways to live (Bonner and du Gay, 1992a, 1992b). In the period since, instruction in ways to live has become much more overt and the injunctions of ordinary television about the consumption of goods and services involve very little of a 'trickle-down' effect between classes. (Indeed, cooking programmes remain one of the few types of ordinary programming where there is any direct address exclusively to the middle classes or any fraction of them.) There is, of course, a difference between the ways that drama and home advice programmes operate, with the former far more likely to operate indirectly and more bound to the markers of the specific class fractions portrayed. It is far from impossible for drama programmes to engage in direct promotion of products, as the development of linked websites selling featured clothing from shows like *Sex and the City* or *Dawson's Creek* demonstrate, but it is still a move away from the television programme. The 1990s saw a substantial expansion in the proportion of television programmes giving direct information about consumption and the increase and mode of their operation require examination.

Nikolas Rose's study of the new ethical politics which has developed over the last decade or so (a period very similar to that which is my concern in this study) considers everyday life and consumption among the sites in which the government of conduct can be observed. His discussion of the way in which consumption and the technologies through which it is mobilized function socially provides an explanation for the increase and the changed way ordinary television addresses its audience:

> Commodities appeared to illuminate those who bought them, to have the power to transform purchasers into certain kinds of person living a certain kind of life. Consumption technologies ... establish not only a 'public habitat of images' for identification, but also a plurality of pedagogies for living a life that is both pleasurable and respectable, both personally unique and socially normal. They offer new ways for individuals to narrativize their lives, new ethics and techniques for living which do not set self-gratification and civility in opposition. (Rose, 1999: 86)

The objects and services that are the content of so much of ordinary television, then, have a prime role in identity formation and its fine-tuning, but also in the production of the ordinary, civilized individual.

Speaking about audience reactions to popular factual programming, Annette Hill has observed that programmes such as those concerned with pets, healthcare and DIY, typically watched by women with their children, were regarded as valuably focusing on self-management rather than management by institutions. The women surveyed used them as opportunities to talk about issues of domestic and community care with their children, discussing ways in which they were like or unlike those being viewed and establishing an ethical viewing position (Hill, 2001). The pedagogies about the respectable life operated by the programmes are here reinforced and personalized by family discussion.

One of the principal ways in which the nakedness of advice to consume more is disguised is through the category of lifestyle programming. This term only became meaningful for television during the 1990s, although similar shows had been screened earlier. Even away from television the term has only had much currency recently. Anthony Giddens notes that a 'lifestyle can be defined as a more or less integrated set of practices which an individual embraces, not only because such practices fulfil utilitarian needs, but because they give material form to a particular narrative of self-identity' (1991: 81). Rose refers to it as a 'habitat of subjectification', a 'belief that individuals can shape an autonomous identity for themselves through choices in taste, music, goods, styles and habitus' (1999: 178). Mike Featherstone, more explicitly detailing how the link with consumption operates, notes of lifestyle, that

> within contemporary consumer culture it connotes individuality, self-expression and a stylistic self-consciousness. One's body, clothes, speech,

leisure pastimes, eating and drinking preferences, home, car, choice of holidays etc. are to be regarded as indicators of the individuality of taste and sense of style of the owner/consumer. (1991: 82)

The list of sites where style or taste is able to be evinced overlaps substantially with the concerns of lifestyle television and obviously reaches into the other discursive sites being investigated here. It is indeed one of the central ways in which the discourses are articulated with one another. Featherstone's reference to individuality, though, needs care, especially in the context of television. Individuality is a complicated matter for television. Desirable because of the way it can be used to underpin an increase in consumption on the basis that individual difference is demonstrated through individualized consumption patterns, yet problematic because broadcast television cannot address an individual and is not interested in individuals until enough of them can be aggregated into a market with shared preferences.

Lifestyle television addresses an individualized viewer with advice about consumption practices ostensibly designed to improve the quality of life in the area addressed by the programme. Actual audience members are addressed only in as much as they recognize themselves and their desires within what the programme is offering, but the fantasies on offer are structured to be inclusive wherever possible. In the overwhelming majority of cases the advice given aims to bring viewing consumers up to date with recent practices and fashions so that they may maintain an appearance reasonably in keeping with their peers. The most common starting point is that the viewer has a problem which can be solved by a product or service; the problem may be straightforward, like not knowing what to plant in shady areas of the garden, and easily solved by naming shade-loving plants, or it may be one tied more directly to self-identity such as worries about appearing out-of-date, which can be solved by advice about contemporary clothing and practices.

The first type of problem is one that is amenable to a single solution, potentially lasting for ever, but the second, centred on fashionability and its meanings inscribed on the viewing self, needs a programme form which provides provisional solutions amenable to constant updating. Even the first case can be redefined as needing revisiting once plants, too, are conceived as being subject to the vagaries of fashion. Having a cottage garden when all one's other appurtenances speak of a trendy inner-city sophisticate is to the eyes of a lifestyle programmer an unacceptable disconsonance requiring advice and correction. Fashionability requires constant monitoring and corrective consumption. Information may be once and for all, but once lifestyle is involved it is always amenable to change.

Lifestyle television does not talk about social differences in terms of class or other markers of social inequality. The differences it acknowledges are ones of taste, seen simplistically as free-floating preferences for one collection of things rather than another, with neither causes nor consequences. A small space is allowed for age-based distinctions since so much of both television and consumption is age-targeted, but otherwise differences are based on 'free choices'. Pierre Bourdieu's analysis of the stratifying function of lifestyles sees matters very differently, establishing as it does the way in which tastes and consumption practices confer distinction on those operating on one rather than another set of routines (1989). Bennett et al. examine how Bourdieu's principles operate in the contemporary Australian situation. They note the greater relevance of age and gender than class and educational attainment on most aspects of taste, but are far from supporting the lifestyle programmes' representation of the world of consumer preferences as one where tastes are completely individual matters. Their examples indicate class-linked preferences in home decoration, and more definite linkages in the ownership of art-objects and in the choice of leisure activities where education rather than income appears decisive (1999: 53, 108–11).

Home-improvement programmes or holiday guide ones can readily be seen as lifestyle programmes, but other types are not as obvious. Health programmes, with their focus on illness and its prevention, may not seem likely candidates for the lifestyle category. They do not seem to fit Featherstone's rubric of 'individuality, self-expression and a stylistic self-consciousness'. Yet the preventative medicine aspect has allowed space for fashion and thus self-expression. Even more emphatically, the shift in the cost of cosmetic surgery procedures that has seen them marketed to the lower-middle classes, together with the popular fascination with transformation, means that such operations and procedures have become a staple of medical shows as well as daytime programming. The typical components of health-based lifestyle programming are celebrations of new forms of treatment and hints on preventing illness and disease. The paradigm shift in public attitudes which has seen a biomedical model of disease and its treatment downgraded in favour of a model of personal responsibility for one's own wellbeing and a rise in the influence of alternative health practices (see Coward, 1989; Hardey, 1998) has influenced both the forms of treatment and of prevention discussed. The individual to whom the advice is directed is conceived as being a body eager to be improved by dietary changes, exercise regimes, cosmetic enhancements and surgical corrections. The body in health programmes is insistently disciplined.

Lifestyle programmes rarely address the young (see Bonner, 2000: 113) who rely on sitcoms for lifestyle guidance. This is even more the case in

Australia where the absence of any programme specifically devoted to clothing, like Britain's long-running *The Clothes Show*, takes out that area most likely to appeal. It is generally the case that programme preference is very different for those under 40 than those over 40, with Bennett et al.'s survey of preferred programme type supporting ratings-derived information to emphasize the desirability of sitcoms and other humour-based programmes to the under-40s, while news and information programmes are generally the preferred domain of those over 40 (1999: 76–7). The success of ordinary television programmes appealing to younger viewers (especially reality game shows like *Survivor*, but also including those with a 'talent' base like *Popstars* or *Search for a Supermodel*) is unobservable in the data from the Australian everyday cultures project, whose television programme categories do not even allow for game shows (ibid.: 73–8). Making the division at 40 is probably a little too high to be precise about the change from leisure pursuits being based away from or in the home, but this is the age on which the various statistics available operate.

FAMILY

The only discourse that challenges consumption for supremacy is that of the family. Like consumption, it is tied to the televisual at a level deeper than programme content. Broadcast television is structured around the existence of the family at the level of scheduling which specifies children's viewing time and time for families to watch together, as well as at the level of programme classification. Just under a quarter of all households both in Australia and the UK are single-person ones, and many others have only single-generation occupants, so families are not necessarily the most typical way of living. Nevertheless, whether or not the viewer lives as part of a stereotypical two-generational family of parents and young children, the availability of free-to-air television is built on the assumption that family life is in need of protection from some of television's offerings and that the way to do this is to schedule certain programmes only after young people can be assumed to be in bed. Pay-television does not schedule in this way, choosing to operate instead through channel streaming, but all countries that operate pay services have dedicated children's channels and most also have ones named 'family'. Television is thus marked out as something organized around families, a mode of address only increased in power by its domestic location. Furthermore, families are seen as homogenous in their everyday practices; all, for instance, are assumed to send their children to bed at more or less the same time.

Brunsdon and Morley, discussing *Nationwide*, the BBC magazine programme of the 1970s and early 1980s which was, in a number of ways, a programme that produced the category 'ordinary television', talk about it as articulated through the domestic and operating to constitute 'a nation of families' through its mode of address and selection of stories (1978: 73–4). For Brunsdon and Morley, as later for Morley and Robins, the importance of this address to families is that it is a first building-block in the creation of communities which then build into nations through the operation of broadcasting systems providing shared experiences and 'knowable' collectivities (Morley and Robins, 1995: 66). Ordinary television as a principal site for the presentation of families, neither fictional nor in duress, is especially important in this.

Game shows are particularly rich sites for examining the construction of the televisually 'good' family. One of the most revealing small signs is that the show called *Family Feud*, in Australia and the US, had its name changed to *Family Fortunes* when the format was adopted in the UK. Though the subsequent production of *Families at War* indicates this is no longer the case; in the 1980s and early 1990s good British families obviously did not feud. In this public opinion guessing game the contestants compete as families trying to produce the answer most likely to be given by a variously representative sample of people. In this they demonstrate Garry Whannel's observation about the public opinion shows that they 'reward normality and penalise deviance' (1990: 105). The shared abilities of the family to approximate (or guess at) typicality is what the show rewards. While the answers given by family members with and without consultation reveal the extent to which they are like other people in their opinions, in their composition and in their demeanour they provide a picture of families themselves. As I have noted elsewhere, they show that the decline of the traditional nuclear family has led to a recognition that membership of a family may be quite diverse (Bonner, 1992: 241–2). As well as wife and husband or parent and child, or multiples of these, families may now consist of cousins, aunts, in-laws and neighbours. They can squabble a bit during preliminary negotiation, but recriminations over wrong answers are not sanctioned; family solidarity must be preserved. Whether or not it is to produce this harmony, some types of family relationships cannot be represented on game shows. Ex-spouses are never acknowledged as family members; and families are insistently heterosexual phenomena.

Game shows here reveal their membership of an older grouping of television programmes (though one has to exempt Julian Clary's *Sticky Moments* which operated from a homosexual perspective to find heterosexuality peculiar). Heterosexuality is not so all-encompassing on some of the newer formats, where homosexual relationships may occasionally be acknowledged (*Love Rules* has had a same-sex item). Many versions of *Big Brother* and other reality game shows have had homosexual participants, but they have only been included singly with the remainder of the contestants steadfastly maintaining their heterosexuality. Homosexual families, though, are more likely to appear as social problems on talk shows and current affairs programmes than as unproblematic ordinary television fodder. A few exceptions can be found in the UK at least. *Changing Rooms Redecorated* was a partial recycling of previous episodes of *Changing Rooms* in which the programme returned to a previous makeover to see what had been retained and what changed. In exchange they offered a small new makeover. In one 1999 episode the return was to two homosexual couples – one gay and one lesbian – who had made over each other's rooms. The lesbian couple were now expecting a child and asked for something for the baby's room. It was treated as unexceptional, but was, none the less, a rarity.

I have already noted how game show contestants are immediately identified by name, occupation and home town and how viewers can add details of gender, ethnicity and age. The short chat with the host, commonly about the family, can occur in a range of ways. For *Who Wants to be a Millionaire?* it usually comes from the host asking who the contestant has brought along to the studio and the camera then focusing on this person who may be asked about the relationship with the person about to answer the questions. This procedure seems designed to increase the pressure on the contestant, since the audience member is allowed to express the tension and worry that is deemed improper for the contestant to show, but its content is usually focused on marriage and what the money (if won) will buy. Mike Wayne argues that the stress on the family in *Who Wants to be a Millionaire?*, which is known to have a reasonable proportion of children in the audience, operates to deflect possible accusations of greed, since it can be suggested that spending of any prize money is for the family rather than the individual (2000: 215). In this programme, as well as for other such shows, questions are predicated on particularly strongly gender-stereotyped views of family roles and a traditional concept of the trajectory of the ordinary life as one in which romance, marriage, children and grandchildren follow inevitably. Since presenters have brief dossiers on each contestant which frequently include reference to some supposedly amusing incident in the contestant's life, the introductory chat, or its continuation as the successful contestant proceeds through the game, can gloss over moments that fail to fit the regular pattern and to stress those that do. Single parenthood and marriage breakdown are still barely acknowledged, though remarriage is happily discussed. The categorization of the programmes as entertainment means that the tone must be happy and light and, in consequence, the picture conveyed by the shows idealizes family life as one of boundless love and support and only the occasional amusing contretemps.

When matters become more serious, ordinary television's role of bringing pleasure and being fun can still continue. In a segment of an episode of *Don't Try This at Home* (tx. 202 99, 6.10–7.10 pm) that is so rich I will refer to it a few times, an instance of a family dealing with imminent death provides a clear example. The item concerned a mother dying of cancer who wrote in to the programme proposing one of her daughters for a stunt to remember her by. The daughter nominated was the thinner and prettier of the two shown, although both girls went to Australia where the stunt took place. In the studio, footage of the stunt was repeatedly intercut with reaction shots of the mother in the audience. The daughter was required to walk across a thin plank between two buildings ten storeys up without a balance pole but with a safety net. She fell into the net, as did presenter Davina McCall when, as the rules of the programme require, she attempted it.

There was nothing special about the young woman who attempted the walk. She was not particularly proficient nor, except in comparison to her sister, all that attractive. In class terms she gave indications of being lower-middle or employed working class. She was, though, absolutely typical of the people who take on the challenges posed by the show. Here, however, she enabled the operation of a double refraction of the programme's premise. Because the challenge had moved out of the casual shopping-centre dare into a premeditated, organized event laden with a range of emotions other than the usual adrenaline-charged terror, its celebration of the extent of a mother's love transformed the programme from one obsessed with the trivial and the humiliating into something heartwarming and socially 'good'. At the same time, by surrounding the fact of imminent death within the family with fun and with the gifts of televisual exposure and a holiday, it transformed death as well. The centrality of the family setting to this cannot be over-emphasized. When ordinary television has to deal with death – and given its fascination with medical matters and with hard-luck stories ('tragedies') it must do this with some regularity – placing it within a ('plucky') family is the principal way in which it manages to do so while increasing its audience.

The shifts in the late 1980s and the 1990s that saw the elevation and romanticization of fatherhood to the point that men could push prams in public with equanimity and sportsmen were insistently photographed with their young babies, had effects on ordinary television too. In the chats before questions are asked or redecoration begins, men and women are asked about their families in approximately the same detail. The primacy of fathers being present at the birth of their children is thoroughly endorsed. An episode of the Australian treasure-hunting programme *The Great Chase*, in which three small teams travel over substantial parts of Australia in search of clue fragments, had one team composed of three people (two is the norm) because the wife of one of them was expecting their second child. Throughout the show, viewers were shown the man phoning his wife to check on progress. When, in the middle of the chase, he heard that his wife had gone into labour, a cliff-hanger throw to a commercial break asked whether he would stay with his mates or return to his wife. There was no question really; of the three competing calls on his attention – trying to win the money, being loyal to his mates and being present at the birth – the last is the one that must now publicly be heeded. It also made for good television since the credits were able to roll over the teammates visiting the new baby in hospital, giving a degree of sentimentalism and noble sacrifice to what was otherwise a succession of desperate bids for money and television exposure.

As is seen here, friendship is allowed a place in addition to the family, though it is definitely ranked second. Again, in *Who Wants ...*, after the associated person in the audience (usually a partner or family member) is introduced and the game gets under way, should the contestant decide to use a lifeline, attention can then shift to the identity of the 'friend' called for help. This person may be either family member or friend, but questioning establishes the basis for the friendship, and if the person is a workmate, discussion is extended until a site for the friendship away from work is identified. In other game shows, contestants are further embedded in the domestic and familial through the prizes offered; here, with money being the prize, such embedding is done through personal connections. Friendship features significantly in programmes involving young adults, too young to have embarked on the marital path, and for game shows like the British *Best Friends* the teams are constructed of university friends or workmates with a shared social life. There is also a major place for friends in *Changing Rooms*. Here it is probably the case that friends rather than relatives are chosen to make over one another's rooms, because family, in televisual eyes, is closer and might be more protective of their relatives' property and their wishes for its redecoration than friends would be. This will be examined further below.

The presence of celebrities on chat shows provides another site where family life becomes the focus of attention. The exchange of privacy for fame that underpins the operation of the celebrity industry, as well-known people promote activities they are connected with by making their private lives available for public interrogation, is ready television content. From the mawkishness of *This Is Your Life* to the abrasiveness of tonight shows, celebrities talk about their partners and children most frequently as a way of demonstrating how, despite their fame and wealth, they are, at heart, really quite like us. Their children also say cute things, they rush to the bedside of ailing relatives and they are sure that the latest romance is forever. Television programmes are much less ready than tabloid newspapers or magazines to dwell on the scandals, misfortunes and dysfunctionalities of the lives of the famous. The most common type of programme dealing with celebrity is the chat show where both questioner and questioned are present together and the restraints of polite interchange between people, modelled on (reasonably recent) friendship, are dominant, so the speculative excesses about 'love cheats', abusive husbands and bad mothers can only be presented as media intrusions that can be exposed as lies to a sympathetic audience. Showbiz gossip does have a small televisual presence on programmes like *Entertainment Tonight*, but otherwise ordinary television operates as a second-level discourse where gossip is a subject in itself asking for discussion and, from the celebrity's point of view, management. The contradictions of deploring media intrusion into one's privacy before an audience of millions, and in all likelihood on an outlet owned by the same company as that bankrolling both the intrusion under discussion and the product being promoted by the exposure, are unexplored. Gossip is constantly massaged back into conventionality by, for instance, noting that while the celebrity wedding may have been represented as extravagant and marred by the behaviour of overly flamboyant guests, what really mattered was that their family and friends were there celebrating together.

For ordinary television, the family is not a diverse structure, nor is it a place of problems and difficulties. Unlike documentaries, drama or news, ordinary television idealizes the family as a social grouping that is shared and desired and which produces harmony and joy. It might seem that talk shows present very definite exceptions here, and certainly the families that appear on such programmes are selected precisely because they do not exhibit the characteristics of the ideal. Their bizarrerie is judged, though, in terms of its departure from the norm; the advice they are given is designed to move them closer to the romanticized ideal of man and woman and their children in a happy, closed unit. This is not to say that the affective economy of the programme endorses this. Audience pleasure is generated by the situation's 'wrongness', by the violence the confrontations on *Springer* unleash and by the excesses of those whose sexual activities fall well outside those covered by the rubric of 'family values'. The advice and the displays of regulation may be in the light of a tacked-on 'moral', there to sanction the display of rule-breaking, but they represent the dominant voice, they are there to produce closure. Even if the presenter recommends ending an abusive relationship it is in conjunction with comments about making it possible for the member nominated as the 'good' one to be able to meet a more acceptable partner for the future. The majority of cases considered, though, are not ones of families at all, rather they are of individuals, but even here the situations quite often are ones in relationships that are seen as potentially family ones or as ones where a family is concerned about the behaviour of one of its younger members.

HEALTH

I have already begun the discussion of health in terms of its relevance to lifestyle, but not all the discourses of health on ordinary television are encompassed by this. The primary areas of content remain new treatments and hints on the prevention of illness. Dedicated health programmes focus almost entirely on these. Science and technology programmes often include segments examining new medical breakthroughs as do news and current affairs shows. Daytime programmes, both magazine-style and talk shows, frequently have segments or whole shows devoted to issues of health and wellbeing, looking both at new products and providing hints on maintaining good health. They, more than any other type of ordinary television with an interest in health, are most likely to include the chief other way in which health issues are addressed – the personal story of the encounter with illness. A standard feature of public health campaigns is the appearance of representative sufferers on shows like *This Morning*, where the pattern of individual testimony combined with expert advice about precautions to take, symptoms to look out for and treatment, if necessary, ensues. Personal testimony from ordinary people about the experience (and preferably its cure) enables such items to be integrated more firmly into the programme by giving a place for the presenters to become involved in the exploration of the situation. Resulting items are longer than the alternative type of segment where a visiting expert simply gives advice to camera.

Health is a more pervasive subject for television than its appearance in dedicated programmes would suggest. Together with law and order on the one hand and sex and romance on the other, it is one of the three largest generators of dramatic material. Hospital series and medical subplots in soap operas and crime shows provide far more continuing discussion of illness and disease than can programmes designed to give advice on health. It is the dramatic potential of the area that makes it so valuable for fictional as well as non-fictional programmes; personal stories of 'miracle cures' and tragic tales of lives blighted by disease dominate medical series far more often than they find their place on ordinary television.

The high personal salience of health and illness, as well as its dramatic potential, underpins the attention paid. The shift from a biomedical model of disease, where medical personnel knew best and looked after us, to our having personal responsibility for our own wellbeing has led to viewers directly addressed by health magazine programmes being repeatedly assured of the need for constant vigilance to maintain or improve our health. Yet this seems in no way to have diminished our desire also for information about medical treatments should we or our families and friends become unwell. The combination winds seamlessly through the programmes: telling us to increase our consumption of broccoli to prevent cancer; reporting on increased use of twilight anaesthetics; and interviewing people who have recovered from life-threatening diseases through intensive, high-technology treatment. There is hardly ever a suggestion that despite our responsibility for our own health we should be admonished when we do fall ill. The 'happy family' tone of most ordinary television (in conjunction with their own lack of visual attractiveness) means that the contemporary diseases for which guilt is most definitely ascribed – those associated with smoking and excessive alcohol consumption – are rarely discussed once they occur; instead they are dealt with only as reasons for lifestyle changes.

The chief exception to this is the programme type which regularly follows a number of ordinary people through the course of their hospital treatment. Exemplified by prime-time programmes like *Jimmy's*, in the UK and *RPA* in Australia, these carry many of the hallmarks of docu-soaps, even if *Jimmy's*, at least, was well-established before the name was required for the category. Firmly placed within a biomedical model and unsuited to product promotion, these programmes can be the final place where the consequences of not following the advice given on other programmes can be displayed, but this is never made explicit. One of the closest instances to this encountered was on an episode of *RPA* in August 2001 when the return to a patient with severe facial skin cancers was introduced in voiceover by the comment 'And now we check up on what is happening with the consequences of Billy's long love affair with the sun.' In Australia, with the world's highest incidence of skin cancer and long-running campaigns about sun protection, there was no doubt that this was a tutelary example. More commonly, the conditions being treated are unrelated to the pervasive advice about exercise, diet and check-ups and are integrated into the flow of ordinary programmes through the persistent placing of the sufferers within family situations. The grimness of the medical situations and the gore of the operations is softened and rendered televisually palatable by the emotional story of the anxiety and relief of the relatives waiting for news. This is not to say that at times the rawness of the emotion is not on a par with the severity of the depicted surgery. Similar daytime shows which are screened in the UK, like the BBC's *City Hospital*, are usually softer, visiting new mothers and talking about baby names as well as interviewing staff about their jobs.

The self-help, preventative side of health coverage means that the combination Health and Beauty is a prevalent one. But this combination is a category title more than an operative single description of items. The two parts of the category usually separate quite clearly when it comes to coverage. As a title, health helps negate the vanity aspects of beauty while beauty helps negate the morbid side of health. Together they imply great desirability and encourage the production of shots of beautiful bodies, yet the actual items are rarely able to bring together make-up advice and ways to combat the common cold. It is more usual for the terms to be linked only metaphorically, as they are for 'healthy skin' or 'healthy hair'. Items on cosmetic surgery and dieting, even if the item is a scare one over eating disorders or surgery that has gone wrong, are the principal ways in which actual conjoining is able to occur.

A recent addition to the health category has been items or special programmes considering what once would have been the difficult area of mental health, often under the more user-friendly rubric of dealing with stress. The BBC's early 2001 campaign entitled 'On the Edge' brought together a range of programmes dealing with topics such as depression and anger, presenting them explicitly as health issues. It did so through the usual modes of self-help instruction and interviews with sufferers, but it was placed together with a more extensive component of investigation than is usual on ordinary television since many of the programmes screened were clearly documentaries.

SEXUALITY

In the last 15 or so years of ordinary television, sexuality has been disarticulated from the love, romance and commitment package where it was previously mostly to be found and rearticulated with fun, transience and willing exposure. The shift from verbal to visual is a feature of the newer shows, although there are still programmes where it is the primary discourse which remains verbal – most obviously talk shows. Gendered differentiation within the shows is much less noticeable than it was, both genders being now presented as eager for sexual adventures. The old standby of mutual incomprehension between men and women being a major factor generating entertainment is less evident, now the main factor is display and the lengths to which people are willing to go to engage in it. Vulgarity, which once was present on television primarily in scripted work associated with comics like Benny Hill, is now so common in programmes requiring the participation of ordinary members of the public that naming it 'vulgarity' seems exceedingly prudish. The appearance of Channel 5 has itself been an indication of a major shift in what is acceptable televisual discourse on sexuality in the UK. No such clear shift can be observed for Australia and it is here, in particular, that the dual influences of UK and US programming are most evident. Sexuality on Australian television is much more in the display of beautiful bodies, scantily clad, in the American tradition, than in ordinary people talking about what they like doing sexually. The nude game show is yet to appear, though nudity is to be found in some reality game shows.

Until the mid-1980s sexuality was not a prevalent, overt discursive trope on ordinary television. It was, of course, present, but in terms of this book's organization would certainly have to have been discussed as a disguised discourse. The major disguise was love and romance leading, of course, to marriage and the production of a family. The other way in which its presence was muted was simply denial of its applicability to standard televisual practice. Pretty game show hostesses walked contestants on to game show sets because that had rapidly become the way things were on television; it gave interest to an otherwise fairly static visual field. What was to become the rich field of dating game shows had precursors in shows like *Mr and Mrs*, where married couples would be quizzed on each other's preferences with the audience's pleasure provoked by revelations of ignorance. The extent to which this was read as revealing incompatibility, male insensitivity (the men rarely knew their wives' favourite colours or flowers), or too much time spent on the physical side of the relationship would obviously vary from viewer to viewer (and maybe contestant to contestant), but it certainly generated a frisson among audiences, cued by studio audience responses. Some of these shows were designed for newly wed couples to be contestants with all the added sexual charge that 'newly wed' had in the days of supposed pervasive female premarital virginity.

Traces of this can still be found in the interchanges between presenters and contestants on the more slow-moving and staid game shows. The briefing papers given to presenters lead them to prompt contestants to tell amusing anecdotes about their past. Disproportionately, often, whether or not it is germane to the focus of the show and even when the contestants are grandparents, these are about their honeymoon. Honeymoon stories, it seems, are still good for a studio audience snigger and for revealing the ordinary people who appear on television as both good sports and just like 'us'. If these chats between presenter and contestant are regarded as microconfessions during which contestants reveal themselves to (and are judged by) presenter and viewers, then the prominence of the honeymoon may be less remarkable given Foucault's assertion that confession has always privileged sex (1980: 61).

Exhibitions of symbolic male–female incomprehension have declined, being replaced by the all-too-literal post-separation game shows like *Ex Rated*, though this opportunity for rancour and revelation about past misdeeds is as yet only seen as appropriate for Channel 5. In its revamp from its precursor *Can We Still Be Friends?* and its shift to a later time-slot, the focus on the sexual side of the failed relationship was intensified. A milder version, though, has been evident for many years in the reporting-back sections of dating game shows where dissatisfactions with the experience feature. Here, since sexual activity was rarely admitted, social niceties were more likely to be the focus.

Sexual confession of a mild kind can also be found on chat shows, especially those later-night ones, whether bonhomous, like *Parkinson*, or sharper-edged, like the tonight show variants. Here the disguise or denial became less, but those involved were rarely themselves ordinary people; rather they were celebrities exhibiting that part of their lives that was less ordinary – not the family person but the famous, desirable figure. For the most part such discussion tended to be phrased in terms of dating and marriage or at least long-term relationships and involved mention of love and romance, but this was not always the case. Male celebrities could talk of pursuit by female fans and joke about sexual topics. I have a personal recollection of Laurence Harvey on a late-night chat show during the promotion of the 1968 film *The Charge of the Light Brigade* joking about bestiality.

The more overt admission of the sexuality of ordinary people came with dating shows, most notably the Australian *Perfect Match* and its British derivative *Blind Date* (which later gave its name back to a revamped version of the Australian show). Here, while one of the long narratives of the series included a desire for a marriage attributable to the programme (and massive on-screen celebrations of those achieved), the weekly stories were, and continue to be, of people wanting to have sexual fun. The marriage narrative was most noticeable through the comments of Cilla Black, the British presenter, in her interrogations of the couples who had been sent off on the date the previous week. Cilla's attempts to get the couple to admit to the possibility of a continuing relationship and her questions about the 'most romantic' aspects of the date sanitize the premise of the programme – setting up people, who had not met previously, for a few days away together. The 'choosing' section of the programme, though, is marked by sustained sexual innuendo and display with which the presenters are complicit. Audience pleasure, as indicated by studio responses (and discussion with other viewers), is generated far more through the revelations of people not getting on and being rude to one another in the reporting-back sequence than of their contemplating continuing to see one another. Like the talk shows just discussed, the affective economy of the programme is at odds with the overt discourses.

More recent dating shows make even less pretence of romantic motivations. ITV's *Dishes* may be seen as characteristic here. In this food-based dating show the choice was based on tasting dishes prepared by those wanting to be chosen and the date was at a restaurant. The reporting-back sequence occurred during the date and was concerned with immediate evaluation of a person's suitability as a dining companion – which was much at variance with the sexual tenor of the studio discussion. In almost all studio-based dating shows currently running in the UK (dating game shows ceased in Australia during the very early 1990s), contestants are asked about the type of person they prefer and usually specify a collection of physical traits. Studio-based dating shows most commonly refuse to allow those choosing to see the people they are choosing between. Clues are given by other means, aurally or gustatorily, for instance, but part of the viewing enjoyment is in watching the choosing contestant pass up the person who best matches his or her physical ideal for someone who looks very different, misled by clues which are not designed to reveal appearance.

Clues operate more to reveal behavioural choices or to act as pointers to personality, and there may have been a reference in the descriptions of preferred types to broad categories of personality – outgoing or fun-loving both being favoured. The *Blind Date* website itself encourages people to become contestants if they have 'a sense of fun, a good personality and enjoy life', and, of course, are 'single and unattached'. 'Fun' is the key word here, as it is used quite widely across ordinary television. For programmes with a strong sexual basis it signifies a readiness to engage in sexual banter with the presenter and other contestants, a willingness to present oneself as sexually knowledgeable and a high degree of imperviousness to embarrassment. It also includes a willingness to 'give things a go' and make the best of things, which may or may not refer to things immediately sexual. Cilla has sent hopeful couples on survival courses when they were expecting weekends in the West Indies. Having a 'sense of fun' requires them to go through with whatever it is that they have won, preferably with minimal complaining – up until the reporting-back sequence of course.

Fun was central to the operation of one of the most influential of the programmes to break the dating show formula, the German format *Mann O Mann*, the many derivatives of which, including the Australian *Man O Man*, are discussed in some detail by Albert Moran (1998: 83–9). In this show a large number of male contestants competed to be voted most desirable by an all-female studio audience with losers being pushed into a swimming-pool by one of an equally large number of identically clad hostesses. That women were interested in men's bodies and that men were willing to preen and pose them to win approval may not have been socially surprising, but on early 1990s television its blatancy was a revelation. Although several of the segments had a dating pretext, including one in which the contestants had to play-act a chat-up leading to asking for a date with one of the hostesses, the winner did not head off on an assignation with someone from the programme; rather they got to choose their own partner for their prize trip and there was no report back. Sex was shown as a matter of visual display by and for ordinary people, devoid of almost all of the trappings of romance, bar the occasional stage prop, and with women as eager to judge men as men were to strut their stuff.

A few newer shows test the sense of fun further by shifting from a dating basis to more of a challenge/dare format. *How Much Do You Love Me?* was Channel 7's attempt to move Australian television into the sexual fun and games of British television by importing Denise Van Outen to present a programme with some aspects of her Channel 4 show *Something for the Weekend*, but toned down for an earlier time-slot, if not also for the Australian market. Only two programmes were screened, but the first one began with the item used to promote it across television and print media, the presentation to a member of the studio audience of her parents on stage in a double bed as the subject of a series of questions she was asked about their sexual life. Van Outen asked the questions (like 'When did you parents last make love?'), the daughter gave an answer, but it was the parents themselves who declared it right or wrong. This took the mutual incomprehension of husband and wife into new territory since the lack of secrets between spouses is part of the mystique of marriage, so their exposure is socially sanctioned, but the maintenance of sexual decorum between generations of the same family is still a powerful force and the public breaking of the taboo required a very high level of tolerance of embarrassment. Embarrassment was indeed the point of the segment, as it is of most of the items within the sexual challenge shows. Contestants are required to face questioning about matters not usually discussed before strangers, not with a view to changing practices around the norms of sexual discussion and privacy, but simply for the entertainment value of seeing how far people are willing to go for televisual exposure in a sexual context.

The newest move in sex-based ordinary television programmes is to go outside the studio on location, taking with it the much greater emphasis on the visual. Channel 4's *Streetmate*, formatted in Australia on Channel 7, has a simple structure of the presenter (in Britain, Davina McCall, who has presented a number of dating shows) finding a single person wanting a date, walking around the location and eyeing up the local talent until a possible person is identified, at which point the presenter asks if a date is possible. If it is, the show follows the pair. Channel 9's *Love Rules* involved various people being nominated by friends or workmates as needing a date, before being presented with a situation in which several contenders perform (for example as male strippers or trainee lifeguards), before one is chosen. Shows like this reveal how much the premise of the *Blind Date*-type shows is that a choice is made *without seeing*. It is as if having to make a choice between options based on voice, sharpness or crassness of wit, and statements of preferences (or in the *Dishes* case, choice of food and competence in preparing it) is more discreet and closer to the norms of ordinary behaviour than basing one's choice on visual evidence. For a visual medium to have valorized the non-visual in these ways is at first surprising. What the unseen choice shows do is remove the body from the equation while the newer programmes put it back in place. When the body is absent one is not, of course, making a sexual choice, but one based on intellect; one is being clever not base. The vulgarity of the newer shows is revealed by their flaunting of this maxim; with them the choice is nothing but sexual, being based shamelessly on the display of the body.

The shift from the verbal to the visual also signals a diminution in the applicability of the term confession to the sexual discourse of ordinary television. Confession is, above all, a verbal activity involving the articulating of knowledge about one's deeds and acknowledging that they could be subject to the judgement of others. Looking at three different men dancing in posing pouches and choosing to go out with the second involves no such frame of reference. The reporting-back sequence which allows for reflection on the experience undergone is rarely a component of these newer game shows, implying that with the return of vision to the choosing process, people knew what they were in line for and revelations about the 'real thing' are less salient. Rather than indicating that there is nothing to confess, this absence attests to the way that the presence and progress of sex does not need to be brought out by the process of confession.

The other new area for sexual display is in reality game shows. These may be founded in a sexual set-up or in some broader mix of compatibility and conniving. *Temptation Island* is an example of the former, being based on discovering whether ostensibly faithful couples will resist the sexual lures of desirable other partners. *Big Brother* (and more particularly its French variant *Loft Story*) has sex as one component of the lives of the resident competitors which is scrutinized by the viewers. That it is not just one of many components but the most important one is revealed by the compilation of sexually charged clips which screen in a later time-slot than the regular daily one under the title of *Big Brother Uncut*. No other aspect of their lives is given this attention. The effect of this treatment is to maintain sexuality as an area of prurient interest: will the couples stay faithful; how much of their body will each contestant reveal; will certain contestants become sexual partners; if they do, what will we see? The dating game shows' situation – that the show will set up a couple of strangers to go on a date – is extended into one in which the show sets up a group of people not only to become sexual partners but also to perform aspects of that partnership for an audience of millions, in the hope of gaining either a direct monetary prize or a career boost. Sex becomes part of the price of fame (instead of being its far-from-secret reward).

The complete dominance of heterosexuality has been fractured in the later shows, although homosexuality is still only rarely acknowledged. If homosexuality has become something very occasionally to be shown as evident among ordinary people in segments on shows like *Love Rules*, the total taboo has become homophobia. This, like racism, is now only admissable as a problem to be addressed, in a talk show perhaps. The practice of placing one homosexual person among the contestants in the endurance types of reality game shows like *Treasure Island* or *Big Brother* provides opportunities for 'tolerance' to be displayed or homophobic statements to be disciplined. This is not to suggest that homophobia (or racism for that matter, since it is accorded much the same treatment on reality game shows) is absent from television, the over-representation of white heterosexuals alone indicates that this is not the case, but the expression of homophobic sentiments is no longer sanctioned. If the rules of a game to be played by two teams require men to hold hands, while that may generate audience laughter at the discomfort it evokes, contestants must comply. At the time of writing, audience acceptance of homosexuality as a sexual practice, though, had not been tested – only one homosexual was allowed in any group and the same-sex others stayed resolutely heterosexual. The first Australian series of *Big Brother* was marked by a very severe difference of opinion between those in the house and the production group, on the one hand, and the most vocal part of the audience, on the other, over the worth of the gay contestant, Johnnie. On more than one occasion, an emerging contestant was warned that their feelings of affection towards their gay housemate would not be well received by the studio audience. Overt homophobia may not be allowed expression on the programme, but its expression by voting viewers can still inflect the show.

The exception to the absence of homosexuality on ordinary television throughout the postwar period, culminating in a few recent token gestures, has been, especially for the UK, a camp style of presentation, which was quite common. The extent to which this actually functioned as a sign of homosexuality (though by no means necessarily of the sexuality of the presenter) is problematic, especially since such campness, until the appearance of Julian Clary, seemed strictly in the service of heterosexuality. With the possibility of a camp style actually being linked on television to the sexuality of its exhibitor, there has been something of a diminution of its appearance, both for game show hosts and for television cooks – though in a late flowering, *Two Fat Ladies* finally showed it was possible for female presenters to operate the mode. The current principal prime-time locale of camp style is among the interior decorators on makeover shows. It continues as one of the available modes for late-night programmes like *So, Graham Norton*, though still largely to discuss heterosexuality (and fetishism).

During the 1990s, a number of infotainment programmes specifically devoted to sexual matters screened in both Australia (like *Sex/Life*) and the UK (*The Good Sex Guide*). They tried to treat sexuality as another aspect of people's lifestyles, amenable like their clothing or their kitchens to remedial advice and handy hints. The subject matter, though, was still somewhat 'sensitive', and while fashion and home shows had a long history of being the subjects of televisual treatment, there were no forerunners of television sex shows to modulate into the lifestyle approach. Programme producers had to learn how to make sex infotainment-style and audiences had to learn how to watch. The Australian programmes took their lead from what had long been the traditional way to discuss sexual matters in public – medical discourse – and chose to model their approach on medical infotainment. This meant that a problem was posed and a solution given; for example, the first erect penis on Australian television was shown in an item on erectile dysfunction in

Channel 9's *Sophie Lee's Sex*, in 1992. The magazine style allowed the didactic aspect evident in this item to be tempered with other consumer-style items – ones looking, for instance, at new ranges of sex toys.

As the title *The Good Sex Guide* indicates, British programmes were not so restricted by a medical model – holiday shows provided a template. Sex here was framed not so much as a sequence of problems in search of solutions, but rather as a fun activity often in exotic locations. Scandinavian orgies and American sexual healing were enthusiastically investigated. Both Australian and UK shows used ordinary people as the subjects of their segments, though some of the sexual problem items were actually re-enactments or dramatizations. They also both employed female presenters – Australia choosing a sequence of young, blonde women, presumably to provide an antidote to the medicalized representation of sex, and the UK using the older comic actor Margie Clarke to reinforce the idea of sex as all a bit of a laugh and to counteract the suggestion that it might be giving the wrong impression to the young. These shows are now much less common. There have been none in Australia for many years, leaving one with the impression that there were only a limited number of problems to be solved or related products to be investigated and that the current audience (or at least the younger segment of it that was the target audience) is now well-informed.

By and large, ordinary television appears happier with using sex as something to joke and speculate about rather than to confront in its practicalities. The reality game shows already discussed used sex as a major drawcard, but it was in conjunction with something else – 'love' was regularly invoked, 'fidelity' was being tested, or the game was really about being able to get along with your fellows while appealing to an audience. An attempt to do something different was *Boy Meets Girl*, a reality game show screened on Channel 4 early in 2001. A group of eight contestants agreed to learn to look and act as members of the opposite sex. Having been carefully screened by psychologists to ensure that the experience would not be harmful for them, they were coached in transsexual behaviour and the four most successful were sent out to 'pass' for a day's activities unaided. The programme stressed the sociological and the educative aspects, talking of 'insights' and 'challenges' to defuse the titillatory aspects like revelations of the underwear needed to strap down male genitals and the hints from actual transsexuals. Only a three-part series, it was primarily concerned with showing the mechanics of sexual difference and the reality game show format gave it a novel way of showing how extensive the range of sexually marked behaviour was and how possible it was to modify it. (*Trading Races*, a similar 'passing' show on the BBC at the beginning of 2002 had black and white participants using make-up and prosthetics to change their race and to operate under disguise in public. There was no element of the game show for this programme, although the participants again spoke of learning much and the show was promoted as providing insights into issues of race in contemporary UK.)

LEISURE

Many of the discourses already referred to are presented under the guise of leisure. Renovating houses and doing the garden are the most prominent, but the principal way in which leisure is represented on ordinary television is through holiday shows. While sporting activities may well be perceived by those engaged in them as participants or spectators as being what they do for leisure, this is not the way television approaches them. For television, there is a separate category called Sport; it is about competition and is the category that ensures that the feminization of television has some limits. Possibly the only sport that does manage to appear on television as leisure is fishing (and British television even occasionally manages a competitive fishing show). The Australian programme *Rex Hunt's Fishing Adventures*, a rare example of exported ordinary television, is very much a leisure programme, devoted to the enjoyment of being out fishing. Soon after he started presenting fishing on television, Hunt was quoted as saying 'Fishing is one of the world's great pastimes. In bringing it into people's living rooms we can also show it's not the last bastion of men. That it's also enjoyable for ladies and kids' (Stapledon, 1993: 34). The importance of linking leisure and the family is very strong here, but that is not inevitable; leisure can be shown as individually engaged in. None the less, the majority of holidays shown on the more sedate holiday shows (not *The Rough Guide to ...* or *The Real Holiday Show*) are family ones, although presenters are generally shown visiting them alone. When *The Real Holiday Show* did investigate family holidays, though, its video diary-derived format meant that actual families and their experiences were revealed and a much stronger impression of what the holiday would be like for ordinary people, as well as of what ordinary people were like on holiday, was given.

Reality game shows complicate the activity of leisure by appropriating many of its components but employing them not as ends in themselves but as activities to be engaged in to win large sums of money. Thus holidays become *Survivor*-style exercises where people are tested on their capacity to endure privation and obey a series of directions delivered in voiceover or by written message. In *Big Brother* enforced leisure is similarly interrupted by a voiceover directing the housemates to perform a sequence of play-based activities designed as much to entertain the audience as to keep the contestants from getting dangerously bored. Leisure activities are redefined as entertainments for those watching rather than for those engaged in them. A variation on this redefinition of leisure was provided by Channel 4's *Watercolour Challenge* which took the common leisure activity of painting *en plein air* and made it both a site of instruction for viewers and a competition.

Pay-TV allows the category of leisure to expand a little more – walking or hiking programmes can be included and these hybridize some of the pleasures to be obtained from holiday and fishing shows. The solitariness of the sport of fishing is combined with extensive shots of landscape into a type of programme too slow for broadcast channels. Slowness and deliberation, which characterize many leisure pursuits, are not perceived as televisual virtues so programmes which acknowledge their place in leisure activities are relegated to the edges of the television world, as with the flower-arranging programmes during the afternoon on pay channels.

One of the principal problems of the category of leisure for television is that watching television itself is one of the principal contemporary leisure pursuits, yet despite television's overweening self-referentiality, this is not something that is alluded to all that directly. As far as television's principal presentation of itself is concerned, watching television should be far more purposive, an active search for information and entertainment, not something inviting the words 'escapism' or 'couch potato'. Travel and holidays, though, are perfect instances of leisure pursuits and shows like *Getaway* and ITV's *Wish You Were Here...?* combine information about potential holiday sites with the display of activities viewers might be able to engage in if they had sufficient money and time. The leisure activity of watching television is here disguised as a purposive search for information to make an informed choice about a separate leisure activity.

THE TRANSFORMATIVE POWER OF TV

As I noted at the beginning of this chapter, television presents itself as an agent in the transformation of people and their surroundings. From the beginning, the inheritance of the Reithian rubric, with its stress on education in addition to information, implied a desire to transform viewers into better educated, more informed, more cultured people. The loss of power of this version of transformation has not resulted in a total loss of mission; television still aims to transform, just not in those terms. Television no longer has a civilizing mission, instead it has the task of guiding us in our quest for a better lifestyle. Fashionability and happiness are the keys.

One of the ways in which television effects a transformation is through the gift of its attention. Since an appearance on television is in most instances a socially valued thing, becoming a participant in a television programme transforms a viewer from just a person into a 'person who has appeared on television'. Such an individual also, as I noted earlier, becomes a person who is knowledgeable about the operation of television through having been there during production. This knowledge, too, has social value. Any material gifts are in addition to this basic enhancing of status. Patricia J. Priest has observed the enhancement of status operating even for those who appear as examples of 'out-group' behaviour on American talk shows. Having appeared on television is so important a marker that it subsumes whatever other marker of identity it was that caused the individual to be recruited for a television appearance in the first place. After shows were screened, participants found themselves being recognized and talked to by acquaintances and strangers alike, 'not as deviant – as many had feared – but as someone "seen on TV"' (1996: 80).

Television's power to transform makes it something of a contemporary fairy godmother, able to dispel dragons and grant wishes. It is a cliché of consumer investigation shows that problems can be solved by the appearance of a camera crew, that recalcitrant service providers become anxious to please and that contracts finally are honoured. The granting of wishes is an even more common theme. Programmes dependent on a continuing flow of participants regularly solicit for them, offering the promise of achievement as part of the deal. People appearing on dating shows arrive with certain wishes – not necessarily for their dream lover, more usually just for fun and a free night out – and the programme grants them. Separated family members can be reunited by shows like ITV's *Surprise, Surprise* or *Trisha*. Talent show contestants want to be 'discovered' and the programmes give them the opportunity. People whose pets have behavioural or health problems consult television vets and the problems are solved. *Dream Lives* shows the fairy godmother operating in a wider field, happily at home offering technological solutions to problems both domestic and work-related. Television pours out a cornucopia of gifts even before we get to prizes. All it asks in return is that we play along with its own importance, acknowledge its beneficence and give freely of our time and emotional life.

The previously examined instance of *Don't Try This at Home* is relevant here too. It is able to actualize the mother's desires by granting her (dying) wish that the two daughters who have cared for her have something to remember her by. It is possible to regard this in a number of ways: as a grotesque belief that televisual presence is so desirable that it does not matter what one has to do to get it and that the display of one's dying self and exposure of one's family members to physical danger is a small price to pay; that the mother lied about her imminent death to increase the chances of her daughter getting on television; or that a dying mother, unable to buy her daughters a holiday, hatched a plan to get them a treat that required the prettier to undergo a smallish risk, and that that was the only way she could manage it. Mawkish or cynical, these readings are all available, but the programme is structured to display a different story – one of a noble mother, a game daughter and a presenter simultaneously not that different from the daughter but, as the representative of the programme, also the bearer of gifts. The fairy godmother who eases the suffering of the unjustly afflicted is one of television's favourite self-images; it is the mainstay of programmes based on fulfilling the wishes of seriously ill children (a major category for the long-running British show, *Jim'll Fix It*), of family reunion programmes, of consumer affairs investigations and, above all, of the charitable makeover special.

This last is a member of a group of ordinary television programmes which, while located in the ordinary, stage special events that testify to television's beneficence and power. Charity telethons and challenges (in the UK usually involving Anneka Rice and in Australia, Angry Anderson) provide opportunities for television to extend its more usual role of fairy godmother to individual viewers into being the intermediary who facilitates individuals doing good deeds for deserving groups. A variant operates in the case of families heavily marked by tragedy, where a channel brings together people who work on a number of its programmes to help out an individual family 'in need'. This latter not only produces an 'extended family' of related programme teams but also functions to publicize other viewing possibilities to viewers who have only previously encountered one of them. It is not only the more obviously domestically focused programmes that engage in the fairy godmother role; financial advice programmes can include items of this nature; indeed, the Channel 9 show *Money* joined with other lifestyle programmes of the same network in a special named *Renovation Rescue* by advising the family being helped about their financial affairs. In addition to the very occasional multi-programme special which can intermittently allow house and garden shows to shift emotional gear in their gift-giving, individual

traditional house and garden magazine shows too, can convert themselves into makeover shows to aid distressed individuals or charities in need. There is a great similarity to Daniel Boorstin's concept of the 'pseudo-event' here (1992: 9–12); these acts of charity only occur because they are televised, or at least only occur at the magnitude they do for that reason. Certainly charities, groups and families benefit as they would not otherwise do, but these programmes, which are very infrequent, provide alibis for the far more common self-serving promotions of greed. In other sites, a sentimental veneer of doing good is often laid over an opportunistic display. The Channel 9 treasure hunt programme *The Great Chase* required its participants to perform a 'random act of kindness' as they raced to be the team to win $20,000.

The recipient of television's bounty is obliged to show gratitude to excess, not to stint in revelations of the private life and, wherever possible, to be amusing without upstaging the host. They need, in the small space available to them, to act a little like a celebrity, because both types of people are benefiting from television's reach. The secret joy of viewers at the makeover recipient who dislikes what is done and who refuses to pretend otherwise and at the person who admits that the transformation was into something worse is a delight at someone who knows what should be said and refuses to go along with the deal. It is a delight at bad behaviour. So evident has the public pleasure at this bad behaviour become that channels now regularly revisit a selection of makeover sites to get the real story. In part, this is to manage viewers' reactions and, by acknowledging them, retain the upper hand, but it also carries aspects of extending a cheap programme even more cheaply, since some footage is already shot and the participants already identified. Furthermore, the space in which the bad recipient is able to exist was created by the programme in the first place, both through the surprise and the practice, most evident in *Changing Rooms*, of disregarding the expressed wishes of the recipient and producing a result more theatrical than domestic. This kind of revisit is not a characteristic of the more mundane makeovers, like the segments in the daytime shows, or of the most dramatic charity extravaganzas. A return to the latter is invariably a celebration.

Andy Medhurst, arguing that lifestyle programmes are the key British television genre of the 1990s, talks about their presenting a domesticated utopia that maintains an element of reality by using readily available products so our dreams can seem more achievable (1999: 27). Utopia, that 'expression of the desire for a better way of being', in Ruth Levitas' phrase (1990: 8), is what is held out by so many transformative projects far grander than the televisual, but for them that other part of the utopian heritage, the 'nowhere', the state of being unachievable in the current situation, is always evident. Televised utopias are most often, as Medhurst notes, 'domesticated', located in the home and presented as achievable step by step. No grand vision or political project is necessary, just refurbish a chest of drawers today, renovate the spare room next month, buy a fountain for the front garden or plan for the facelift, things will get better and television is there to help. Thus the transformation television engages in is far from that envisaged by Lefebvre, as discussed in Chapter 2. Television's transformation is a conservative one based substantially in the contemporary concept of 'cocooning' – retreating to one's personal space and investing time and money to produce it as a bulwark against the unpleasantness of the surrounding world.

THE MAKEOVER

One of the prime types of programmes specifically devoted to transformation is the makeover. Whether transforming the person or their surroundings, the basis of these shows is the unsatisfactoriness of the original state and the greater desirability of the new. This can be seen as a particular application of Nikolas Rose's concept of the 'continual enterprise of self-improvement':

> The individual is to adopt a new relation to his or her self in the everyday world, in which the self itself is to be an object of knowledge and autonomy is to be achieved through a continual enterprise of self-improvement through the application of a rational knowledge and a technique ... the norm of autonomy produces an intense and continuous self-scrutiny, self-dissatisfaction and self-evaluation in terms of the vocabularies and explanations of expertise. In striving to live our autonomous lives, to discover who we really are, to realise our potentials and shape our lifestyles, we become tied to the project of our own identity and bound in new ways into the pedagogies of expertise'. (1999: 93)

Such self-scrutiny can be observed as foundational to talk shows, but it is valuable to trace its operation away from therapeutic discourses in the practical arena of lifestyle makeover programmes with their aim of bringing self and appurtenances into harmony.

Internationally franchised hit makeover shows like *Changing Rooms* and *Ground Force* are recent additions to the repertoire of ordinary television. The idea of the makeover, though, is not. The transformation of the unsatisfactory into the improved has a long history on and off television, but this history is one divorced from the link to lifestyle and self-improvement. 'Before' and 'after' shots have long been found in a wide range of print magazines from ones devoted to cars, through home and garden ones, to those dealing with fashion. Cooking programmes, already noted as among the earliest instances of ordinary television, have long transformed ingredients into finished products and gardening shows concluded by demonstrating the results of hard work and mulching. Among the most dramatic, yet formulaic, of the before and after shots are those associated with weight-loss programmes and these, which are to be found in just about all visual media forms, as both editorial material and advertisements, are arguably the first to have linked the change to the matter of identity.

The 'pedagogies of expertise' mentioned by Rose refers to the way in which ordinary people take on knowledge and attitudes from professionals, internalizing them as codes of conduct (1999: 92). Rose's emphasis is on therapeutic expertise, but it also can be seen applying to practical expertise, though, when passed through televisual forms, in a rather equivocal way. People, rooms and gardens are transformed on television shows by the application of expertise as much as a new product. Yet this practical expertise is a vexed issue, since while the pretext of almost all of these examples is that the ordinary person can effect the transformation his/herself, once they have been shown how, the 'showing' is nearly always inadequate. The point of making the transformation the subject of television time or magazine space is to disseminate information about how whatever it is can be done. Yet contemporary television audiences cannot be assumed to have followed programmes from their starting point, building up knowledge and practising their skills between episodes; they cannot even be assumed to have watched much of a single programme. The audience is indeed, as John Hartley has pointed out, unknowable and hence most easily treated as if childlike (1992: 107–8). The consequences here are that ordinary people are seen as needing instructing again and again and the expertise which is passed on each week, supposedly diminishing the distance between amateur and professional, evaporates by the beginning of the subsequent show where once again the expert passes on knowledge. There is also, customarily, an illusion of ease conveyed by the expert who advises 'just' doing this and 'just' following it with that, in a way that denies the complexity of the tasks. This denial is abetted by the speed at which programmes are now expected to operate. It is not just that tasks shown fail to observe the real time the job would take, but that whole steps can be omitted in the knowledge that most viewers will never attempt to emulate the expert and that for those that do, more detail can be provided in the associated magazine or book.

While most programmes operate on the contradictory assumptions that the viewer can follow the experts' instructions and that they never learn what has previously been shown, occasional programmes are predicated on a different state of affairs. The lack of knowledge or incompetence of the lay person is overtly the basis of the BBC programme *DIY SOS* where the transformation involves the correction and completion of handyman projects begun by viewers but botched or not completed. Delia Smith's *How to Cook* did actually start from extremely basic information about eggs and assumed a loyal base of viewers who improved (slightly) as the series progressed. Daytime BBC car restoration show *Real Wrecks* differs in that it operates somewhat closer to real time in taking several episodes spread over a number of weeks to bring whatever motor vehicle is being rescued back from decrepitude.

The old before and after presentations did not involve surprise as part of the public component – however, much of it may have been there privately. Now this is central and the production of the surprise is built into the show by, for example, incorporating video footage of the person whose garden is being made over, shot while they are away. The narrative builds to precisely the moment of revelation and it is probably this as much as the existence of the magazine or other related instructional materials that makes it possible to skimp on the details of how effects are achieved. More than how to make a pergola, viewers are led to focus on the surprised recipient's reaction to the pergola. The leading of the surprised garden owner around the site at the end of *Ground Force* resembles a child having to endure the gift-giver pointing out the important features of the newly unwrapped present. No such sustained and detailed admiration of the gift is required in *Changing Rooms* which is much more blatant in its sadism. It is the decorator who is asked to reflect, to identify which is his or her favourite feature. The home owner is required only to be shocked, pleasantly or otherwise, and more sustained consideration is saved for the possible future 'revisit'.

The narrative of gift and surprise and the importance of the deadline make the new makeover shows viewing for the whole family. Children who would not normally be interested in home advice programmes can happily watch a rapid transformation that is being kept a secret from the owners of the property and revealed to them dramatically at the end. Since almost all of the makeovers result in rooms or gardens far brighter and more dramatic than they were previously, the theatricality of the transformation has an appeal to children too.

Rachel Moseley's investigation of British makeover shows concentrates on the individual appearance makeovers, especially BBC's *Style Challenge* and *Looking Good*, but she too notes the importance of the surprise, detailing the withholding of the mirror in *Style Challenge* until the end of the show as the 'climactic spectacle', at which point 'the private experience and the public display collapse and merge' (2000: 307). This latter observation has much more point for the style makeovers, nearly all of which are based in studios designed to replicate intimate spaces like bedrooms, dressing-rooms and beauty salons, than it has for the house or garden ones. The structure of the style programmes fragments the presentation of the person being made over, focusing on their hair, their make-up or their shoes, so that the sight of the complete transformation in the mirror is not only the first look at the whole effect for the participant, but also the first clear look for viewers as well. The prior exposure of parts of the make over, indubitably public though television has made it, has not actually been display in the way in which this revelation of the whole transformed appearance is. Significantly, the moment includes viewers in an assessment of the success of the change, at the same time as it distances them to judge the private affective response: whether the participant is satisfied with the result?

Despite the greater impersonality of making over a house or garden, something of the same applies, as Moseley herself observes. Her concern is to argue that the moment of surprise or revelation is an opportunity for viewers skilled in reading facial expressions to observe 'authentic' responses on a medium where they have been become rare, and she cautions that this 'excess of the ordinary' has the potential to make viewers uneasy with the collapsing of public and private spaces (2000: 314). I consider rather that the extent of this moment is carefully judged in terms of its not becoming excessive, that it is held just to the point of discomfort and then cut. In contrast, the excessiveness of talk shows is held so long that the question of authenticity and the practice of disavowal is raised to cope with the unease. These judgements, though, are not hard-and-fast ones; they vary over time and across cultures. The discreet withdrawing of the camera from close-ups on the family reunions at the end of Cilla Black's *Surprise, Surprise* in the late 1980s and early 1990s would not, I suspect, have been considered had the show been devised in the late 1990s. Moseley's argument does not allow either for what I have earlier termed the 'bad recipient' and our joy as viewers in their not producing the proper response.

Observing the operation of the public and private spaces on house and garden makeovers is revealing, though, especially in terms of the shifting inclusions of ordinary people and the distinctive break of the moment of revelation. A camaraderie is produced among the people working on the transformation, whether they are ordinary people, television performers or trades professionals, through all being together working against the clock. The togetherness delivers an intimacy which, in conjunction with the 'secrecy' of doing the procedure without the recipient knowing what is going on, produces an illusion of the private. Public exposure and display then occurs when the person or couple for whom it is being changed sees it. Viewers, privy to the makeover from its on-screen beginning are thus positioned with the makeover team knowing what is happening privately; aware, for instance, that the new coffee table was constructed of cast-offs salvaged from a skip, and that the paint on the pergola won't be dry until filming has stopped. The makeover goes public when it is returned to the person who owns it. The garden programmes are more obvious in this as the teams become more formal in relation to the space which, from the point of the revelation and handover, is no longer 'theirs'. The surprise, then, is part of this re-inscription of the space from the intimate yet semi-public space we have watched being changed, through to a more public space which is displayed to its owner whose response is the climax of the programme, after which it returns to the fully private as we, and the makeover team, withdraw.

Carol Vorderman's Better Homes does not operate in quite the same way since there is no involvement of ordinary people in the makeover itself, although they are on screen to request the specific changes to their houses, the programme does visit them sequestered away from the project and there is a moment of revelation. The principal difference is that the surprise, even if it is the climax, does not bring closure; instead this comes with the announcement of which improvement has increased the value of the house the most. This shift away from the personal into the formal world of real estate valuations removes this programme from the affective regime of most recent ordinary television since the pleasure the winning couple shows in their extra cash prize is an old-fashioned way to close a programme, no different from a game show and totally lacking in the risk of bad behaviour or the excessive emotion of the 'real' makeover programmes.

Medhurst's interest in prime-time house and garden makeover programmes and cooking shows, stresses the importance of the reaction shots, but observes also how central 'neighbourly vindictiveness' was to the pleasure generated by *Changing Rooms* (1999: 26). He argues that they are less glamorous versions of ITV's talent show *Stars in Their Eyes*, where ordinary people are transformed into versions of the performers whose songs they are about to perform (1999: 27) – an observation Moseley makes too. The domesticity of the transformation is the key to the house and garden programmes' success, though, since it is on the possibility of getting hints that part of the popularity rests. These makeovers are designed to draw on the individuality of the recipients' tastes which are elicited either directly or from friends at the beginning. The results are shown to give ideas to viewers ostensibly for their own subsequent customizing. The performance makeovers reduce individuality and are judged on the success of the impersonation – the 'gift' is much more focused on the single recipient (unless we imagine a nation of would-be impressionists).

One other characteristic of the makeover programmes that needs attention is the importance of the deadline. All of the key makeover programmes allow limited time for the makeover to be completed. Most show the team racing against the deadline and conclude with a speeded-up sequence in which the final arrangement is completed. While a deadline certainly adds narrative interest and provides an excuse for the often slipshod techniques adopted (stapleguns and glue are wielded far more freely than good practice would encourage), it also operates to mark these programmes out from earlier house and garden shows. The earlier ones, like Channel 9's *Our House* usually had, and continue to have, craft segments that assume viewers have ample free time in which to perform embroidery or master French polishing. This may be the case for some viewers, but the newer programmes assume otherwise, insistently using short-cuts and, in their self-imposed race against the clock, reflecting a world in which there is never enough time for what has to be done. Furthermore, in the short-cuts and temporary expediencies they employ, they acknowledge the transience of the fashionability they espouse. The look that has just been used to revamp a dated room will itself have only a short life before it too needs changing.

Medhurst argues that British makeover shows are 'deeply rooted in white, English suburbia' (1999: 27). When they are screened in other countries and when the range of transformation sites is extended further, something of this is modulated, but the sensibility remains predominantly a white, lower-middle-class one. Cooks, like Ainsley Harriott, Dorinda Hafner and Tony Tan, disguise this somewhat, but since all operate in programmes where it is food that is transformed, and thus ethnicity is a privileged category, this is only a slight modulation. While a few of the ordinary people who appear may be other than white and the extent to which middle-class people dominate those chosen varies across programmes and time-slots, presenters are overwhelmingly white and leaving their working-class roots, if any, rapidly behind. The most glaring instances of the dominance of middle-class whiteness may well be the clothing makeovers that are a staple of US talk shows. It is evident even when Ricki Lake is conducting a makeover for black, working-class women before a predominantly black studio audience. Presented with the 'problem' of fat women who dress unsuitably (in tight, sexy clothing),

Lake's experts transform them into more demure figures by putting them into looser clothing so that both their physical contours and their class origins are less obvious.

Makeover programmes are the most overt signs of the way television perceives itself to be engaged in a project of advising its ordinary viewers about their transformation into happier, more satisfied, more up-to-date versions of their selves. Most of the transformative practices advocated involve consumption of identified goods and services; even the spiritual transformation that the new-style Oprah encourages has its associated paraphernalia of books, tapes and courses. The idea of lifestyle has been a very fruitful one for ordinary television, enabling as it does the articulation of many disparate practices into a singular expression of identity located in taste. Such fracture lines as can be seen in the unity this promotes across disparate programmes are located primarily in whether the viewer is targeted as an individual or as a family (actual audiences are, of course, larger and more varied than television can take account of). The newer programmes targeted, by and large, at younger viewers are less likely to conceive of viewers as located in families; the older shows can only conceive of viewers as individuals if they are also perceived as problems (elderly and alone). The atomization of the young and the forced familial grouping of the over-40s are the opposite sides of television's inability to deal with actual individual diversity and its need to set up fictions of what its audience is and wants. There are exceptions to the homogenization into older family consumption or younger individual consumption as some of the sex-based shows reveal, but the dominant discourses are surprisingly harmonious on all matters other than those inflected through the age bifurcation. To perceive a more fractured view it is necessary to consider the discourses which have been in various ways, and to varying extents, disguised.

Disguised, Quarantined and Absent Discourses

The expansion of ordinary television under the rubric of infotainment has led to certain discourses, which had had important legitimating roles under the previous regime, having to be minimized because they militated against entertainment. Chief among these was education, once a key member of the 'inform, educate and entertain' triumvirate. Jeremy Tunstall's attempt to re-insert education in the portmanteau replacement term through the coinage 'edinfotainment' to refer to programmes like BBC's *Tonight* and *Antiques Roadshow* did not even survive to the end of the chapter in which it was introduced (1993: 80–2). As far as the rhetoric of television programming is concerned, education is now an undesirable word, best avoided and used only for programmes specifically made for designated instructional purposes, broadcast at unpopular times of the day. They have nothing to do with 'real' television. Certain discourses closely linked to education – like scientific and historical ones – have suffered much the same fate, though these have not been quite so thoroughly expelled.

The principal other discourses which will be considered here have not followed the same trajectory. Law and order has always been one of the primary discourses for fictional television as well as for news and current affairs. Its absence from ordinary television was a sign that crime was only entertaining in fictions. As a result, as far as ordinary television and its precursors have been concerned, its presence has been quarantined, in the UK in *Police 5* or *Crimewatch*-type programmes or, in Australia, emulating the US, in *Australia's Most Wanted*. Work and employment have never been a particularly productive discourse for television, because however ambiguously television may situate itself as a leisure pursuit (as noted in the previous chapter), it certainly establishes itself in opposition to work. The remaining discourse, economics, has been and continues to be much more complicated. When this book was being planned in the mid-1990s, there was no question that its importance to ordinary television was disguised, but now it is far more overt. I have chosen to retain it in this chapter since the *extent* to which it pervades ordinary television does remain disguised.

EDUCATION

The fundamental assumption of education is that its recipients are improved by the skills and knowledge it imparts. Its centrality to the Reithian conception of public broadcasting underlined the civilizing mission the BBC, and to a lesser extent, the ABC, saw themselves as embarked upon. British commercial television operated for many years in a system where public broadcasting was the dominant form, and when Channel 4 was introduced it too had an 'improving' function, even if it was not in terms Reith would have recognized. In Australia the commercial channels were dominant from the beginning and the introduction of SBS was initially based on catering for the 'home' languages and cultures of an immigrant population, so education and 'improvement' were less central to public rhetoric about television in general.

As well as 'improvement', evident now only in the way it has been appropriated by lifestyle television, in such sites as 'home improvement' and where it refers primarily to fashionability, the other key term for education was 'seriousness', if not always in terms of delivery, certainly always in terms of intent. Education was a serious matter requiring application and effort. All of these terms are inimical to entertainment and thus to the thrust of ordinary television.

Until 1990 the importance of education was enshrined in the ÙK's *Broadcasting Act*, but amendments in that year removed ITV companies' duty to screen educational programmes. Under self-regulation, the companies are required to meet a 'quality' threshold which includes up to two hours a week of programmes with clear educative purpose supported by fact sheets. In 1999 a number of government working parties and advisory groups recommended a greater use of television, especially prime-time ITV, for adult education. The stress on ITV was because the 8 million British adults deemed functionally illiterate and innumerate are far more likely to watch ITV than they are to watch BBC and Channel 4 which do still carry some programmes targeted at improving basic skills. In responding to these calls, the Independent Television Commission claimed that screening such shows in prime-time would dent advertising revenues and that they were meeting their obligations by screening *This Morning*, which provided 'Items on health education, parenting skills, what's going on in schools, but also more kinds of life-styley, leisurey stuff [sic]' (unnamed spokeswoman for Independent Television Commission, quoted in Kingston, 1999: 13). *This Morning* regularly promotes its fact sheets, and in 2001 started referring to them as booklets, although the range of subjects remains more or less the same (recipes, home decoration and make-up are the staples but there are also occasional one-off specials; for example, for the first quarter of 2001 there was one on fears and phobias). In what might be seen as a gesture to a greater educative role, the programme's website promotes the services of Learn Direct, the training arm of the University for Industry initiative. The availability of fact sheets in conjunction with websites in the UK thus serves a purpose in addition to those like the advertising of services noted in the previous chapter. The effect is to move the focus on education off television screens themselves.

That the ITC could so publicly assert that the reason they were lax in abiding by licence requirements was because it would dent advertising revenue (and succeed with this defence as far as one could tell at a time when licences were not up for renewal), is itself telling. It speaks of the diminution of the perception that there is something special about broadcasting, that it is in the public interest to put constraints on the unbridled operation of the market. With the major increase in the number of channels, the profitability of television companies is no longer so easily assured and their compliance with the view that discourses other than those associated with profit maximization should influence their operations has declined, if not disappeared altogether. The introduction of self-regulation to broadcasting – now the most common form of regulation internationally – acknowledged that governments had retreated from most aspects of the belief in the importance of public interest in determining the terms of operation.

Not even such minimal regulatory requirements apply in Australia where there is no 'quality' threshhold for licences and renewals are effectively automatic. The presence of any reference to education on Australian television outside ABC Schools programmes and the early morning ABC Lifelong/Open Learning programmes is even more vestigial than is the case in the UK.

If one does regard the information provided by ordinary television in lifestyle programming on subjects like cooking and home improvements as educative (as the ITC obviously does) then ordinary television is significantly educative when supplemented by print materials. The problem, though, is that education and information are not the same and it is information that has supplanted education. This is not because the field of information has grown, so much as that the growth of entertainment has pushed information into the space where education might once have been.

In addition to the instruction provided by lifestyle programmes, there are a number of shows where teaching or training is more overtly part of the on-screen activities. Talent shows, like *Stars in Their Eyes*, coach amateur performers in professional presentation skills, though these are often offered as 'tricks'. More recent variants, like *Popstars* and *Search for a Supermodel*, progressively reduce the number of contestants over the run of the show, in part by seeing how readily they can learn the skills required of professional singers or models respectively. It is corporeal rather than intellectual knowledge that is being imparted and there is no suggestion within the programme itself that viewers too could be being instructed in what might once have been termed deportment, but instruction is happening and its immediate recipients are regarded as having been improved by the process.

A more significant instance of this occurs in the BBC's *Faking It* (imported into Australia for Channel 9). In this programme, individuals skilled in one area were coached so that they could pass themselves off as practitioners in another. Cameras followed them for the month of intensive training before the final test. During this month, as well as the kind of appearance makeover also deployed in the talent quest programmes, three tutors worked to impart the skills and knowledge necessary to succeed in the test. As well as professionals in the designated area, it is usual for one of the tutors to be a teacher of the fundamental skill. The individual concerned is depicted studying the necessary material and practising the required skills. It is the process of education that is being shown, yet very equivocally. When the individual succeeds in the impersonation (as is usually the case), it is not presented as due to the teaching skills of the mentors, nor to the amount of learning a highly committed individual can achieve in an intensive one-to-one educative situation. Instead, it is advanced under the title of the programme as fakery, as a con-job, managing along the way to denigrate the years of dedicated training of those who earn their living by whatever practice is being 'faked'. On the one hand, the skills of the target activity are shown and treated seriously, whether they be nightclub bouncing or the practice of contemporary art; on the other, the time taken for their being acquired in a way that would enable them to be exercised on a regular, continuing basis, rather than for a single display, is dismissed as irrelevant.

Despite all this, education does have a discursive place on ordinary television beyond the remnant spaces on BBC2 and Channel 4. Formal education is evident as a frame for programmes like *University Challenge* or, in only a slightly different way, *Blockbusters*. Knowledge game shows themselves have education always present as a silent partner in the procedure of asking questions and judging them right or wrong. Though Anne Robinson is not silent about lapses in contestant's formal education in *The Weakest Link*, Cornelia Frances, playing the same minatory presenter role in Australia, has so far made no such comment. The departure of *Mastermind* removed the most likely place to find those employed in education among the competitors and it is now rare to hear any game show contestant admit to being a teacher or lecturer. *Who Wants to be a Millionaire?* does sometimes reveal a person formally engaged in education as the person nominated as the 'phone-a-friend' lifeline. It is notable, however, that while the introductory chat with quiz contestants can ask about their occupation, which might reveal their being teachers, it does not seem possible to ask about their educational qualifications. It is instructive to ponder on why it is that this seems taboo. It seems most likely that it is because educational qualifications are seen as divisive in revealing some people as possibly advantaged in a situation where all are to be considered equally likely to win. Educational qualifications, though, are not of themselves completely unable to be mentioned since they can become relevant when the person concerned is cast in the role of expert (not usually the case on game shows, though Carol Vorderman's Cambridge qualification is an exception).

When there are post-programme interviews with successful contestants, as there have been in the wake of the popularity of *Who Wants ...*, the discussion may ask about how they came to succeed. Here the focus is on the very short term, with the question being most often the bald 'How did you prepare for the contest?', which elicits answers like 'By reading reference books.' In an exception to this on one Australian celebrity *Who Wants ...*, film actor Rachel Griffith commented at the outset that she was nervous because she did not want to let down the nuns who had taught her. (She didn't.) Education is not normally much of a topic for celebrities in their interviews on chat shows unless they are British comedians who started their careers at Oxbridge, and even here the focus is on the extra-curricular.

There are other ways in which education can be a significant component of television discourses and the most common of these is when the programme concerns itself with particular academic disciplines like history or archaeology. Both these are most likely to be dealt with in documentary programmes that cannot be described as ordinary television, but in the UK in particular there are a number of programmes that have devised ways in which to be educative and involve ordinary people without shifting into the populist so far that any element of education becomes unlikely. Channel 4's *Time Team* is the most outstanding of these, but even quite small afternoon programmes like BBC2's *House Detectives* provide detailed historical information and guidance in using archival material as experts help homeowners trace the history of their houses.

Time Team has been running for six or so years and has developed a following both on and off screen with clubs and activities and a range of publications. Each episode records a dig at a site of archaeological interest which may be very old (a Roman fort, for example) or comparatively recent (the crash site of a World War II bomber). Viewers or *Time Team* clubs nominate sites and the Team, comprised of regular members as well as a changing number of experts and a group of volunteers from the local area, dig to unearth information. For the last few series they have also commissioned an object to serve as a memorial marker when they leave. The programme operates to a three-day deadline, a relic of its originating in a live show broadcast over a bank holiday weekend, which gives it the racing-against-the-clock character of makeover shows. The various personalities among the team, like presenter Tony Robinson and regular character Phil Harding, with a trademark hat covering long straggly hair, interact with local informants and the ordinary volunteers to transform the didactic into the highly entertaining, while not diluting its ability to educate regular viewers both about their own heritage and about the ways in which archaeological knowledge is developed. The theme of the programme is that it is possible to discover information about the past from material traces and that doing so is fun. At times there are echoes of makeover shows in the joyous display of men having fun with big pieces of equipment (the deadline means that the arguments about proceeding with traditional archaeological caution versus using an excavator almost always are won by the advocates of the big machine). Nowhere was the play aspect more evident than at the end of the programme on the bomber when all the ammunition that had been unearthed was piled together and a (male) team member, celebrating his birthday, was allowed to push the button to explode it all. One episode, though, could be advanced to counter the view that the programme shows archaeology as easy and fun. A visit to Cheddar Gorge produced a show in which nothing was discovered.

House Detectives is not quite so benign a form of education, even though it does instruct viewers in the history of particular areas and provides them with the tools to conduct their own research. The owners of the house that is the focus of each episode's investigation start off with high hopes for the centrality of their dwelling to whatever is the high point of local history. The experts investigate and, usually, people's hopes are dashed and the popular knowledge on which they have been drawing is proved false; Bonnie Prince Charlie (or another famous figure) could not have hidden in the house. The entertainment of the programme for viewers is often in the display of the owners' eccentricities and the persistent exposure of middle-class aspirations for aggrandisement through ownership. The consistent educative theme of the programme, though, is that age does not guarantee importance; most buildings that survive centuries are quite mundane and it is in that very mundanity that their interest lies. It also demonstrates regularly that popular wisdom about historical events is based more in wish fulfilment than fact. The buildings investigated by the 'house detectives' reveal local social history and can be used to teach how fascinating that is, but rarely allow the retrospective enactment of recent gentrification. This is rather a harsh lesson for a medium that operates more happily as a fairy godmother, which perhaps explains why *House Detectives* is an afternoon BBC2 programme.

Another programme that managed to combine an educational thrust with entertainment and the participatory practices of ordinary television (and even incorporated an element of disenchantment with romantic nostalgia) was Channel 4's *The 1900 House*. Here highly detailed social history about domestic life at the turn of the last century was made palatable and engaging for a contemporary audience by choosing an ordinary family from a number of volunteers to live in the house for three months and to discover for themselves and the viewing audience just how much hard work and privation (by modern standards) was involved. It took from the reality game show format the confession closet in which each week family members told how horrible the experience was and revealed various other secrets. The voiceover commentary, too, drew on this form with its forecasting of difficulties to come throughout the programme rather than just in the final 'coming next week' fragment. The ordinariness of the life being detailed and of the family chosen, together with the incorporation of confession and constant narrative signposting to maintain viewer interest, means that this discovery of how to produce prime-time education, albeit on Channel 4, is likely to increase the amount of programming that carries an educative discourse. Little more than a year after the programme screened, *The 1940s House* went to air. Unlike the earlier programme, which showed segments from a continuous three months, the wartime programme collapsed time into five momentous occasions from the year. In both instances the times chosen ensured that the endurance aspect of the period was able to be highlighted. This, too, was an importation from the reality game shows like *Survivor* and *Shipwrecked*, where much of the anticipation is in seeing how people from today cope without the comforts they expect. This means that one of the prime themes becomes how lucky we are to live in the commodity-rich present. Even though, for instance, people may return from their adventures claiming to be fitter from their healthier diet, junk food features repeatedly as something eaten before immersion, longed for and seen as a reward.

In Australia, *The 1900s House* screened on SBS, indicative of the perception that this was where it would have most appeal. The viewer profile of SBS is even more substantially educated middle class than it is for Channel 4. Although *Time Team* has not screened in Australia, somewhat related programmes, like *Meet the Ancestors*, have, and also on SBS. *House Detectives* seems most unlikely to have any Australian resonance and has not been purchased. The result is that this grouping of imported 'educative' programmes is seen as of minority (and middle-class) interest. No similar Australian-made programmes exist.

The three programmes examined all combine history with the local and then incorporate ordinary people to produce both education and entertainment. That two of them are so domestically focused that they have 'house' in their titles is also relevant. Similar domestically related educative material can be found elsewhere. Given the opportunity afforded by a celebratory special entitled *Fifteen Priceless Years* to explain their practices, including the providing of two valuations – auction and insurance – *Antiques Roadshow*'s Henry Sandon explained:

> There is no real value in a piece – it's what people are prepared to give or take. You usually suggest to a person if you want to buy this at auction or send it there, or sell it to a collector or dealer, then I think the value is X, but if you want to insure it, it should be for a value higher than that because perhaps if you need to replace a particular thing you are going to have to buy at the top of the market, you're going to have to buy at an expensive auction, you may have to pay much more than if you sold it, you have to pay the dealer's mark-up, perhaps, or the auctioneer's charge. So the usual thing is to suggest it can be 25 per cent or even 30 per cent higher for the insurance safeguard. It's an ordinary necessity. (tx. 28/3/93, BBC.)

The clarity of this exposition indicates very well the way in which the educative mode continues to operate within ordinary television and the way in which such programmes can be most powerful conduits for economic precepts. None the less, things are rarely this explicitly directed to economic education, for the educative thrust is directed more obviously to the antiques; the viewer is shown the signs that the experts call on to make their identifications and is informed about the processes of production involved in the creation of the artefacts.

When it comes to science and technology programmes matters become slightly more complicated. The technology magazine show has long been a staple of television schedules and I have argued elsewhere for *The Inventors*, an Australian technology programme of the 1970s, being a precursor of lifestyle programming in its stress on the domestic and its use of a personality panel to judge inventions submitted by members of the public (Bonner, 2000: 103–4). More recent science and technology magazines like the BBC's *Tomorrow's World* or the Australian-produced *Beyond 2000* retain significant educative components which probably are implicated in their being inflected or replaced by programmes with more popular participation, demotic delivery and everydayness. *Dream Lives*, the BBC prime-time technology programme, is one way in which this is achieved. The visit of the team to an ordinary person with a problem amenable to a technological solution combines the local with the discipline concerned and with ordinary people. It also provides an opportunity, as noted earlier, for a fairy godmother moment.

As far as making science and technology entertaining is concerned, the principal recent instance most certainly is *Walking with Dinosaurs* which, with its large budget, slow production time and complete absence of ordinary people or on-screen personality presenters, is anything but ordinary.

One of the extra channels available since the introduction of digital television is BBC Knowledge, a new digital channel running primarily factual programmes, especially documentaries, and promoted as 'feeding the mind'. The word 'education' is not used of this channel. That term is reserved for the offerings of BBC Learning which is an internet-based service guiding both school- and mature-age students to relevant radio and television programmes. Digital television is starting slowly in Australia and while there ABC channels for 'Kids' and 'Youth', education is not promoted as a component of them.

ECONOMICS

Until the beginning of the 1990s, television programmes explicitly dealing with economic or financial matters were specialist ones restricted in their appeal to those few of the population who understood such arcane concerns and were wealthy enough to have investments. BBC2's long-running *The Money Programme* operated in prime-time but not as a highly popular show; indeed, it could probably have been seen as one of the channel's more educative offerings as it found it necessary each week to provide viewers with basic information to explain terms like 'derivatives', which were central to their lead items. The extent of such explanation was limited in order for it not to be off-putting to the core audience of financially knowledgeable viewers and none of the devices ordinary television has at its disposal to popularize issues were deployed. In Australia, Channel 9's *Business Sunday*, running from 8 to 9 am, did not even go this far; it unashamedly catered for an audience of businessmen with long, talking-head interviews and to-camera pieces by commentators discussing economic indicators and takeover bids.

In the late 1980s, though, the salience of economics and its place in the public sphere changed. It became the dominant political discourse as economic rationalism became the creed of choice for governments across the globe, market forces became the explanation and alibi for both actions and inactions and entrepreneurs became popular heroes (see Turner, 1994; ch. 2 for a discussion of some of these in the Australian context). Formal economics programmes proliferated – *Business Breakfast*, at 6 am, weekdays on BBC1; *Working Lunch*, at 12.30 pm, weekdays on BBC2; Thames had *The City Programme;* and Channel 4 had *Business Daily*. The ABC started a weekend business programme, *The Bottom Line*, and in 1995 ran a late-night Monday version of it. Most of these have ceased to operate, but the much greater interest in economic matters and the spread of share ownership much more widely through the population of both countries has led to a growth of more popular forms of programmes concerned with financial matters using all the techniques of ordinary television. Probably the first of these was the Channel 9 show *Money* which began in 1993, scheduled at prime-time and very quickly becoming a top-rating programme. Ostensibly innovative, it was and continues to be basically a compilation of household money hints in a breezy magazine format with a regular presenting team and a populist approach; indeed, its closest predecessor was the money tips segment of the Channel 10 lifestyle show *Healthy, Wealthy and Wise*. The Channel 4 programme *Dosh*, which began in October 1995, was similar. Their address to viewers is (or was, for *Dosh*) primarily a domestic one, talking to a consumer concerned with value for money and using examples of real ordinary people and their financial practices as illustrations. *Money* has continued to rate well, its print magazine rapidly gained a high circulation and in the last few years it has incorporated a much greater interest in the share market than it had at the beginning. Australian television has seen few other financial programmes apart from a hybrid between *Money* and *Business Sunday* called *The Small Business Show*, another magazine-style programme which gives advice to people running small businesses and incorporates some ordinary people into its items. A much greater number of different British programmes have advised viewers on looking after their finances, investing in the share market and starting their own business (like Channel 4's *Real Deal*, which uses a more innovative format than its Australian equivalent).

The range by which financial information is made entertaining even includes game shows. *The Stocks and Shares Show* was a short-lived British programme of the 1980s, but more recently Channel 4's daytime *Show Me the Money* has proved highly successful with teams investing an imaginary £100,000 in five actual companies, one of which has to be traded live on the show each week. Any team whose portfolio drops below £90,000, something that regularly happens, is replaced by a new team. A financial adviser and the chairman of one of the companies concerned both help decision-making, and the team with the most valuable portfolio at the end of the series wins. The programme is designed to appeal to the share market novice as well as the knowledgeable and is regarded by the channel and the Royal Television Society as part of the educational remit. *Wheeler Dealers* was a short BBC series in which teams dealt in goods and services in specified areas (cars, art), again with the winners being those who profited most, and with a design which combined the game show format with an informative brief. Its relationship to business programmes was enhanced by its presenter previously having appeared on *Working Lunch*. The use of weekday daytime for these programmes, while making the educational aspect less problematic, is a further sign that share ownership (or the expectation that this is something attainable by all) is now widespread.

Another change evident in these programmes is a gendered one. The older programmes saw finance as overwhelmingly a male concern, the newer ones incorporate women almost equally. *The Small Business Show* even goes further to acknowledge a point it made in one of its earliest episodes – that the majority of small businesses are established by women. The programme has been presented since its inception by Janine Perrett, and the programme logo is a feminized one in soft green and gold with the programme name in a curly script. The business world it depicts is, similarly, a more feminine one, with regular items on the economic value of childcare and stories of successful businesswomen and how they accommodate families without diminishing their financial achievement. While matters are not quite the same in the big business shows, women's financial competence is now so accepted that they can be used as interviewers to ask about macro-economic issues and be interviewed to pronounce on them. Economic concerns are now indeed presented as everyone's interest. The real estate valuation improvement that is the culmination of *Carol Vorderman's Better Homes* links this programme also to the overtly economic ones.

Where once there had only occasionally been documentaries dealing with companies' economic states, now there are prime-time series like the BBC's *Blood on the Carpet*, devoted to detailed analyses of particular firms' tribulations, and Sir John Harvey-Jones has become a celebrity figure. The BBC programmes are produced by the Business and Adventure unit, although they are more generally categorized as Business and Work, and most of them are grouped under the 'Trouble' label. This reveals the very major transformation of the finance and economic area in the last decade. Who would earlier have conceived of the yoking of Business with Adventure? Who would earlier have considered investigations of the financial affairs of troubled organizations as entertaining? Most of these programmes are on BBC2 and remain far closer to documentaries than to ordinary television, but their presence in the schedule indicates how explicit economic discourse on television has expanded into far more sites and has been able to draw more viewers. In tandem with the growth of popular money programmes in the infotainment genre they could be taken as signs that economic discourse on television is no longer disguised or a minority affair. In addition, the common concerns which television addresses in its fairy godmother mode (discussed in the last chapter) can now be articulated in terms which seem to share much with the companies in trouble genre. *Dream Lives*, the BBC1 prime-time science and technology show, describes the community problem which its technology experts help redress each week, most frequently in terms of financial woes, as was the case with their visit to a convenience store proprietor concerned about his competitiveness who was given a computerized stock control system as part of their suggested solutions.

It might seem, then, that to discuss economic discourse in this chapter is a little strange, but not only are many of the programmes mentioned above not ordinary television, but even were they to be considered so, they do not constitute the majority of non-fiction sites in which economic discourse proliferates. Obviously, news and current affairs, too, are now much more dominated by financial and economic stories, but so too is ordinary television. The way money and its circulation is talked about here is inflected by the more formal sites (whether news or documentary) and by the general increased importance of the field. Crudely put, the viewer alerted to the greater importance of discussions of money (the days when it was a taboo topic for sociable interchanges are now gone) is more aware of and receptive to comments and prescripts about it in more accessible programmes.

The forms of ordinary television most relevant here because of their persistent but relatively disguised economic content are game shows, antiques programmes and practical advice shows including travel, cooking, gardening and motoring programmes. Game shows are particular significant, even when they are not themselves based in trading goods or shares. The period in which economic discourse has become publicly more prominent is also the period in which the British regulations on the size of prizes in game shows has been lifted. (There have been no regulatory controls on the size of Australian prizes.) It was once the case that the size of game show prizes was a major distinction between British and non-British game shows. British shows would reward winners with small household appliances and losers with souvenir stickpins or similar memorabilia. Referring to pressure to ease the restrictions on the size of British game show prizes towards the end of this period and quoting an article from the *Daily Mirror* of 21 May 1988, Garry Whannel first mentions a Thames executive wanting to offer houses or Porsches as prizes, then notes: 'Others have even more grandiose ambitions. Jon Schofield of Central says: "If someone was going to win a million, it would clear the streets. People would be glued to their seats"'(1990: 200). This did indeed prove to be the case. With the removal of the rules (the last restriction went in 1993), prizes became more than just an adjunct to the great desideratum of appearing on screen. Until 1995, the big prize in both the UK and Australia was signified most potently by a car, displayed but not available in each episode (of, for example, Channel 9's longest-running programme *Sale of the Century*). In 1995, however, the ITV game show *Raise the Roof* offered a house each week and then, in 1999, *Who Wants to be a Millionaire?* went to air. The ratings soared when Judith Keppel became the first contestant to play for and win £1 million on British television in November 2000.

Mike Wayne has argued of *Who Wants …* that the move to monetary rather than object prizes was part of a bid to get more upmarket audiences for the game show genre (2000: 210). Object prizes, like nests of marble tables, clearly designate particular taste cultures and make it difficult to appeal across classes. Large sums of money appeal far more widely and Wayne also notes how the very title of the show was chosen for its aspirational quality (210).

The principal types of game show are knowledge quizzes, whether intellectual (*Mastermind*) or populist (*Sale of the Century* or *A Question of Sport*), word games (*Catchphrase*), games of physical skill or nerve (*Don't Try This at Home*), public opinion (*Family Fortunes*), consumer knowledge (*The Price is Right*), dating games (*Blind Date*), combinations of physical and mental tasks (the long-gone *The Krypton Factor*) or of knowledge and strategy (*The Weakest Link*). More recently these have been augmented by reality game shows. With the exception of dating game shows, the purpose of the show is for contestants to win goods or money, and even with dating shows the date itself is paid for by the production company – and, on shows such as *Blind Date*, quite an expensive holiday can be won.

Whatever the type of response rewarded, objects, rather than cash, still dominate as prizes as far as the bulk of shows is concerned, though cash dominates in the highest-rating programmes. In televisual terms objects are more desirable since they can be shown more readily and their display meshes seamlessly with and augments commercials. They are also less of a charge against the programme's budget (and against the provider's advertising budget). In shows where cash and objects are both available, opportunities to exchange cash for objects or to risk accumulated cash are frequent. The standard economic story of game shows is that knowledge, skills or dignity can be exchanged for goods, but with the increase of programmes in which contestants gamble with the points or cash they have won, the story changes to become one in which a person who is not the most knowledgeable can still win through betting 'wisely'. The share market games are ones where knowledgeability is seen as the basis for the bet (called, of course, in these instances an investment). Betting in these instances involves backing oneself; it is self-knowledge that is rewarded. Fiske explains this differently, claiming that it allows the intervention of luck which is important since it is an ideologically acceptable explanation of success or failure in a competitive democratic society (1987: 270). Even were this the case elsewhere, luck can rarely be found operating alone in British game shows – indeed, the now defunct regulations required skill of some kind to be exhibited before prizes could be won, precisely to remove the taint of gambling and winning just on luck – and their influence continues in this regard. The combination of academic and/or human knowledge, self-knowledge and luck is the one shown to be successful.

The newest game shows, like *The Weakest Link*, combine knowledge and a form of manipulation of one's fellow competitors that is a far cry from the knowledgeability of others which rewarded the ability to guess the most popular response to a polled question (in shows like *Family Fortunes/Feud*). The older form is more social, the newer defiantly antisocial. The Channel 10 answer to *The Weakest Link* revealed in its name the starkness of the new economic regime. Formatted on an American programme for Fox and designed there to take on *Who Wants to be a Millionaire?*, to which it bears some resemblance, it was called *Greed*. In its Australian version, perhaps through its choice of presenter,

Kerri-Anne Kennerley, it lacked some of the fierceness and innovation of *The Weakest Link*. Kennerley would say how sad she was to see contestants leave and while the contestant who chose one of his or her fellows to eliminate was asked why the particular choice was made, losers were not subject to an exit interview. The signs of the new regime were in the reiteration of how desirable greed is ('There's more than a million reasons why greed is good' was one of the lines used to throw to an ad-break, referring to the prize being in excess of $1 million), the size of the prize and the possibility of leaving with nothing.

The new high-rating programmes which ignore object prizes and concentrate on large sums of cash generate all or most of their prize pool through the premium rate phone lines which would-be contestants call. In 2001 there were a number of news stories in both the UK and Australia about people who had made hundreds and even thousands of calls to ensure that they did get chosen to appear on *Who Wants* .... Apart from being further evidence of how desirable television appearances are (for a significant part of any prize money would already have been spent, even assuming the person survived the on-air elimination round), the stories revealed in their tone and in the discussion they generated some of the equivocations around the changes in attitudes to economic matters. *Who Wants* ... is 'new' primarily in the size of its prize. The absence of consumable objects and the rapid elimination of contestants other than the person in the hot seat could be found on *Fifteen-to-One*, for example. The reception of the stories of the extremities to which would-be contestants went split between those who thought it showed unreasonable desperation and those for whom it indicated the necessary 'right stuff' for success in today's world. It is the latter attitude that is rewarded in the very newest shows, not just *The Weakest Link* but also reality game shows like *Survivor*.

Most of the shows that are focused upon physical skills are of the stunt or dare type and in these it is the willingness to make a fool of oneself that is traded for gain. For some, like *Don't Try This at Home* or its Australian original *Who Dares Wins*, there may be an aspect of personal competence involved, but usually the desire to show an ordinary person operating under duress ensures that the skills necessary are exhibited by the expert demonstrator rather than the contestant. The dare variation of shows like *Don't Forget Your Toothbrush* or segments of the various British programmes presented by Noel Edmonds did not involve skills, simply revelations of how much ordinary people were willing to give up – from dignity, through their childhood stuffed animals, to their cars, – rather than forgo an opportunity to be for a moment the centre of televisual attention and perhaps a chance at a prize. This is not just a phenomenon of the late 1990s – *Game for a Laugh* was a similar ITV show of the early-to-mid-1980s, and the expectation that audiences would derive pleasure from the extent to which ordinary people were willing to accept humiliation to be on television has an even longer pedigree.

Contemporary reality game shows which can call for extended narratively based exhibitions of survival skills or sexual display seem to be operating slightly differently in that for some of them experiencing humiliation does not seem to be in the repertoire of the contestants chosen. Everything is sanctioned by the desire to win with the opportunity to capitalize further through spin-off celebrity and the only negative aspect is the possibility of losing. It is no longer the case that the desire to be on television is satisfied within the boundaries of the initial show; now this constitutes the stage on which to make a bid for a little more exposure, a taste of celebrity, with a view to this being the 'big break'. The appearance on the game show, then, can now be part of a career plan involving programmes other than those which are designated talent shows. Early signs of this could be seen in the late 1980s among the contestants on *Blind Date* who performed routines ostensibly to attract the choosing party but with more than an eye to a watching talent scout.

My assertion of the televisuality of objects as opposed to cash, as well as the need for more than luck, may seem to be contradicted by the televising of lottery draws. While in Australia this is simply two minutes devoted to the selection of the winning numbers, rather like the slightly longer UK midweek draws, on Saturdays in the UK it is a more complicated performance. Following the introduction of the National Lottery at the beginning of the 1990s, it was a 15–20-minute variety show-inflected attempt at the televisual impossibility of a regular special, event, but more recently it has transformed first into a 35-minute, then a 50-minute, game show incorporating various lottery draws. In all instances it is undoubtedly ordinary television with its entertainment structure of presenters directly addressing the ordinary viewer. The British programmes incorporate the on-screen presence of ordinary people both in the current game show format and in the earlier versions where there was a regular ritual enactment of the disbursing of a fraction of the profits to 'good works' in an attempt to give respectability to state-sanctioned gambling. The representatives of 'deserving' causes were not very adequate substitutes for the ordinary punters whose lives were just waiting to be transformed by good luck. The moment of delirium which is the necessary climax to the draw was forever deferred – the presenters tried to get excited over the announcement of the winning numbers, the charitable cause was suitably grateful and, if present, some of the previous week's (lesser) winners calmly told of their plans; but the moment of revelation, of the epiphanic bringing together of winner and won, was unrepresentable on the *National Draw Live*. *National Lottery Jet Set* – the first of the game shows surrounding the draw – attempted to compensate by offering prizes of a week of the life of the rich and famous, and having this miniature sign of the glories and excitement of the real winners evident before the viewers' eyes. It demonstrates quite clearly the televisual desirability of material objects and for the need for the presence of actual contestants/winners. One or the other is necessary for any prolonged programme designed to extol the economic desirability of winning. Early in 2001, a lottery-linked game show called *Cash Bonanza* began in Australia not linked to the lottery draw but drawing its contestants from winners of instant 'scratchies'. The announcement spoke of the programme as designed to help counteract the competition lotteries were facing from alternative forms of gambling (Ellicot, 2001: 4). It did not last long.

Whether lottery or game show, the message of these programmes is of the acquisition of possessions without work. Even when significant preparation for appearing on a programme has been engaged in, even when a person challenged to climb Mt Kilimanjaro has had to go into training for months to become adequately fit or has devoted a year to fine-tuning a broad generalist education for a quiz show appearance, these are regarded as pleasurable hobbies rather than as labouring for the chance of reward. The erasure of work from the world of television is one of its most consistent themes, with even those paid to appear on screen being required to act as if they are just having fun playing. If they are celebrities, it is part of their job to engage in activities like attendance at first nights or participation in pro-am golf tournaments, but these must be treated as if they were not work.

The receipt of something for nothing thanks to the beneficence of television continues on *Antiques Roadshow*. Like game shows (including those British ones where the knowledge tested is itself of antiques) and unlike *The National Lottery Draw Live*, this programme is able to show the moment at which people discover whether they are major or only minor winners. The programme is a succession of moments of such revelation, but with the great oddity that the winner is already the owner of the prize and what they have been given is its commercial valuation. It is, in effect, a reversal of the normal game show exchange in that here, people have objects and are given knowledge. With very occasional exceptions the objects are domestic ones and the programmes include varying amounts of historical information, so *Antiques Roadshow* can be regarded as another of the mildly educative programmes that combine localism, domesticity and ordinary people into an entertaining whole.

Antiques are no more at the centre of the economic life of a society than antiques programmes are central to broadcast television schedules. Both can be regarded as marginal, the former certainly as luxuries. The major analysis of *Antiques Roadshow* will occur in the next chapter; at this stage, however, I want to conclude this section by noting how the economic discourse which pervades the programme has continuities with game shows and the overt economic shows. The story that persists is one of capitalizing on unrealized assets (knowledge, abilities, possessions) so that improvement in the material conditions of one's life is possible. There are two main consequences of a sizeable valuation of an object on *Antiques Roadshow*: a discussion of insurance and an assumption that the piece will be sent to auction. The latter is particularly the case for the very large valuations, but the way all valuations are given is to provide probable auction prices. In part this is because the experts most commonly are drawn from the large auction houses, but it keeps in the forefront of the programme's discourse the way in which the 'value' given to the owners is based on their selling anything recognized as worthwhile. 'Sentimental value' is recognized primarily as a compensation for negligible economic worth. Circulation not accumulation is the prime economic virtue recognized by ordinary television.

ETHICS

Nikolas Rose has noted how reference to ethics in public discourse is expanding. He warns about this not necessarily involving increased debate about the evaluation of self-conduct, but rather a disguise for old strategies of discipline and morality (1999: 191–2). Something of this is evident, not so much in the content of ordinary television, but in the public discussion about it and what that discussion in turn reveals about the way television acts as a site where ethical discourse is negotiated.

Ordinary television is particularly subject to allegations of ethical impropriety. Reality game shows and quiz shows like *The Weakest Link* are charged in newspaper columns or on talkback radio with encouraging antisocial behaviour and with providing bad models for children. While these shows attract most attention, a whole panoply of the programme types considered here are also accused of rewarding greed or showing off, leading people to expect 'quick fixes' to problems, advocating 'shallow' interpersonal and sexual relationships and destroying community sentiment.

While it is easy to see how these ideas may be generated and, indeed, to sympathize with some of the allegations, a number of writers have argued that the programmes do encourage socially desirable ethical positions in their viewers, though they may do so in unconventional ways. The most common of these is by the very display of unethical behaviour. John Hartley argues that contemporary television teaches neighbourliness and civility, not only directly (through soap opera narratives, for example), but also through such virtues being the required touchstone against which to judge the unneighbourliness and incivility displayed in both dramas and such ordinary television programmes as the clip-shows featuring various kinds of bad behaviour (1999: 160).

As mentioned in the previous chapter, Annette Hill draws on her ethnographic studies of British viewers of popular factual programmes to argue that such programmes as those dealing with pets, healthcare, DIY and police/crime, which are watched by women and children together, should be seen as positive programmes, with happy endings providing practical knowledge. They focus on an ethics of care, especially within the home environment where they can be seen to enhance family life, but the care can be extended outwards to include, through the police/crime programmes, community surveillance. She notes how families use the material in the programmes to discuss overlaps with their own situations. In a similar way to Hartley, she reports families also using the programmes to distinguish themselves from those depicted, arguing, for instance, that they are not as stupid as those shown engaging in some castigated practice (Hill, 2001: n.p.).

This use of the programmes to trigger debate about the bounds of acceptable practice can be found quite pervasively; it is one of the major ways in which discussion of reality game shows is conducted. Unlike the pet programmes, for example, where the right way to care for those dependent upon you is on the surface of the programme, the ethical discourse of the newer programmes is presented more indirectly. Deceit, selfishness, boastfulness and greed may be rewarded by the rules of the games, but they usually appear in conjunction with more conventionally valued demeanours. While discussion occurring in the programmes' reception is not, strictly speaking, the concern of this examination, it can feed back into television content in various ways. The various promotional appearances of people associated with one programme on other shows (most often morning shows or chat shows) provide sites for the discussion of these kinds of issues in ways which are invariably designed to show the programmes in the best possible light. With programmes like *Big Brother*, the inclusion within the range of badged shows of one or two where 'experts' discuss aspects of the show regularly include not only psychologists discussing the interactions of house members, but also others (including television scholars) talking about reception and providing guides to reading the show precisely as an ethical one. It provides a further example of the 'working through' discussed by Ellis (1999, 200).

Even without this kind of integrated meta-text, the programmes themselves are at times explicit in exposing the undesirable nature of particular types of behaviour. The 2001 series of Channel 9's *Search for a Supermodel* followed two contestants who were best friends at school and who had entered the competition together. When at the beginning of the third episode one was eliminated, it showed how the successful girl immediately embraced one of the other successful ones and ignored her rejected friend who was shown leaving the room alone, uncomforted and crying. Perhaps mindful of the large teenage and younger audience, the voiceover provided a comment about the transience of friendship in such a situation. When, later in the same episode, the successful one failed to survive the next obstacle, there was an obvious gap in the commentary where sympathy would more regularly have been expressed. Friendship may seem an unusual virtue to stress in a competition when all but one is eliminated, but whether or not it was discussed to disguise the 'true' nature of the programme, it provided a persistent ethical theme throughout *Search for a Supermodel,* as did the castigation of bitchiness.

WORK/EMPLOYMENT

I have already noted how the idea of work is kept away from ordinary television by disguising it as play or leisure. The early game show *What's My Line?* may have trivialized work by choosing bizarre jobs as those to be mimed for the panel to guess, but it did acknowledge the centrality of work to the lives of ordinary people in its very design. It is very difficult to find spaces where this happens on contemporary television. Indeed, quite the reverse, work is shown to be easily disposed of. Contestants on reality game shows have to be ready to spend up to three months on isolated islands, contestants on quite mundane game shows need to arrange absences during regular working days and the title of *Don't Forget Your Toothbrush* alluded to the fact that the successful contestant of that programme would have arrived at the studio as a member of the audience only to be whisked out of the studio after an hour or so onto a plane for a week's (or more) holiday. Families seem readily to arrange themselves for television's convenience. The children in *The 1900s House* were enrolled in new schools, the wife took leave from her job as a schools inspector and the husband's employer's willingness to have an employee appear at work in historical costume (he was in the armed forces) presumably aided their being chosen from the many applicants.

In as much as docu-soaps can be considered ordinary television, their frequent location in the workplace (as in *Airport* or *Driving School*) does provide a place where work is the subject matter of a programme, but these are equivocal members of the grouping, using ordinary people, but keeping much of a documentary approach especially in their lack of an on-screen presenter and reliance on voiceover, as well as their extended treatment of the single situation. Even so, John Dovey's examination of the grouping reveals how partial a picture of work is provided, noting how 'work is only screened as it functions within the economy of consumption, travel and leisure. There is a massive skew in topic selection in favour of shopping of all kinds, on travel, tourism, sport and recreation' (2000: 140). Despite the documentary inflection and the overt engagement with the world of work, then, the continuities with the emphases of ordinary television are still evident in docu-soaps. This is much less the case with the more thoroughly documentary business programmes like *Blood on the Carpet* which centre on work practices in particular companies.

The set-ups that are common to various surprise-based programmes, from *This Is Your Life* to *Love Rules*, often involve surprising the person at work and taking them away to another site to make the programme. Given that the usual workplace for a *This Is Your Life* candidate is within the entertainment industry, and the programme can be regarded as good publicity, it may not be so surprising that companies are compliant, but can the same be said of an office manager whose subordinates decide that her sex life needs help and contact the presenter of a television programme to appear in the workplace and remove the manager for a day's filming in a male strip club? In a continuing display of television's self-importance, the arrival of a television crew is never treated as disruptive, or the loss of an employee's working day (or week) a matter of concern. Presumably some places do object, but instances of this are not broadcast and so the impression is maintained of the unimportance of work compared to the great desideratum of having fun on television. Since few employers these days would be willing to countenance nonspecified time away from the workplace, it seems that it is a casualized workforce that provides these unpaid television workers. Laura Grindstaff talks of the skewing of the sample that appears on American talk shows in terms of those who can arrange absence from work and for whom a trip to New York for filming is a treat (1997: 176–7). Again it is a casualized workforce or an unemployed body of people that supply the raw material for the programmes.

Appearing on television as a contestant or a testifier or a witness does not itself count as work even though a regular supply of participants is required. The most probable role to be seen as 'working' during a television appearance is that of expert since it is usually the case that professional expertise is called upon, yet the more regularly an expert appears, the more she or he is absorbed into the televisual world where all is play. The professional gardeners on *Ground Force* are shown having such fun or grumbling as do ordinary folks for whom gardening is at most a chore rather than work, that we are discouraged from perceiving them as just about their professional business. Nor are we encouraged as viewers to see the many appearances of celebrities on ordinary television as part of their work (although it frequently is part of their contractual obligations).

In drama programmes the mundanity of work is almost always the background to something more exciting like emotional tensions or exceptional emergencies. On the news, work is most newsworthy when industrially disrupted or when abstracted into employment statistics and in ordinary television work is transmuted into pleasurable diversion. In 1973, Richard Dyer observed that built into the definition of light entertainment was 'that it must provide an alternative to the world of work and of general drudgery and depression' (23). Little seems to have changed. The relentlessness with which television displaces work gives added force to Lefebvre's previously quoted comments about the way television 'divert[s] the everyday by ... offering up ... its own spectacle' (1987: 11). With Lefebvre's belief that leisure time is inevitably part of the whole panoply of the repressive everyday, the insistence with which television presents itself as not work and does not show work as worklike in its repetitive routineness, can be more readily comprehended. Work is best forgotten and television is a prime mover in such amnesia.

LAW AND ORDER

Matters of crime and law enforcement are similarly troubling for ordinary television. No matter how valuable they are as the subject for dramatic treatment or the content of news bulletins, they sit uneasily in fun-loving ordinary television since the principal way in which ordinary people encounter them is in the position of victim. For this reason law and order is quarantined into special programmes rather than being a discourse that appears across a range of sites. It can be called on for comic effect, but this is most likely to be the case in sketch comedy. Game shows – whether reality or traditional – chat shows and lifestyle programmes pay no attention to it. *Antiques Roadshow* may advise owners of valuable objects to keep them in a safe if they decide not to send them to auction, but house makeovers do not spend time on security features and reference is never made to any of the ordinary people flooding through the nation's television studios ever having been victims of crime, let alone having spent time in prison; indeed, reference to their ever having had a parking fine is rare.

Yet programmes that discuss crime, and which do so in ways that incorporate the ordinary person, exist and are increasing in number on British television, no longer just *Crimewatch UK*, but now also ITV's *Ratrap* and *Police, Camera, Action*. They quarantine ordinary television's concern with crime into specified spaces and rarely intrude into the domains of other programmes, as is usual for most ordinary programming. The viewer of such crime programmes is most commonly positioned as a possible witness to a crime that happened in the real world and an actual witness to its re-enactment. Unlike the overwhelming majority of ordinary television programmes, the address is not to the viewer as consumer or 'good sport' but, atypically for the grouping, to the viewer as citizen. It is as an old-fashioned citizen that the viewer is invited to participate by helping solve crimes, deploring their commission and applauding activities aimed at catching criminals. So aberrant is the solemn, serious and public-spirited address of these programmes, that it is also possible in them for work to be acknowledged as tedious, repetitive and exhausting – although the term 'painstaking' is preferred.

Crimewatch UK is the longest running and most prestigious of the programmes and the one which most firmly follows this model, describing and re-enacting crimes and calling for viewers to help in their solution. ITV's *Ratrap* used hidden cameras placed in likely crime spots to record the activities of vandals, bike thieves and other petty criminals. Here the viewers were overtly addressed as victims wanting to know how to protect themselves from the offenders, the eponymous 'rats'. The observer here is not positioned as a potential police witness but is framed by the 'reality TV' mode as a voyeur, closer to viewers of surveillance video-based clip-shows, of which ITV's *Police, Camera, Action* is a comparatively sober example.

Anna Williams' study of *America's Most Wanted*, from which *Australia's Most Wanted* is formatted, notes how the set from which the presenter addresses viewers represents a clerical workplace with props signifying police work (1993: 100). Her main concern, though, is how the programme establishes the white, middle-class family as the most imperilled by crime, focusing on violent crimes, especially those against women and children (99). Both its dramatizations and its interviews with victims are structured by melodrama and stress the family both as the site of crime and the group most traumatized by it (110). Williams observes how doing this means that the programme's discourse is shattered, since while it prefers a representation of the criminal as an aberrant individual outside family structures, a focus on families means that domestic violence is inescapably a crime featured (109).

This representation of crime is evident in the only other site of ordinary television where it is regularly to be found – talk shows, though here, both for the US and the UK, the families involved are much less insistently white. Williams examined the extent to which the investigation of crime and its solution was presented as a masculine activity, something that applies also to the Australian programme although not to the British ones, where *Crimewatch UK* has long been presented by a male/female team and *Ratrap* had a solo female presenter, Mary Nightingale. Talk shows, though, are much more frequently presented by women and focus on the concerns of women. Women advising other women to leave abusive situations or confessing to predominantly female audiences that they were abused as children present a different picture of crime, one that focuses much more on the healing of the victim than on the catching and punishment of the offender. Williams argues for *America's Most Wanted* having a therapeutic approach to crime on the basis of a single episode where a violent convicted criminal talks of the need to treat others like him (ibid.: 104), yet this approach is much more regularly to be found in shows like *Ricki Lake* and *Trisha*.

RACE

Unlike the other disguised or absent discourses, that around race is not simply rarely present or quarantined, it is silenced. Tokenism and a reliance on the visual seem rampant as devices to stop the discourse erupting. The selection of ordinary people incorporated into programmes is overwhelmingly white in both countries, but black and Asian (in the various meanings the term has in the two countries) faces do appear from time to time, especially in those programmes aimed at younger viewers. However, when they do (as when they do not) race cannot be spoken.

One way to consider this is that it is through the force of sociability being the communicative mode. Under the rules of sociability, as mentioned earlier, potentially disruptive issues cannot be raised and distinctions of all kinds must be put aside (Scannell, 1996: 22–3).

It is unclear whether the silence is to be read as race being itself unmentionable or that a pretence is engaged in that assimilation has happened and that this is a difference that makes no difference, but the displacements engaged in are varied. The primary one is to show but not allow to be spoken. The second British *Treasure Island*, in creating its diversified grouping of contestants (a classic World War II film's 'bomber crew' of social types), included a gay, black Scot, but left his blackness as a purely visual effect. The first series of the Australian *Big Brother* included a woman identified as being born in Papua New Guinea and interviewed her parents so viewers could see her white father and black mother, but from then on even her 'exoticism' was downplayed. The social dislocation that such shows set up by removing contestants from their normal settings to produce them as individuals of equal status and opportunity allows little space in which race can be discussed and the editing smooths the screened material into an acceptable collection of highlights.

The most ordinary of televisual places (apart from in a studio audience) is as a contestant on a gameshow. Overwhelmingly these contestants are white, even more so in Australia than in the UK. When they are not, especially for knowledge quizzes, then the alternatives follow the lines of prominence in formal education – Asian faces (in both countries' terms) more commonly than African, West Indian or Aboriginal. A typical 'show, don't speak' approach could be seen on an episode of a team-based quiz show when a group of young contestants of Chinese background was introduced as having the (sole) common thread of their all being at university together.

Alan McKee has discussed what he calls, after Baudrillard, banal Aboriginal identities, referring by that to the experience of Aboriginality in the everyday (1997: 192). The main site in which he finds such banality is game shows and he discusses a few instances in the early to mid-1990s when Aboriginal men competed in *Sale of the Century* and *Wheel of Fortune*. The latter instance was a celebrity special and involved the actor, comedian and television presenter Ernie Dingo. In neither instance was Aboriginality completely 'unspeakable'. The 'ordinary' contestant was introduced as 'the first Aboriginal head teacher in Victoria', but this was not then subject to discussion. The host on *Wheel of Fortune* introduced Dingo with a comment about his tie, prompting Dingo to remark, jokingly, about its Aboriginal design (ibid.: 197). In both these instances Aboriginality is marked verbally as well as visually, but it is announced and then abandoned as irrelevant to the process of chat and of answering questions. McKee argues that the banality of the game show situation and of the identities of competitors is completely at odds with the common recognizable Aboriginal representation on Australian television, which is linked with poverty on the one hand and spirituality on the other.

Discourses around race appear very differently on American daytime talk shows where the presence of African-Americans and Hispanics as presenters, guests and studio audience members is significant to the point of their being in the majority on many programmes. Not only is there visibility, but various issues associated with race are the subject matter of shows. Jane Shattuc notes of the newer shows which developed in the wake of Ricki Lake's that they repeatedly deal with the unhappiness of lower-class women and most especially those of colour, but warns that this is testimony rather than politics, since it is without any wish or gesture to improve their lot or suggest that improvement is possible (1997: 141). To presence and subject matter must be added an element of style since instead of the middle-class modes so dominant elsewhere, '[d]ecorum and civility are not the mode of new talk'; instead the gestures and dialect of poor Afro-Americans and Hispanics take centre stage (165). This is certainly the case on *The Jerry Springer Show*, but it is always returned to decorum and civility by Jerry's own closing homily which renders the extremities of the behaviour which he has just provoked, characteristic of his guests and their milieu – not his. When these programmes are screened in Australia and in the UK, the extent to which their approach to racial representation is subsumed under their overall foreign American-ness, or is capable of transferring to local conditions, is questionable. The absence in Australia of talk shows of any kind other than American means that all of their characteristics are seen to be those of the form generally, rather than its American version. British talk shows have been running long enough that they now have their own norms and, despite having a black presenter on the most popular, *Trisha*, these norms involve a substantial diminution of the presence of racially marked participants and subject matters.

Stereotyped conceptions of the financial acuity of people of Indian sub-continental or Chinese background mean that Asian faces are more frequently found on programmes relating to money than on other ordinary types, like makeover ones. This applies both to the transient ordinary member of the public chosen to talk about their experience with some monetary issue and to the reporters chosen to delve into an issue. In Australia, where Chinese faces are overwhelmingly the ones more likely to be selected, all such reporters are female. Given the frequency with which media representation eroticizes Chinese women, it leads to the suspicion that, despite their undoubted expertise and competence, their use as reporters on traditionally dry matters of finance is intended to provide extra pleasure to male viewers. Only on the far-from-ordinary 'high'-finance programmes like Channel 9's *Business Sunday*, where specialist commentators from Hong Kong may be used, is there a link between Chinese-ness and the area reported on, otherwise the customary silence pertains.

When it comes to racially marked presenters and reporters away from the financial area, matters can be a little different. Since both roles are accorded much greater screen time and appear repeatedly, a total silence on the issue is rarely possible. If the people concerned become celebrities, then the requirement to talk about their private life in exchange for greater exposure operates. Here discussion about the consequences of being racially marked does occur, though usually comments about its negative consequences are placed safely in the past, as things that happened at school rather than matters which had to be overcome to achieve success in the workplace. Chat shows, which are one of the prime places such discussion occurs, require as much as other ordinary television (with the exception of talkshows) that discussion be predominantly both happy and inconsequential. The highest-profile indigenous person involved in ordinary television in Australia is Ernie Dingo, mentioned above, presenter of Channel 7's holiday show *The Great Outdoors*. An actor with a background in stand-up comedy and experience in film and television, he is able to meld aboriginality and a laconic Australian 'Bush' masculinity into a highly usable persona. The use of Dingo in a programme associated with the outdoor life and often with the Bush itself follows from this. He can, at times, refer to his race as being suited to certain locations or particularly exotic in others (as when he visited a NASA launch site). The political bite of his comedic persona is abandoned in the newer role and the comedy muted to suit a presenting persona. This is evident in his commenting as he sat beside a digeridoo duo: 'You've heard of the three tenors, well we've got the three blackfellas', before closing a segment on an outback holiday.

In all this bland and happy world where some people 'just happen' to have different coloured skins which have no meaning attached to them, the cooking programmes, where race and ethnicity are allowed to have meaning and consequences, stand out. They are still dominated by pleasure and even excitement, but difference is important and Dorinda Hafner or Madhur Jaffrey can both talk of 'we' and not include white viewers. The positive value of ethnic cuisine transcends the 'unmentionableness' of race and difference here. Stranger instances arise from the common practice of sending cook-presenters off to foreign locations. Both Ainsley Harriott and Dorinda Hafner have made series exploring the cuisine of the United States. Neither the black British Harriott nor the African-born, sometime British now Australian resident, Hafner have actual links to the US, but the programmes play with the combination of their visual similarities to Afro-Americans, their emphatically non-American voices and their highly extrovert personae to unsettling effect.

CLASS

Like race, class is not overtly a subject, but is readily identifiable on British television, though much less evident on Australian. Given the way in which class in the UK is revealed by speech (and linked in various ways with regionalism), it is audibly a factor whenever ordinary people are present – and usually also for presenters and guests. Other class markers, like occupation and dress, underpin speech-based identification in the UK while providing the major indicators in Australia, where immigrant British dialects are frequently to be heard on television, but are not 'placed' by audiences who lack the practice which supports the British obsession with the identification of speech cues.

Class can be and is a subject in drama, and especially in sitcoms, in the same way that race is, but it shares the characteristic of not being spoken about in the sociable interchanges which help constitute the ordinariness of ordinary television. It is possible for presenters and celebrities to raise the matter in their autobiographical comments. The ladette performances of Denise Van Outen required acknowledgement of her working-class Essex girl placement (which may have contributed to the Australian audience's incomprehension of her persona when she presented Channel 7's *How Much Do You Love Me?*).

As I noted earlier, the tendency to construct homogenous groupings of people in programmes obscures the consequences of class identification. Upper- and upper-middle-class accents are rare away from programmes on stately or otherwise historic homes, though food programmes, money programmes, antiques shows (which I will discuss in this regard in the next chapter) and, to some extent, science magazines are regularly constructed to be comfortable for their exercise. With the disappearance of quiz programmes like *Mastermind* and, most especially, *Connoisseur*, game shows are overwhelmingly home to working-class and lower-middle-class contestants, though the substantial increase in the size of the prizes on offer has altered this a little.

The most fascinating of the recent programmes in terms of its refusal to mention the class basis of its premise has been *Faking It*. A reality game show which stands with *The 1900s House* as demonstrating that the form is not ineluctably concerned with humiliation and selfishness, the programme trains a person from one professional background to be able to masquerade for a single performance in another, at such a level that they pass a test set by experts. Ostensibly, the programme involves cross-trade 'passing' and the mastering of a body of unfamiliar skills. Unacknowledged in its design, though obvious to the audience, is that the masquerade is also class-based. The middle-class' cellist who had to learn to be a club DJ also had to learn to operate in an overwhelmingly working-class (albeit wealthy) environment. The Liverpool painter and decorator who passed as a contemporary artist shifted the other way into a much more middle-class milieu. Both these examples are ones where the economic differences were not particularly significant in the shift, but those involving cultural capital, deportment and lifestyle were substantial. These are not ignored practically, since the person passing is tutored in the necessary knowledge, dressed and styled appropriately, but they are represented and spoken of as tied to the occupation, not the class of those customarily engaged in it.

The only programme to have class issues as overtly a substantial part of its subject matter is *The 1900s House*. Safely located in the re-enacted past, the contemporary family and, especially, its womenfolk, are able to talk about what people 'of their class' would do. It becomes especially evident when they decide to take on a servant. The maid of all work is chosen by the middle-class wife and mother to help with the heavy housekeeping load and it is represented to the contemporary viewing audience as both Edwardian verisimilitude and necessary because of the onerous nature of keeping the house clean without modern appliances. Not discussed is the way the class divisions continue to exist (and the way the shift to a service economy has brought back an analogous performance of domestic labour by those other than members of the household). The mistress of the house was, in the present day, a middle-class school inspector married to a military officer, her servant a working-class woman who had substantial late twentieth-century experience as a cleaner, employed with no greater job security than she would have had 90 years earlier. She is eventually 'let go' because her employer cannot handle the middle-class guilt of being a proper Edwardian mistress and cannot confront her maid with her failures face to face. Verisimilitude loses out to sentimentality. The servant's lamenting of her loss of a job, though, is convincing simultaneously in period and contemporary terms.

VALUE

The smoothing of difference and the reduction of variation into a meaningless matter of taste can make it seem as if there is a flatness of judgement on ordinary television. 'New' is equated with good, though objects sufficiently 'old' can be made good by judicious renovating touches or by acknowledging their economic worth. While one new object may be preferable to another in terms of individual taste, it often seems difficult for ordinary television to say that one is better than another on any dimension other than newness. Much of this follows from the previously noted power of 'fashionability' as the basis on which change is advocated. Makeovers are absolutely predicated on the new version of house, garden or personal appearance being better than the old, but this is primarily in terms of their appearing up to date. As noted in the previous chapter, comparative assessments of simultaneously available options are rare, and when they are present, the evaluations are generally couched in an 'If you want this effect choose A, if that choose B' mode which returns us to a relativity of taste rather than a judgement of worth.

Ordinary television constantly makes recommendations, but they tend not to be comparative ones. The processes by which certain products rather than others are chosen to be mentioned occurs off-screen where they can be influenced by sponsorship or other forms of less visible promotion. Either a single brand is named or (more rarely) a small range is mentioned as interchangeable, but the detailed examination of which of the available options represents better value for money or is likely to be more lasting is rarely a televisual approach.

Cultural products are differently treated, with film review programmes like SBS's *The Movie Show* and the British equivalents so long associated with Barry Norman readily willing to approve or dismiss films and to rank those available at any one time. The same applies to shows dealing with books or popular music. In the awards programmes that, despite their presentation as special events, are regular features of the programming schedule, evaluations extend to nominating certain products as indisputably the best of the year. The acceptance speeches, however, most frequently return proceedings to the undifferentiated and ordinary with thanks being given to the many collaborators and often to the competition. This is, however, more a feature of those awards operating firmly within popular culture; it is rarely evident at the Booker Award ceremony.

In this, cultural products appear less like objects awaiting use and more like appurtenances of the people involved with their production, since the reluctance to judge comparatively applies not so much to people as to objects under the domain of the powerful discourse of consumerism. This distinction is, of course, illusory since cultural products are commodities too, subject to the same consumerist discourse, and that, as John Frow has demonstrated, regardless of whether they are high or low (1995: 22–5).

When it comes to people themselves things are very different, especially when those people are in some way contestants. The very term implies competition and winners and losers and that is indeed the case in both game shows and talent quests. Tests are applied and some succeed while others fail. The basis for judgement may be popular (an audience vote) or factual (the answer is or is not correct) and the subject area significant beyond the programme or not, but judgement is made and some individuals are judged better than others.

This is most especially the case away from traditional game and talent shows and in the unscripted newer variants. Programmes like *Popstars* and *Search for a Supermodel* start with hundreds or even thousands of would-be performers and discard all but a few. Reality game shows, like *Survivor*, *Big Brother* and the like, similarly eliminate people until a winner remains. In both instances choice is made through using either popular response or professional judgements. The massive elimination that precedes the start of reality game shows (having many thousands of applicants is now considered normal) occurs off-screen but stories about it circulate in attendant media stories giving greater cachet to those chosen to appear at all. For these programmes, as for their apparently more traditional game show descendants like *The Weakest Link*, the process of becoming the last one standing is not merely a matter of submitting oneself to external judgement of one's worth, but also one of conniving to influence that judgement. The rules of these games are designed to favour the most manipulative. This is the person most valued, not just for their capacities of endurance, but also for their value as entertainment.

The realization that nice people are not always the drawers of the largest or most desirable audiences seems to have changed the bases for televisual evaluation. A far more open acknowledgement of the value of the individual whom viewers love to hate has developed, not only for drama where the worth of a soap opera's 'queen bitch' has long been recognized, but also in more ordinary situations. The value of a 'heavy' on a judging panel has long been known institutionally by those running talent shows, whether traditional, full programmes like *Opportunity Knocks* or segments like the 'Redfaces' one on Channel 9's now defunct variety show *Hey, Hey It's Saturday*, where Red Symons obliged as the hard-to-please judge. They, however, were outnumbered by the other judges and the presenter, and their inclusion as a standard part of the design of the programme was not publicly discussed. With the shift of the role to the contestants, the more 'ordinary' side of the equation, the operation became more evident since the rules supported it, the commentary underlined it and the results endorsed it. Manipulative skills to the point of extreme self-centredness and all-round meanness no longer disqualified one from winning or being recognized as 'best'. Value here is to be judged explicitly on winning at all costs.

Ordinary television, then, does not explicitly conduct a discussion of value, but in its persistent elevation of the new and fashionable over the old and dated, as well as its design of the more recent programmes to value winning to the extent that overt scheming, deception and undisguised selfishness all appear perfectly acceptable practices, it is possible to detect consistent bases on which judgements of value are made.

THE SELF VERSUS THE TEAM

This brings us to an overarching if somewhat disguised discourse of the newer programmes: the importance of the self rather than the collective. Television's equivocal relationship with individualism mentioned earlier has here been clarified. The rhetoric of individualism, albeit still in conflict with the pragmatic necessity of appealing to large groupings of like minds, is no longer restrained by sociable niceties about co-operation and group harmony. Teams become temporary groupings aware that the dominant member will sacrifice them ruthlessly to his (or very occasionally her) advantage. This discourse is disguised both by the continued use of the term 'team' and by the continued existence of a large number of coexisting programmes still operating by the sociable niceties of collective behaviour.

The clarity of the new regime is nowhere more evident than on *The Weakest Link*. Here, instead of their being two opposing teams, the whole group of contestants is described as a team, but act as one only for the disruptive purpose of reducing their number by voting off the eponymous member. The comments made after the departure of an individual are not in terms of strengthening the remaining group, but rather involve expressions of personal dislike and assessments of how the departure of that particular person has improved the speaker's chances of eventual success. The ABC sports comedy programme *The Fat* adopted this procedure for its special programme filmed during the 2001 Melbourne

Comedy Festival, voting off panellists deemed too clever or too peripheral to the show's core values. Unlike the more serious (and more ordinary) programmes they were emulating, contestants on this did not see the female contestants as more disposable than the male. Those shows closer to the real world through using ordinary people rather than operating with (minor) celebrities relentlessly mirror masculine dominance of public space, a practice only slightly concealed by using *The Weakest Link*'s Anne Robinson or Cornelia Frances as the presenter and displacing the apparent aggression onto her.

Popstars, internationally franchised from its New Zealand original, and aiming to produce a musical group as its end point, has no need to adopt quite such a ruthless approach. Decisions about membership are taken outside the group of contestants and include among their criteria the ability to work together. However, another criterion requires each person chosen eventually to be distinguishable – the sexy one, the 'kooky' one and so on. In this way, although the 'team' remains necessarily valued for musical harmony, the individual's distinctive marketable virtues are asserted.

Big Brother's tactic of requiring the selected housemates to live together for a while, before calling for the initial nominations for exclusion from which viewers are allowed to vote one out provides a further variant. The Australian version featured in its first 'selection' episode a succession of reluctant people explaining how they hated to choose anyone because they 'loved them so much' (after five days) but that they nominated X because he or she was the one they 'clicked' with least. A lack of rapport was here given public primacy, only one contestant saying that he nominated another person because they seemed the biggest threat. This was, however, at an early stage before those who had survived nomination (and thus had experienced the group turning against them) had begun to alter the warm and fuzzy dynamics of the hedonistic situation. As the group of survivors became much smaller the protestations about disliking nominating a fellow returned, accompanied by resignation about this being what was required.

An odd exception to the relentless selfishness encouraged by the rules of the newer programmes occurs when contestants on shows such as *Greed*, *Big Brother* or even *The Weakest Link* are asked about how they would spend their prize money. The most common answer given is that the would-be winner would take a group of friends off on a trip or out on sustained and lavish partying. Older responses, like paying off the mortgage, are now very much minority responses. Whether this is a result of the reduction in age of the contestants or of their being not as firmly inscribed in the workforce is unclear, but the tendency for the admitted fantasies to be for experiences rather than material objects, and for these experiences to be shared ones, is clear. The fantasies expressed are then in much greater accord with the ethical positions endorsed by viewers who discuss the programme in terms of acceptable and unacceptable behaviours. As long as the rules require it, contestants will adopt selfish behaviours, but this is tied to the programme. When talking of what they would like to be seen wishing for, unconstrained by the rules, they exhibit generosity.

There are then a number of discourses which are disguised, quarantined or absent. Education, economics, work and employment are obviously opposed to the organizing principle of entertainment, as is their dark side, criminality. Race, class, value and selfishness operate differently, but are linked together by the difficulties they pose for sociability, the dominant mode by which ordinary television conducts itself. The newer forms like reality game shows have a more complex relationship to sociability, in part because of their explicit organization around an economic objective to which sociability is sacrificed. Older game shows also organized around an economic objective did not and still do not require the sacrifice of sociability because they allow little if any interaction between contestants, all talk and action is mediated through the host, allowing the maintenance of a veneer of 'proper' behaviour. When contestants are allowed either to interact directly or to comment on their own and other's manoeuvres, the unsociable aspects of competition can no longer be disguised.

The Global and the National Ordinary

One of the constant refrains of television studies for the last decade or more has been a concern with globalization. Television is seen as prime evidence for the loss of national distinctiveness as all the world watch *ER* and *Oprah*, or Rupert Murdoch's satellite-delivered signals penetrate yet another part of the globe. Much of the argument has transferred from the older theories of American media imperialism, although now transnational companies are less necessarily located in the US and whether they are or not, the global dispersal of production may result in a very different pattern from that of the older theory. Television, or media and telecommunications more generally, has played a central role in theories of, and arguments about, globalization. It is often called on as particularly hard evidence of the existence of a 'world system'.

There have been many approaches to disputing the extent or the impact of the proposed homogenizing of culture. Marjorie Ferguson has argued for the utility of regarding the principal tenets of globalization as myths with ideological rationales rather than strong evidence in support (1992: 75–88). Stuart Hall has talked of global mass culture as 'a new field of visual representation ... [which] is centred in the West and ... always speaks English' (1997a: 28), but he insists that the global is 'the self-presentation of the dominant particular' (1997b: 67). Like most of the work contesting theses of globalization from a cultural perspective, Hall's concerns are with local and marginal cultures and identities, which, in a global system marked by diasporic movement, represent a local which has no necessary geographic locale. One of the most ambitious attempts to map this in the 'complex, overlapping, disjunctive order' that is the 'global cultural economy' notes: 'because of the disjunctive and unstable interplay of commerce, media, national policies and consumer fantasies, ethnicity, once a genie contained in a bottle of some sort of locality (however large), has now become a global force, forever slipping in and through the cracks between states and borders' (Appadurai, 1996: 41). It is, in part, from this kind of realization that the powerful term 'glocalization' has arisen, insisting on the place of both the global and the local (see Robertson, 1995, for example).

While acknowledging that the local does represent the most intransigent (and fascinating) alternative to the arguments about global homogenization, my focus will none the less remain on the unfashionable national since this is the frame within which free-to-air television operates and which it persistently acts to call into being and maintain. It is also the site of empirical work which contests the simple American-dominated view of contemporary global culture. Stuart Cunningham and Elizabeth Jacka, for example, have examined the Australian television industry as an example of a 'significant trader' in an international mediascape which they argue to be far more diverse than crude globalization arguments would allow (1996: 246). This does not mitigate Hall's West-centred, English-speaking argument at all, though I would like to modulate his 'dominant particular' term to name not the global grouping but the more particular national fictions: 'Britishness' and 'Australianness'. The ordinariness that I have been discussing throughout this study represents an inclusive, idealized version of this particularity, its dominance evident primarily in what it over-represents.

This is not to ignore the extent to which Channel 4, and even more, SBS, complicate the picture by their recognition of the presence and distinctiveness of many 'locals' within the national. It is SBS's mission to produce a multicultural national out of the many local particulars. So persistently has it maintained this role that it is possible to suggest that there is now a 'multicultural ordinary' evident in the broadcaster's own programming. The first episode of its lifestyle programme, *Nest*, examined the interiors of the homes of a range of Australians – an Italian-Australian couple, one of whom was part Indian, a post-World War II Polish refugee and his wife, an Aboriginal man and, its sole Anglo, a lesbian prisoner nearing the end of her sentence. So far from appearing tokenistic and improbably united by its thematic focus, it appeared characteristic of how this national broadcaster sees the nation comprised. The more popular networks retreat from this viewpoint producing a less differentiated version of what the national particular is, and because they are more numerous as well as more watched, their versions can readily be held to be more powerful.

Even though it would be difficult to argue that as far as television content is concerned, the British or Australian national is produced in opposition to the American, America remains perceived as the main threat for non-American television industries since it is the principal exporter of programmes while simultaneously being the smallest importer. This has led various nations to enact legislation to protect their television industries by requiring quotas on local content. Australia requires that 50 per cent of programming be Australian-produced (and there are extra provisions mandating that certain amounts of this be documentary and drama). The European Community has a similar requirement for content made by Community members, although many countries exceed it considerably.

The programming that is most commonly imported from the US by nations around the world is drama, the most expensive type of content, with the possible exception of news. As has been noted repeatedly so far, ordinary television is not commonly imported. Exceptions fall in two main areas: talk shows and cooking programmes. Other than that, programmes are formatted or compiled by mixing segments with locally derived materials as is the case with most clips-shows, though some of these, especially those with titles like *Worlds' Most Dangerous Wildlife,* may be imported in their entirety for late-night, off-season screening. Importing British compilations into Australia may be less contentious if they are hosted by the expatriate Clive James, though this in no way allows the material to qualify as local content. Reality game shows provide another area where some programmes are imported, although they do not constitute the majority of the type in most countries. It is not just the industry that is being protected by these measures and the rhetoric about them is not primarily couched in industry terms, which would be fatal given the tenor of the Global Agreement on Tarriffs and Trade. It is because television is seen as a central site for the expression and maintenance of a nation's cultural identity that local content regulations are able to be maintained, though American attempts to contest them are regular occasions for the rhetoric to be exercised yet again. France is the nation most assertive in its international campaign to protect its cultural identity, though its principal focus is on cinema rather than television. Australia, initially seeing television as a site to rebuild skills for its film industry, has had Australian content provisions since the earliest days of television, and once more, in early 2001, trade negotiations with the US involved discussions about whether more equitable access for agricultural products to US markets could be gained by allowing in more American television shows.

HOMOGENIZING VS DIFFERENTIATING

So how is it that ordinary television talks about the nation, and does it do so differently from drama in all its forms, from sitcoms through soaps to series and serials? It is probable that ordinary television provides a less romanticized view of the nation than drama does by its very inclusion of ordinary people and its greater mundanity, but it is also likely that ordinary television shows a more diverse nation and does so deliberately. British drama affords more space (in part because there are so many more programmes) for the different peoples that make up the contemporary nation to be represented than Australian drama does, but even so allegations about domination of television screens by white people from south-east England can still be encountered and the matter of stereotyping of all but Anglos applies in both countries. While ordinary television in both countries also over-represents dominant groups (and in Australia probably allows less space for Aboriginal Australians than even drama does) its hunger for bodies in audiences and as contestants or contributing voices enables it to be more representative of various particularities in certain areas. Elderly people are undeniably the major component of studio audiences since they are most likely to have the available time, but they are also, for the same reason, well represented among contestants on game shows.

Aware of their role in representing the nation to itself, television networks and those who make programmes for them are conscious of the desirability both of being representative and of catering for dominant myths about the nation. In Australia the disproportionate importance of rural areas and the disregard for the fact that the overwhelming majority of the population are urban dwellers are highly influential. The tendency for the nation to be represented by those resident close to the major television studios needs to be counteracted by a number of deliberate strategies. One is active solicitation of more contestants from further afield. Studio audiences do not normally reveal their geographic location, though if there are parties from rarefied locales, presenters may single them out or floor managers may allow the waving of identifying banners, but contestants and others identified on camera are always placed in terms of where they come from. Across a range of programmes, presenters in their opening or closing comments may pick out a different particular town to greet – individualizing the show, marking for one night viewers in that town as favoured by being personally addressed, but in the regularity with which another night brings another town, local difference is erased into a national identity which incorporates the various locals. The people in Cootamundra are no different as Australians viewing the Australian *Sale of the Century* for being hailed by the female assistant at the end of one night's show, than those in Cairns the night after, but Australia becomes a country that recognizes including both places.

Occasionally, the programme itself travels to incorporate itself more closely into the geography of the nation. Except for those like *Antiques Roadshow* which are always on the move, these occasional forays add to the budget but are justified through operating both as publicity for the programme and as demonstration of its 'truly' national approach. So important is this procedure that the name of the programme is often adjusted to indicate the special character of the show (most commonly by adding 'Live' to the title) and if this is not the case, then the presenter's opening comments ensure we are immediately informed of the changed locale. This is reiterated with every return from a break, whether for advertising or for a prerecorded segment. Even when going on location, it is rare for any programme to venture far from major centres of population, especially in Australia (though Australians would certainly see there being no alternative in the UK). Most commonly, programmes visit related festivals: *Burke's Backyard* goes to the Melbourne Garden Show or *Gardeners' World* goes to the Chelsea Flower Show, *Good News Week* used to visit various Writers' Festivals, pet programmes continue to go to Crufts. The British instances do not involve much of a geographic translocation, but the festivals themselves signal national concerns and those interviewed can represent a wider range of home territories. The Australian instances allow state loyalties to be noted. One of the most wide-ranging programmes in terms of presenting a geographically and culturally diverse nation is the SBS programme *A Foodlover's Guide to Australia*. This magazine presents brief items showing food from ingredients to finished dishes and speaks to those associated with growing, selling and cooking it, drawn from far more areas of Australia than most inhabitants would ever be able to visit. The items in each episode are linked graphically by a map indicating to where the next move is, but no attempt is made to present a unified picture of the nation, the format and its production by the multicultural broadcaster makes doing so impossible and also undesirable. It is another instance of the multicultural ordinary mentioned earlier, and ideologically its message is of plenitude and infinite variety.

The nation, though, is televisually constituted by more than just its geographic and demographic variation; it is also called into being by practices within the programmes, which far more often do try to present a unified vision. Gardeners are told about 'typically English' styles of planting, would-be holiday-makers are asked for feedback in terms of what 'you, as Australians' think would be a useful kind of place to investigate? The direct address to the nation through hailing viewers as nationals is a minor modulation of the practice of news bulletins and current affairs shows speaking to an audience of citizens, and emphatically one of the range of practices Michael Billig refers to as 'banal nationalism' whereby 'established nations are reproduced as nations, with their citizenry being unmindfully reminded of their national identity' (1995: 155). It does not characterize all ordinary television by any means. If there is any chance of the programme being sold to another country, it would have an undesirable alienating effect and so is downplayed. Perhaps because of its echoes of jingoism, it is more likely to be found in programmes targeted at an older audience, like gardening shows. Programmes aimed at a younger grouping offer themes of unification if they do this at all, around the figure of youth in opposition to (middle) age. Nation can still enter a programme through its subject matter when other nations need to be named. Thus the second series of the reality game show *Treasure Island* sent its contestants off to an island in the Pacific Ocean and worked to ensure at least one foreign sale by incorporating a few Australian contestants in with the majority British contingent. Although it had chosen one emphatically marked 'outsider' – a black, gay Scot – much of the commentary and the evaluations of the contestants was in terms of 'the Brits' and 'the Aussies' and their supposed national characteristics. Similar situations occur with travel programmes, even those that are pitched to the younger traveller, as the foreign setting produces a national out of the presenter or reporter no matter how un-British or non-Australian they may be able to represent themselves as being on home soil.

IMPORTING PROGRAMMES AND LOCALIZING THEM

Despite the importance of local content regulations to the Australian situation, a very substantial part, especially of prime-time, is filled with imported material. Screening the cheaper imported programme may reduce the extent to which Australian television looks distinctively 'Australian', but does not mean that for the time that programme is being screened the audience is rendered the same as that in its place of production. Both Appadurai and Hartley refer to the 'indigenizing' that occurs when television or other cultural products and practices are taken up by local or national groups other than those among which they originated (Appadurai, 1996: 32; Hartley, 1991: 34). Hartley's article refers particularly to the Australian practice of watching television outdoors, but while he does not use the word in his later work, he continues to observe how imported programmes are rendered local by their context (1999: 156). His recent concept of DIY citizenship modulates this to reduce the significance of nation in a formulation with echoes of glocalization, but he acknowledges that such citizenship is a possibility in the process of becoming (168–9). I do not think that the nexus of television and nation is yet broken given the dominance of network free-to-air television in determining how television is popularly conceived, especially away from the US.

Not only is the actual design of the schedule, as noted in Chapter 2, nationally distinctive, but the advertising and the surrounding programmes all function to produce a different effect from that achieved in the home territory. Viewers, too, make meanings in terms of their own everyday experiences and understandings, something Kirsten Drotner has encouraged realizing and exploring (1994: 354). The standard practice of British channels screening Australian drama made for prime-time during the afternoon makes their audience a different one, differently positioned in the television day. Cooking programmes provide a very particular example of re-inflection in the new context. As noted earlier, it is characteristic of the presenter-led programmes to explore food in foreign countries. When these programmes are screened outside the country making the programme, the extent of otherness can expand, since both the presenter and the country whose food is being showcased are foreign to the nation in which the programme is being screened, but the way in which food seems 'naturally' to encompass exoticism makes this often a positive characteristic. When, however, the 'foreign' presenter visits the country into which the programme is being imported, as when Keith Floyd or Rick Stein visits Australia, matters become very different. In these cases the valences of national and foreign reverse and the mode of viewing shifts entirely into judging the foreign presenter, observing what she or he thought important or characteristic or got wrong. This shift can happen for any kind of television programme, drama programmes and garden shows both intermittently go offshore, but it is probably most common for cooking programmes given the interest in examining ethnic food in its home locale.

Australian or British viewers watching American talk shows are permanently outside looking in, never able to see themselves mirrored in the programme for the combination of American referents, and the bizarrerie and excess of the performances and situations estranges rather than interpellates them. It is not that the entertainment value is negated, it may even be enhanced, but these programmes speak very emphatically of a different nation with different modes of operating, as British talk shows like *Trisha*, with very different morés for audience participation and different frameworks for intervention in subjects' lives, make clear. In Australia the foreignness of all talk shows means that the form itself says 'We are not like this; this is not to be taken seriously.'

The case of reality game shows is worth considering separately. As a new type of programming, the popularity of these types of programmes and the willingness of both national programme-makers to test the market and of local talent to expose itself to the conditions designed for the show may have been thought to be uncertain. In these situations it was possible to find three possible responses operating together: imported versions were screened to prepare the way for local ones; formats were bought; and original ideas were tested out. While many of the reality game shows originated in Germany or Holland, these countries are not sources for much imported programming in either the UK or Australia, except for a small amount of drama on SBS. The early imported programmes were American and then, in Australia, British, but this latter was in conjunction with locally produced shows. Part of preparing a segment of the audience for participation involves their learning how to operate on particular types of programmes, and this is done in the first instance by watching similar types of show or even imported versions of the format that is to be franchised.

That both British and Australian individuals are more restrained than American ones is a cherished part of both national myths and is one of the reasons advanced for there not having ever been a successful Australian talk show. Given the opportunity to try out for local versions of reality game shows, it rapidly became apparent that would-be contestants were eager to reveal a lack of restraint. The initial attempts by Australian programme-makers to produce local versions, like *The Mole*, rated well enough (though not outside the younger age group) but failed to get all the elements of duplicity, scheming and technologically-mediated viewer involvement together in the first instance. Not just contestants but also network promoters and audiences had to learn how to work with these programmes.

There were two breakthrough shows for Australia. The first was the formatting of an Australian version of the New Zealand-originating *Popstars* and the second the importation of the American version of *Survivor*. In both instances it was publicity which changed reception. A thoroughly integrated internet presence encouraged the production of a fan-base able to interact beyond the time and space of each programme itself. *Survivor* demonstrated the value of heavy promotion of the personalities involved, so that being unable to join in conversation about the programme in terms of its competitors became a social handicap across a wide range of demographic groups. Although *Popstars* was more tightly targeted in age terms, its non-televisual component made it distinctive and newsworthy. A major investment from Warners (in Australia a music production company, not a television one) in the first series of *Popstars* helped fund personal appearances of the group as the promoters tried to ensure the five members would move from substantial television exposure into the music industry. Warners' desires were probably focused more on the musical spin-offs than the televisual or the arguably more successful magazine and website extensions. In the case of Bardot, the group from the first Australian series, musical strength seems to have peaked with the first song, heavily promoted during the show itself, but maintained at a much lesser level since (They disbanded early in 2002.) The second series, made without Warners' money, was more closely tied to the television product alone. None the less, as the highest profile of the early Australian-made reality game shows it was significant in showing how viable local versions of formatted shows could be.

The ability of some imported reality game shows to attract audiences lies in the aspects they share with the other programme types which survive importation. They display otherness as much as likeness, they pose ethical problems which may not have much local applicability and they are frequently set in exotic locations. Australia itself became the exotic location for the American *Survivor II* and this caused problems which had not been evident with the local showing of the first series. The heavy publicity which generated an international 'buzz' about *Survivor* drew in an eager Australian audience and the promotional tour of the first winner to coincide with the announcement of the Australian setting for the second series set up anticipation only slightly dinted by the total failure of the touring winner as a celebrity contestant on *Who Wants to be a Millionaire?* However, having the local used as a site for an imported programme with claims on reality proved a mixed blessing in ways more extreme than those effecting the reception of British cooking presenters making shows in Australia. Various revelations about the depiction of Australia as far more dangerous than its residents know it to be, together with the identification of sub-tropical rainforest as the outback, not to mention something of a furore over the on-camera slaughter of a feral pig and the illegal removal of coral during a diving expedition, all figured both as publicity and as complaint. The reduction in the importation of reality game shows and the substitution of more formatted ones may be a consequence of this or may have been in train already. 'Indigenizing' is not as possible when the country being represented as dangerously 'other' is one's own. One watches more to see the wrongness, and the lack of ordinary Australianness in the contestants becomes more marked. Subsequently, the Australian *Big Brother* went to air very successfully, showing that format adaption for reality game shows was now fully understood and that Australian participants knew what was expected of them. Such imported reality game shows as continue to be screened in Australia are scheduled after prime-time and are the more extreme American kind that continue the representation of the US as excessive and other advanced by the talk shows.

Indigenizing may be adequate for drama programmes and those pieces of ordinary television like talk shows, clip and cooking programmes where, for various reasons, foreignness is desirable, but where ordinariness is more central to the appeal of the programme it is insufficiently powerful. National conditions are not referenced, national myths and locutions are not deployed and recognizable local types are unseen. In these situations either a brand new programme must be devised or a format purchased for local production.

FORMATTING AS ACKNOWLEDGING THE NEED TO LOCALIZE

Purchasing a format and making a local version of a successful programme has many advantages. The programme becomes eligible for counting as local content, the formula has been tried and found to be successful and the development costs of an untried original concept are avoided. Furthermore, buying the format gives access to the 'bible', the guide which provides information about its likely appeal and the terms on which that appeal is judged to be based. All in all, formatting is regarded industrially as a desirable practice, though, oddly, one which is not much acknowledged publicly. At times when sufficient variation can be incorporated to make legal challenges avoidable, the niceties of format purchase will be avoided too. As Moran makes clear, although no successful case has been made against illegal use of format, defending such a case is expensive, so it may be cheaper to buy rights (1998: 17). Legal skirmishes over perceived infringements are endemic. In Australia, in 2000, GMG Endemol sought legal advice with the intention of launching a case against Channel 9 over *Backyard Blitz* which they claimed violated copyright on *Ground Force* (Danielsen, 2000: 5). Both were garden makeover shows and both continue to run, no news of a legal case emerged, so despite statements that the case would help clarify precisely just what does constitute a format, it seems once again that format protection was left as a grey area. Such cases are not uncommon and happen in most territories: in the UK, Target Distribution, which handles *Popstars*, spent part of 2001 in dispute with Pearson's over *Pop Idol*, arguing that the name change (and, presumably, the shift from group to single artist) was not sufficient to render the programmes different; at the same time in a domestic dispute in the US, CBS alleged Fox's *Boot Camp* copied elements from the *Survivor* franchise. The challenges all seem to relate to ordinary television where the UK, the US and Australia all buy and sell formats. In neither the UK nor Australia is the buying of drama formats common, though both sell them, especially British sitcoms, to American producers and Australian soaps to German and Dutch ones.

In making local versions of foreign-derived programmes, it is the ordinary aspects that are most likely to be adapted. The ordinary people involved become the local ordinary, presenters are chosen to exhibit local variations on those characteristics of the original host that are held to be important and the voiceover takes on local intonations. Arguably even more powerful are the lateral links to other pieces of ordinary television which can make national versions of formatted shows distinctive more reliably than calling on unpredictable ordinary people who might turn out to be foreigners anyway. The choice of a presenter is often the simplest example of this lateral harmonization. Presenters bring with them the memory of their previous, or continuing other, work. It is likely that not all of this will be formatted and thus a more definite national component is carried over. When *The Weakest Link* moved to Australia, Anne Robinson with her links to *Watchdog* and a persona derived from her own, was replaced with Cornelia Frances, an actor who 'plays' the Anne Robinson role but, even so, does this with the supporting background of her succession of 'bitch' roles in soaps like *Sons and Daughters*. (It is worth noting that the American version of the show cancelled in 2002 retained Robinson herself, but not only is there less need to 'fix' elements pointing to foreign content in a country where so little is imported, but the cinematic tradition of using non-Americans for villains supported her role.) *The Weakest Link* is a very tightly formatted programme with the BBC retaining a high degree of control, not just over the rules and the set, but also over quite minor details of the appearance and demeanour of the presenter. They were apparently party to a decision about whether the Dutch presenter would or would not wear glasses.

For *This Is Your Life*, also a very tightly controlled format, lateral harmonization occurs not so much through the choice of presenter but of guests, especially since the requirement for the availability of clips of the guests' lives makes guests more likely be those who have had some kind of televisual presence which can then be replayed. In a similar way, celebrity guests on chat shows or special celebrity editions of game shows are frequently television performers and they too bring with them their other televisual 'place', stitching the programmes together into a particular national quilt.

There is considerable variation in terms of how tightly a format is followed. As far as can be detected, *Who Wants to be a Millionaire?* follows the format very tightly across the more than 40 countries where it is screened. Certainly the British, American and Australian versions use the same set, the same rules, the same music and the same scheduling practices (intermittent stripping across the week, occasional celebrity specials). The principal variation, apart from the nationality of the contestants (though at least one contestant has competed in both Australia and the UK), lies in the selection of the host. According to the website, only in Canada is the presenter female, but the style of male chosen to ask the questions further localizes the show. It is a prestige role, given how valuable the property is. Single-handedly, the American version is credited with saving the free-to-air networks from being relegated to second place behind pay-TV in terms of audience size (see Boddy, 2001: 81 for details of how profitable the show has been in the US). The host there is Regis Philbin, previously a morning chat show presenter and maintaining the soft, avuncular manner proper to that, very different from British presenter Chris Tarrant or the Australian Eddie McGuire. Tarrant, with his background from radio and in youth-oriented programmes, has an edgier style than the others. When he pushes contestants to decide whether they really want to proceed with an answer, viewers and contestants alike know he cannot be trusted to be on the contestant's side (as traditional quizmasters once were). The BBC's design of *The Weakest Link* to challenge the dominance of *Who Wants ...* picked up on the implied nastiness of Tarrant to modulate into Anne Robinson's approach. British presenters are generally much less bland than Americans and most Australians; 'niceness' may be required of daytime ones, but at least half of the evening presenters are allowed a different persona: abrasive, zany, camp, sly, even morose.

Prior to his taking the helm of the quiz show, Eddie McGuire, who started as a sports journalist, was the presenter of the Melbourne edition of the comedy-inflected sports panel programme The *Footy Show*. (The geographic observation is a meaningful distinction in a country where the dominant code of football changes from state to state. McGuire is linked to the Australian national code, closest in international terms to Gaelic football.) He is less convincing in attempts to mislead contestants (Philbin barely tries) and his sports background gives him rather a 'blokey' approach which is a very saleable commodity in Australia where he is the highest paid television personality. Both Tarrant and McGuire also carry the specifically desirable aura of men who have worked their way from employee to company owner, both are people who have, from ordinary beginnings, become millionaires.

A more typical relation between original and format is present for the two versions of *Changing Rooms*. Although recognizably the same programme, with two couples making over rooms in one another's houses under the direction of visiting interior designers and with the aid of both presenter and handyman, there are differences produced in large part by the specific conditions of each country. The variation here is emphatically in the most 'ordinary' part, as the houses and the people owning them localize each show in ways not possible for the small studio exposure of quiz show contestants. The panel from which the experts are chosen bears some resemblance in each version, though no Australian designer comes close to Laurence Llewellyn-Bowen. The possibility of doing up rooms in French holiday houses is missing too. Overall, the distinction is that the Australian programme is more casual: the presenter, Suzie Wilks, is younger than the British Carol Smillie, has a more outdoor persona and nearly always wears shorts; and there is even less likelihood of showing viewers how to actually do some of the renovations shown. It uses professional terms or refers to complicated processes very much in passing, secure in the knowledge that watchers who are interested in the production of the effects rather than in the narrative of the programme either will have the knowledge or will gain it from related print sources (as is the case for the British show as well). The Australian show was initially shorter, with the evaluation sections, where designers reflect on the experience, absent. Now a great success, it has moved a little closer to the British version by lengthening to 40 minutes and including the reflective moment when designer and presenter discuss the transformation. From the beginning, the tendency for the makeover to produce a more colourful, theatrical result has been shared. Still, the non-studio location in the houses of the participants remains a powerful force in differentiating the two versions.

A much looser format example can be seen in the relationship between the British *Have I Got News for You* and the Australian *Good News Week,* where the name change is the first sign that things are very different. Both are current affairs-based celebrity panel game shows, but the points of similarity are as limited as the points of difference for *Who Wants*.... *Good News Week* changed further in its move from being a half-hour ABC programme into a one-hour Channel 10 one, which altered again during its run there (it has now stopped production). Unlike the two previous examples, here the structure was changed, perhaps because the programme could not immediately be made more relevant to the new country by the inclusion of ordinary people, although it was filmed in front of a live (usually studio) audience. The British format of teams of two with both team captains male comedians and the presenter an actor known for comedic roles, was varied in Australia to allow for three-a-side teams with one male and one female captain, both comedians, as was the presenter. The immediate consequence of a regular female presence was to reduce the emphatically male view of the world, so notable especially in the comments of Ian Hislop, and the aura of the public schoolboys' debating society. In Britain there is much greater continuity available from BBC radio comedy programmes that comment on topical events and the programme's lines of descent are obvious. Radio 4's *The News Quiz* is acknowledged as the specific forerunner. The bleakness of the world view of *Have I Got News for You* is derived largely from Hislop's *Private Eye*-nurtured extreme cynicism about other people's motives and Paul Merton's mordant humour. The cynicism evinced on *Good News Week* was much milder and more often generated by guests than a signature of the regulars. The most downbeat sections of the show came after the shift to Channel 10 when the inserted lugubrious monologues from The Sandman (a character played by Steve Abbot) were carefully marked out from the show proper. Australia does not have either the radio panel game tradition or the satire magazine support that underpin the British programme's approach and hence the show was inflected more by gregarious stand-up comedy where the Australian tradition is rich.

In both programmes, panellists were chosen precisely because they were not ordinary, the British mix of comics and political figures was extended in Australia to allow the occasional celebrity from another field, though the main sources remained. Model and some time actress Kate Fisher was a frequent panellist while the show remained on the ABC. Publicly derided as a bimbo and supporting this by ingenuously revealing her dependence on the autocue, she was retained by the programme-makers because she delivered two extra ratings points whenever she appeared. The Australian version of the show was thus both more feminist, through team captain Julie McCrossin, who was unashamed in her politics, and more sexist than the British one. Fisher was never put on McCrossin's team, although there usually was another woman member on it. Many of the ways questions were framed and the games played were drawn from the British programme, but the background of the presenter, Tim Ferguson, as a member of the sometime singing comedy team the Doug Anthony Allstars, meant that musically based interludes were always possible. With the shift to the commercial network and the longer time limit, breaks away from the question-and-answer format became customary and despite the retention of its political core, it began to approach a variety show. The British show's characteristic 30 minutes of clever repartee and stream of verbal abuse was much more varied in its Australian version, at times incorporating not only music, but physical humour or independent 'turns' by guest characters.

The topicality of the programme in both countries was central to its appeal. In Australia it was recorded two days before broadcast and in its ABC version its twenty-eight-and-a-half minutes was the result of cutting down a live hour and a quarter. The structure of the programme was tightened around the work of the writers, who devised the questions and the presenter's lines, and the editing focused the unscripted guests' responses into a tighter, wittier whole. In the process the guests were further removed from the ordinary, but the need to have visuals to cover the edits meant that more shots of the audience's reactions were incorporated, placing the programme solidly in the domain of the ordinary viewer.

An example of a format loosely adopted but moving the other way, from Australia to the UK, is provided by *Who Dares Wins*, which was transformed into *Don't Try This at Home*. (It could not continue under the same name since that had already been used for a comedy sketch show.) An already existing catchphrase was appropriated, the show was doubled in length and scheduled earlier in the evening, an extra reporter was added as was a hierarchy of stunts and a surprise element reminiscent of the formatted *This Is Your Life* was intermittently incorporated. In Australia it had a male host with a female subordinate who had to do the dares if the ordinary person failed; in the UK it transmuted into having a female host, Davina McCall, who is herself the default darer, but who has two location reporters, one male and one female. The British programme not only has a greater budget than *Who Dares Wins* but also displays the richer tradition of British game shows of asking ordinary people to do stupid things (like *You Bet*), which I suspect is the principal reason for the longer length. It also, of course, has the memory of Michael Lush, the ordinary person killed when doing a stunt for Noel Edmonds' *Late, Late Breakfast Show*. This seems to me the explanation for the British show requiring the ordinary volunteer to give verbal consent to doing the stunt on camera, rather than any real likelihood that tension is generated around the person possibly backing out at the last minute.

In both versions the ordinary person is most commonly someone shopping who is young and reasonably personable. They are approached, asked to do something silly and, while some are shown refusing, some accept. Most of the more substantial dares, the ones with some risk (other than that of humiliation), ones that also require preparation and training, involve the person doing the stunt having a partner or family member present in the studio. This acts televisually to give a focus and voice to supposed audience anxiety and to wind up tension by cross-cutting. It acts to construct the ordinary person as part of a family or a heterosexual couple in the same way that similar practices do in *Who Wants to be a Millionaire?* Looking at the episode of *Don't Try This at Home* already examined in Chapter 4 reveals not just the strength of the family motif considered there, but also the hybridizing with other ordinary television programmes. *This Is Your Life* provides the framework for the opening of the segment, but the sentimentality evident in the references to the dying mother's wish has more in common with the British *Surprise, Surprise.* Perhaps because this latter is not quite standard (it certainly was not part of the Australian format), the fairy godmother aspect is rendered implicit as opposed to being foregrounded, as it was in other sites like *Jim'll Fix It* or *Hearts of Gold.* Once again, the localizing aspect comes in the lateral harmonization across British ordinary television where there are more wish-fulfilling programmes.

THE IMPORTANCE OF THE ORDINARY TO THE NATIONAL

Despite the way in which imported material is 'indigenized', for a country like Australia, where the majority of drama is imported, ordinary television is particularly important to the representation and constitution of the national on television. Sport and the news (probably in that order) are equally important, but sport is so masculine and the news generally so negative that without ordinary television a very different image of the nation would be available. The greater proportion of domestically produced drama in the UK means that not quite as much emphasis is placed on ordinary television there; but, even so, its function of providing a continuous picture of the uneventful and the sociable aspects of the nation is hard to overestimate. Drama requires momentous events to attract audiences, even soap operas feature weddings and kidnappings, death and crime to lift them above the everyday. Ordinary television is of the everyday and the occasions when it includes the exceptional (like an attempt at answering a £1million or $1million question, or the revelation of which contestant is the winning survivor) are much less common than the cliffhanger grandstandings of drama programmes.

The 'imagined communities' that in Benedict Anderson's famous formulation are how nations are constituted (1991) require evidence from which to be built. Television is a principal provider of this evidence in telling us what other people in similar and in different situations are like, how they live, how they act in public, what they aspire to, what they fear and how they react under unusual conditions. Televisually, some of this can be drawn from drama programmes and some from news, but the ordinariness of imagined communities, our sense of what our fellow nationals are like, beyond the bounds of our first-hand knowledge of them, is far more likely to be drawn from contestants on game shows, the vox-pops of programmes like SBS's *Front Up*, the people being made over on *This Morning* or the agitated interjectors of *Kilroy*. It may be that the great differences in the viewing habits of younger and older audiences modulate this. Younger viewers, learning about the world and their place in it, and less focused on the nation, construct an imagined community from wider-ranging materials and draw more heavily on drama, especially sitcoms, and on reality game shows that speak of possibilities rather more expansive than those available to conventional game show contestants hoping for some new furniture for the house. Their imagined community may be more one of the young, backpacking around the globe, so the house and garden shows, for example, are not a source from which they recognize their place in the nation. For older viewers ordinary television in general and the more conventional shows within it in particular may play a larger role.

THE DISTINCTIVELY NATIONAL

For a number of years it appeared that the talk show form was distinctively American and that other nations could not produce their own versions. The British *Kilroy* programme, which did use ordinary people to discuss ethical matters, seemed too different to be advanced as an equivalent and it was only with the arrival of ITV's *Trisha* and the BBC's *Vanessa* that it became possible to resoundingly reject the idea of the essential Americanness of the form. Some programmes, however, seem quintessentially of one nation either in that they are not found elsewhere or that they are so marked by the national that when adapted for another country they need to be changed radically and, even so, usually fail to have a similar success. *Antiques Roadshow*, my British example, is broadcast in Australia on the Lifestyle pay-TV channel, but its audience there is, as far as it is possible to tell, overwhelmingly comprised of the expatriate British. There is no Australian programme with any similarity. *Burke's Backyard*, the Australian example, is not exported. Furthermore, both programmes play a particularly assertive role in constituting an impression of Britishness or Australianness in their respective national broadcasting systems.

Whether or not they are dedicated viewers, I suspect that most British or Australian people are familiar with the relevant national one of these shows, since they are very much the type of television we watch without necessarily being all that aware of doing so. We see it incidentally, when someone else, say an elderly relative or a child, is watching. In both cases the programmes have been around long enough that they form part of much of each nation's childhood viewing, both being emphatically family viewing.

THE MOST BRITISH OF PROGRAMMES: THE ANTIQUES ROADSHOW

Antiques Roadshow has been broadcast since 1977 on BBC1, usually at around 6 pm on Sunday afternoons. It involves a group of experts in the field visiting a different location each week to which local inhabitants have brought various objects that they consider interesting. The display, identification and valuation of these constitute the programme.

The arguments for its national distinctiveness begin with its scheduling at Sunday teatime. Former host Hugh Scully introduced the anniversary programme 'Fifteen Priceless Years' (tx. 28 March 1993) with the comment that 'a cup of afternoon tea and the *Antiques Roadshow* seem to have sat comfortably together on winter afternoons for the last 15 years'. This points immediately to the characteristic romanticized Englishness (more even than Britishness, despite its regular visits to the other parts of the Union), as does its overt focus on the past and on culture. Further emphasizing its positioning are its overwhelming middle-classness, its whiteness, and its celebration of regions and certain kinds of achievements associated with them. Finally, the programme repeatedly and explicitly calls on the Nation itself, usually in ways which mark the importance of the programme through identification with the national interest. The famous people whose biography helps distinguish the places the Roadshow visits and from which the programme is broadcast are either important names in political or military history, like Gladstone, or important to the antiques trade itself, like Sir Josiah Wedgwood. The romanticized Englishness operates as a certain distinctive 'cosiness' which enables it to call on residual ideologies to disguise the blatancy of its exhibition of the dominant ones.

Situating *Antiques Roadshow* among other British programmes

The precursors of *Roadshow* will be detailed below, but it exists within a great number of other programmes, either directly about antique objects or about old houses, which extend its influence (since it is undoubtedly the leader among them) further and harmonize its place in the schedule. As of early 2001 these included two daytime programmes – BBC1's *Bargain Hunt*, in which two teams are given an hour to find the best bargain at an antiques fair and, on Channel 4, *Collector's Lot*, in which presenter Sarah Greene visits the homes of collectors to talk about their objects. These reveal two lines of association: the first is one where antiques are treated as tradeable commodities; while, in the other, they are subject to an inquisitorial gaze for educative purposes. A variant kind of programme which links to this is another Channel 4 show, *Revealing Secrets*, which traces information mainly from personal written records, but also from objects to produce stories of the past.

While antiques programmes can also be positioned with other home-based shows, and the *Roadshow* is found on the BBC website in such company, it is rarer to find antiques being considered as domestic objects, except in those programmes devoted to visiting stately homes. *The 1900s House* on Channel 4 is an important exception, not only because of its attention to the authenticity of the objects furnishing the house but also because the romanticized approach to the past which the mother of the translocated family exhibited at the beginning of the programme (and which was modulated as she came to experience the drudgery of being a full-time housewife in the Edwardian era) is regularly to be seen among those who visit the Roadshow when it arrives in their locality.

Although there is not always an example on air, game shows centred on antiques are reasonably common on British television. Intermittently, a revamped version of the precursor to *Antiques Roadshow* – the game show, *Going for a Song* – is given a brief run and a newer game show, *Going, Going, Gone,* has also been screened. Both of these, and the *BBC Homes and Antiques* magazine, called on the same group of experts as the *Roadshow*, indicating something of a unified field. Antiques are not a category of apparent interest for ITV channels, though they are considered on lifestyle pay-TV channels.

History

The display and description of antiques on television began firmly within the educative mode. Items were shown and discussed often as part of programmes about historic figures or stately homes or, even more explicitly, the National Heritage. Their ownership and value were usually kept in the background, rather taken for granted, unless it was that a mundane artefact had been given worth by association – Nelson's hairbrushes, for example. This kind of ownership was located in the past, therefore current ownership seemed irrelevant – whether or not they were the property of museums, they were treated as if they were. Economic discourses were out of place in programmes like this, which were dominated by aesthetic and historical concerns.

The next way in which antiques were incorporated into ordinary television (from the beginning they had a place in costume and other dramas) was in game shows. These were initially quizzes of experts, which meant that they were concerned with informing and entertaining, rather than with winning prizes. Because the knowledge required to compete in these programmes is specialized, even when members of the public are involved, they can hardly be regarded as ordinary people and thus, until very recently, prizes were not the focus of the programmes. (There is a parallel here with sports quizzes.) Thus *Connoisseur* operated during the 1980s under *Mastermind*-like conditions, with weeks of heats, no prizes for losers and just a trophy for the single eventual winner; *Going for a Song*, even in its recreation, teamed minor TV celebrities with members of the public but chose the latter from the antiques trade, and, while each programme had a winning team, no-one gained anything but exposure. *The Great Antiques Hunt*, however, uses knowledgeable members of the viewing audience to compete for smallish prizes. All these antiques programmes are screened on the BBC.

Concern with the monetary value of the objects as well as their identification began with the introduction of the quizzes. In a 1972 *Listener* column, Raymond Williams expressed disdain for *Going for a Song* compared to *Collector's World* because he detected within the programme the drive to the top of the market and the production of viewing pleasure through the contemplation of high prices (1989: 173–5), both of which were to become standard in *Antiques Roadshow*. Points were given in *Going for a Song* not for identification but for valuation, which then closed the discussion of the object under consideration.

Antiques Roadshow was something of a departure from the quizzes and the tours of aristocrats' homes. It developed from viewers' letters to *Going for a Song* and the phenomenon of auction house valuation visits to areas of potentially saleable objects, the whole being made possible by technological advances in outside broadcasting. Experts continued to be used, but the contest element was modulated since the expert was pitted against the object and there was no adjudicator. Winning was no longer the result of possessing knowledge, since the knowledgeable figured as disinterested advisers; winning actually came from being ignorantly in possession of a valuable object. Still, the stories which together make up *Antiques Roadshow* are the same as those of quizzes like *Going for a Song*. The mini-narratives in both pose as detective stories by opening with the enigma posed as 'What is this object', but reveal, by their culmination in a valuation, that the enigma is instead 'What is this object worth?'

Popular knowledge about the show

Even those few Britons who may never have watched the programme are likely to be familiar with some of its tropes, since they have an existence in what may be regarded as the 'folklore' of British television. Here 'folklore' refers to certain aspects of intertextuality, certain reading practices which operate both naively and knowingly across popular television programmes. There is a form of popular knowledge about televisual conventions that is frequently made explicit in comedy programmes, which then further disseminate this awareness. In these terms, *Antiques Roadshow* operates on a premise that people naively bring along objects, the value of which is unknown to them, and then are astonished at what they are worth. In contrast to this, we all 'really' know that people take objects to *Antiques Roadshow* in the hope of being told that they are worth hundreds of thousands of pounds and that the valuation they had done on the item in the previous week is going to be shown to be an underestimate (and comedy sketches can be based on this premise – there is one, for instance, by Victoria Wood). Owners who appear on the programme, however, must play along with its terms and exhibit astonishment at how much their object is worth. In this their demeanour, like other ordinary people on television, moves from lack to gratitude. Disappointment is not a permissible reaction – losers must be 'good'; as makeover subjects must be overjoyed at the transformation, so owners given a lower estimated value than that which they had hoped for or told they have a fake must be cheerful none the less.

The other side of this unspoken contract is that as the owners must perform gratitude, the experts need to perform reliability. Even though they have allegiances with the more prestigious auction houses or with very expensive antiques shops, at least for the duration of their televisual appearance, they are to be devoid of self-interest. That *Antiques Roadshow* can appear the place for an honest valuation is based as much on television being a public site as it is on the *Roadshow* not involving the sale of items. It is similar to the way consumer programmes can act in the public interest; in both cases 'public' indicates a position closer to the individual than to a business.

Other shared pieces of popular knowledge about *Antiques Roadshow* include: its structuring, which ensures that if a really valuable object is discovered in the course of a visit to a particular location, this discovery is the last item in a show, which thus can end on a satisfying high note; and the way in which the voiced hopes of the owners are centred around a few well-known names, whose popularity may owe something to the *Roadshow*'s, as is the case with pottery by Clarice Cliff. The final piece of folklore about the programme is one that is more likely to be exchanged as a juicy piece of inside information – that it is watched by thieves, both for the immediate identification of a desirable piece and its owner, and for longer-term educative purposes.

Characteristics

One of the most striking aspects of *Antiques Roadshow* is the contradiction which runs through it over the matters of use and value. This dogs the history of antiques on television and is a further indication of hegemonic ideological shifts occurring postwar and culminating under Thatcherism. Antiques had figured as things to be learned about and appreciated, or, if they were possessions, to be used and cared for. Problems arose when the economic value of an antique was acknowledged as primary at the same time that more possessions were realized as having the potential to be recognized as antiques (or at least to become 'collectable'). Value and use then came into collision. The more an object is used, the more a reduction in its monetary value is at risk. *Antiques Roadshow*, addressing an audience composed both of those still holding the older beliefs and those hoping for a windfall from an old household item, regularly confronts this problem. Over the years of its existence it is possible to detect a substantial move from favouring caring and use, to advising maximization of value. Even the phrasing of the valuation has changed from 'If you wanted to send it to auction, you should expect ...' to the blunter 'At auction, you should get ...'. Televisual discourse is, however, habitually pulled towards a sentimental register when the domestic and familial character of its perceived reception chimes with domestic and familial content (as is the case with *Antiques Roadshow*). This makes it difficult even now for the programme to admit that its logic should lead people to stop using and possibly even regret caring for their possessions. In this context the exaggerated fondness the experts have for making admiring comments about patina can be explained by its constituting one of the few signs of use that add value.

The most fraught and, in consequence, the most informative moments in terms of the use/value opposition occurred in 1992 during the first children's roadshow. Presenters from *Going Live*, a programme described by Stephen Wagg as representing consumerist children's television in distinction to the old bourgeois view of children's programming found in *Blue Peter* (1992: 168–9, 173), joined *Antiques Roadshow* experts to assess toys brought in by children in a joint programme called *Antiques Roadshow Going Live*. These are now regular events with the title of *Antiques Roadshow: The Next Generation*. Despite Wagg's assertion, the addition of children's television mores, even in their more consumerist mode, made the ideological contradictions of the *Roadshow* starker. It is not uncommon for children to appear on children's television as collectors, being advised about or showing off their collections. With *Antiques Roadshow*, where the end point is valuation, the situation is transformed and can become quite difficult when the object concerned is not even a collection, able to be discussed in terms of the allocation of pocket money, but an individual, beloved toy. The awkwardness of telling an adult that having chipped a vase has wiped 80 per cent off what it would have fetched at auction is as nothing compared to telling a child that loving its teddy has rendered it valueless, yet this is what the experts had to do. The construction of key moments in the programme which enabled it to make the necessary didactic point – for cuddling one's teddy *does* decrease its economic value – without deterring viewers was notable. The teddy problem was addressed directly with a large group of children clutching their bears meeting the expert, Bunny

Campione. Having declared several bears as of little value or of good British manufacture and some small monetary value, she was presented with a large and quite dilapidated example. She took hold of it, manipulated its unusually long limbs and pronounced it a rare prototype of a Steiff standing teddy and, if X-raying confirmed her suspicion that it had rod-joints, worth £3–5,000. All was thus made well; a loved toy had been discovered that was still valuable.

The point about use decreasing value was made most pointedly by a different segment about a non-cuddly object. A child had brought along a Dinky toy. These often appear on the adult version of the show as collectables, so the audience for the programme was well aware that the presence of the box in which the toy was sold substantially increases the value of the object. The point was made again. The child in this instance had taken three versions of the same toy – one that his father had played with when small that continued to be used, one that his uncle had not played with that was for display with the box and one which had not even been removed from the postal wrapping in which it had been sent. Even the expert, in this case Hilary Kay, appeared to find the latter excessive and admitted that her valuation of £150–200 for it was unreliable, unlike her confident pronouncement that the used one might bring a pound and the display one £80–100, but it certainly strengthened the point.

Most objects that are the focus of television content are new – in ordinary television as well as in advertisements and as significant plot devices in dramas. Use is something envisaged as in the object's future, after which comes the next stage, that of replacement. This is not the case with antiques and certainly not with *Antiques Roadshow*'s ideal object – the unrecognized treasure that has been in the family for several generations. Similarly, the value of the new object – economically and socially – is at its peak at the moment of purchase and declines thereafter, while the ideal *Antiques Roadshow* object has a value-in-waiting and a stratospheric trajectory. The programme might thus be seen as operating in opposition to the contemporary. Ironically, *Antiques Roadshow* is more a representation of post-industrial production. In watching the programme we see knowledge in operation as a technology, adding value to and thereby transforming ostensibly worthless objects. Following this initial transformation, furthermore, the object tends to require the attentions of a number of service industries – restoration, insurance, auction houses – most of which act similarly.

The transformation effected by knowledge operates on the status as well as the value of the item and can completely transform the relationship between owner and possession. In a show broadcast from Northampton in 1990, a woman brought in a ceramic owl drinking vessel. It was examined by the British ceramics expert and chief *Roadshow* character, Henry Sandon, who performed the ritual questioning of whether the owner had any idea of the worth of the piece. (One of the pleasures the programme offers its viewers is that of deciding whether the owner is being genuine when she answers no – as she must – at this point. This particular woman appeared genuine.) Sandon then asked if she was sitting comfortably and told her the owl was worth £20–30,000. In the anniversary programme, this, unsurprisingly, was one of the moments replayed. Sandon then commented to camera:

> She was last seen taking a taxi home. But what are you going to do with Ozzie now? You can hardly put him on the mantelpiece and put flowers in him, because some fool is going to knock him over. They very wisely sold him, and Stoke-on-Trent Museum happily bought him, and if you go to the museum you can see him now in his own special cabinet. We've found it for the nation and I think that's great.

This is a particularly rich moment in the programme's discourse, showing an object transformed from something that had a domestic utility into a commodity unable to be used as it had been up to the pronouncement of the knowledgeable expert and, indeed, unable any longer to be properly ('wisely') retained by its owner. The commodity status of the object is, however, brief because it is removed both from private ownership and from circulation by being declared a heritage object. The phrase 'We found it for the nation' is especially redolent, both for its construction of the programme as discoverers acting on behalf of the nation and for its vision of valuable objects lost to or endangered by the ignorant.

The last major example from the anniversary programme is the one that concluded it; the one that those structuring the programme chose (from 150 programmes) as a final encapsulation of their activities as they like to represent them. Hugh Scully, closing the show, calls it 'the best story of all' but introduces it by commenting generally: 'The essential ingredient is the character, humour and stories of the people who come along to our shows. It's the people who make the programme what it is.'

There is then a cut to a section from a programme originally broadcast from Liverpool in 1989. A woman with a strong regional dialect is showing expert John Battie a teapot and telling him, as is standard, about its history within the family. Battie asks the ritual question about whether she has an idea of its worth and also whether she would sell it? She answers no to both saying she loves the teapot too much, and is given a valuation of £5–6000. The programme then returns to the present where Hugh Scully is watching this replay on a monitor with the same woman at her home. He questions her about why, having said she would not sell, she subsequently has – for £14,000. She explains that she 'bought the council house, yes. We'd lived here for 30 years and we'd been paying rent all that time, and it was lovely to think that Joe was retiring and we could buy the house and live rent-free, and we've had a couple of holidays out of it too.' Scully then asks her if she is still a fan of the programme, and she continues:

> Yes, I love *Antiques Roadshow*, absolutely not for the value of anything, Hugh, but the atmosphere. You know, when you go there you're standing next to the expert and he's telling you about it and he tells you what it was used for in the olden days and your friends are saying come and see this and you want to see what is happening and you don't want to miss anything. It's a full day of excitement; it's marvellous.

This is indeed a stunning example of having one's cake and eating it, as the programme shows itself as having identified significant value within a mundane object and also as having helped a worthy individual to a better life (but still within her proper class location), while simultaneously disclaiming its being primarily about money, since it is about information and 'excitement'. Analytically, it is important to recognize that *Antiques Roadshow* constitutes, in Arjun Appadurai's term, a commodity context, being a social arena 'that help[s] link the commodity candidacy of a thing to the commodity phase of its career' (1986: 15) even though the exchanges that occur there are neither of goods nor of money. The programme effectively announces the arrival of an object in the market-place, regardless of the emphasis in the anniversary programme on saving things for the nation – as well as the ceramic owl, the programme featured a painting by Richard Dadd which was bought by the British Museum – for this is not the most common destination of objects identified in the programme. Rather, they retain the commodity status they have been endowed with and move into circulation.

Stories

Despite Scully's statement that the programme is about the stories of (ordinary) people, the stories in the regular programmes are focused upon the objects. People who bring their objects to be valued are asked to talk about them. The general direction is 'Tell me how you got it.' In professional terms, they are being asked to give information to aid the experts in their assessments, to provide details predominantly of provenance (though the term is never used); in televisual terms they are being asked to provide human interest. None the less, the stories provide a succession of biographies of things, to use Igor Kopytoff's term and criteria (1986: 66–7). The basic opposition is one between inheritance or gift and purchase (and the programme clearly prefers stories of inheritance or, as they phrase it, 'family'), but the story can be a more elaborate one involving commissioning, production, siting within the house, passage through generations and preferences. The distinction between inheritance and purchase is an illusory one anyway, since the objects must have been acquired in the first place, though stories of inheritance usually omit this on the basis of its having been forgotten. What the distinction establishes for the programme is whether the object can have a naive owner and what kind of story can be told about it, or whether it has been bought recently, in which case it can be assumed that the owner is knowing and might even have bought the object as a commodity. This last, while not providing the favoured story (none of the examples chosen for the anniversary special were of this nature), does have a place within the programme and a ritual response: after the valuation is given, the expert announces whether the purchase was a wise one, often phrased as 'Well, you had a good eye there', but basing this assessment on a significant increase in the object's monetary value. The major exception to the inevitability of acquisition occurs when the object has been made by a member of the family. Not many of these occur, but there have been several instances of china or furniture decorated by amateur painters and the first edition for 1995 concluded with a woman whose mother had taught the painter Laura Knight to enamel, showing some enamels by Knight, a piece of Art Nouveau jewellery made by her mother and a brooch that was a joint effort. This is another rich instance, providing in the programme's terms a fascinating family story and a famous name and in other terms a detailed biography of the objects plus solid provenance.

The story of origin is the only major discursive form available to the owners, the non-experts. Their comments apart from this can only be brief answers to questions. Yet even the experts tend to present their judgements in stories about the manufacture of the object or about the detective work that enables them to make an identification. This demonstrates that conversationalization, to use Norman Fairclough's term again, is so dominant that too substantial a tutelary exposition must be recuperated into the informality of the programme. Thus after expert David Battie gave a very cogent and informative explanation of the marks on the back of a plate, the presenter commented: 'David's description of the Chelsea red anchor period was about the best few minutes on that I've heard', thus marking it out as an atypical, but still valuable, moment.

It is within the biographies of things that the colonial discourse which has diminished somewhat is located. During the 1980s there were frequent instances when the biography of an object began with the statement that it had been 'brought back from the East by a relative'. The relatives were identified as soldiers, missionaries or traders and the objects were overwhelmingly Chinese, Indian and Japanese – ceramics, metalwork, carved ivory, the kind of thing regularly described as of 'exquisite workmanship'. The biographies of these things began with their entry into European hands; they were objects treated as *terra nullius*. Yet their situation within the programme has always been quite complex. To begin with there was the geographic specificity of the objects – they rarely come from settler colonies or from Africa, in part perhaps because objects from these places tend to be termed 'ethnographic' rather than 'antique' and are not often brought in. Colonially marked objects were usually presented to the experts as mementos and souvenirs, though the details of their acquisition were not part of the story. The imbalance of knowledge, power and economic resources that was probably part of the 'colonial' object's acquisition is in some ways re-enacted on the programme as ignorant owners who do not recognize the worth of the pieces they have are encouraged to put them onto the market where they can resume their commodity paths. In the more recent editions that I have looked at, the pieces from the East (still overwhelmingly Chinese, Indian and Japanese) have all been ones that have led to substantial discussion of the export trade, including the commissioning of pieces of Chinese manufacture by titled Englishmen. Discursively, colonialism seems to have been replaced by educative disquisitions on an ostensibly equal trading relationship.

Here, and throughout the programme, there is a constant theme of objects being misrecognized and undervalued. They need to enter circulation for this to be rectified. This is underwritten by a common visual element of people appearing with battered cardboard boxes or old plastic shopping bags from which they remove a jumble of objects wrapped in newspaper. Out of this mess of casual waste is produced an item of great beauty and value. The expert, recognizing what is valuable, can return the object to its proper place in the world and restore order.

Taste

The whole matter of taste, class and distinction which permeates the programme must be considered since it is endemic to the antiques trade, a difficulty for a mass medium like television and overdetermined as a characteristic of Britishness. Taste on *Antiques Roadshow* is treated as a personal thing and is usually subservient to monetary judgements. An expert's positive aesthetic judgement is expressed in terms of liking or loving something and can disregard value; negative judgements can only be admitted in conjunction with an economic positive, as in 'I don't much like this myself, but it is doing very well at auction now' or 'This is very popular with American collectors'. At times owners disclaim objects in ways which reveal apparently class-based insecurities about their taste. A high valuation seems always to soothe these worries. Class is never directly referred to on the programme, although, as another aspect of the show's Englishness, it is rarely in doubt.

It is valuable to employ Bourdieu's work on 'habitus' here. Characteristically, the experts are possessed of cultural capital, the display of which meshes with the programme's need to discover unsuspected treasures. But this display can neither talk about nor even consider the proper fit of object and owner. When the object is appropriate to the class location of the owner, knowledge does not transform it into a commodity. The programme, however, is premised on a mismatch of object and owner that is resolved by the object's becoming a commodity and the owner presumably acquiring money to be spent on a more suitable possession – like the council house, or a couple of holidays. Alternately, an owner may retain an object precisely as a demonstration of distinction – the object in these cases needs to be treated differently, hence the experts' stress on physical transformation, on the removal of the object from current use. This transformation occurs along a sliding scale linked to the assessed value of the piece and its current place in the household. If in use, they recommend removing it and putting it on display. If it is already on display then perhaps it should be moved from open display to a glass cabinet, but they may further suggest it should be protected from light. They do not, however, suggest that the object should be put in a safe. It is a conceit of the programme that objects are at risk of damage from clumsiness, fire or neglect, but not from thieves. Insurance, although it is mentioned at almost every recent valuation, is always against a generalized 'loss'. Mentioning a safe comes too close to acknowledging the possibility of theft. If protecting an object from light (i.e. hiding it away) is insufficient, then the suggestion is that it should be sent to auction. Implicit here is that adequate security as well as appropriate levels of appreciation are available further up the socio-economic scale.

The main class location of the owners who appear is lower- to middle-middle class. Exceptions of course occur. One that was particularly informative was the case in a 1992 programme of an elderly man who brought in a gaming table. It was adjudged a superb example of early eighteenth-century furniture-making and the expert valued it at £10–12,000. He then chatted to the owner about how long it had been in the family and how it continued to be used regularly. The owner, giving all the signs of a habitus long-based on money rather than cultural capital, laughed deprecatingly at the valuation and pre-empted any comment about its needing to be removed from use by acknowledging that he might ask his bridge partners to be a bit more careful with their drinks, but showed no signs of noticing that his table had been transformed, since it had not. It was properly located, it was unlikely to become a commodity and the only aspect out of place was that the owner had appeared on the programme. He had no place on ordinary television – the televisual place for faded upper-class gentlemen is not in non-fiction at all, but in drama. His naivety was not so much about his possession, as about television. People like him, and I recall a small number of others, are the only ones who can dispute the experts; they cannot dispute the experts' knowledge, only their right to instruct them in the disposal of their possessions.

Despite my assertion that *Antiques Roadshow* is the most British of programmes, I am not suggesting that antiques are central to the British psyche. The programme, though, is important as an instance of the power of national television to speak locally and ordinarily from within a globalized television culture. As well as drawing on the cosiness and heritage-consciousness of the older British self-image, it is completely contemporary in the economic story it tells. The conflict between old and new Right ideologies within the programme has considerable potency. The stories of inheritance, of keeping possessions in the family and the belief that objects are not personally owned but are 'in trust' for one's heirs, and thus can only be sold with dishonour, characterize the residual, old Right perspective, while those advocating putting the family silver on the market are the dominant New. *Antiques Roadshow* provides a prime place where contests within conservative economic discourse can be pursued, disguised a little for public consumption. The changes in the programme over the years that have made far more acceptable the displays of greed and exaltation at high valuations are indications of the entrenching of a much broader drive to commodify and that become much starker in other programmes across the schedule.

QUINTESSENTIAL AUSTRALIA: BURKE'S BACKYARD

Arguably the most potent myth for Australians – one that can be called on in many different situations and which despite its Anglo-Celtic origins is amenable to a range of modulations, and that has even served to aid recognition of Aboriginal land rights – is that of the Bush. The myth of the Bush is widely agreed to have had its genesis in the late nineteenth century, but its folkloric derivation from the actual stories of bushmen themselves is generally rejected in favour of its being a product of urban dwellers romanticizing their rural past. Graeme Davison has traced the genesis in the situation confronted in the 1890s by the radical intellectual writers for the influential magazine *The Bulletin* moving into the 'sleazy urban frontier' of inner-city Sydney from smaller country towns (1982: 111–12). Despite the particularity of this, the consistency with which life in the city is regarded as an unsatisfying substitute for the 'real' Australia can be traced through the whole range of Australian cultural products. Graeme Turner has talked of how Australia is represented in terms of a basic opposition variously figured as 'the country versus the city, rural versus urban, nature versus society' (1993: 25). While the first of these terms is repeatedly the one preferred, there is an ambivalence at its heart given that the core theme is the difficulty of survival on the land (28). From this comes the most powerful mythic Australian figure, 'the battler', readily found in all manner of environments but maintaining a rural 'bush' ethos. Turner suggests that the Australian experience is repeatedly represented, especially in populist texts, as being a 'harsh but worthwhile' one in which a 'pragmatic resourceful self' battles against isolation and powerlessness and that this underpins a politics of acceptance and subordination (143). Televisual texts usually fail to get to the end of this chain of reasoning in any overt way, but certainly can be seen to celebrate the resourceful self dealing with harsh conditions in various attempts to produce a satisfying life.

Despite living in one of the most urbanized countries in the world (approximately 85 per cent of the population live in cities) the dominant Australian self-image is a romantic one of rural roots and outdoor competence. The popularity of 4WD vehicles as town cars, of rural outfitters as providers of trendy casual clothing and of authenticating the holiday experience by reference to having endured low-level privation, were embraced earlier and more enthusiastically by Australians than by other nations, even the British or the Japanese. Yet these are occasional and expensive ways to exhibit and explore the 'Bushness' of being Australian. Television's evocation of this aspect of the national imaginary is widespread but fraught. Wildlife or nature programmes display the actuality of the outback, dramas can cater to the nostalgic pull and holiday shows take television viewers into their own vicarious interactions with the Bush; but one programme has operated successfully for many years to rearticulate the Bush ethos in the urban present and to integrate it with a number of other powerful myths of Australia, like egalitarianism. That programme is *Burke's Backyard*.

The sentimental nostalgia for the Bush focuses on the outback or the farm but actualizing this is an impossibility on a day-to-day basis for the ordinary urban and suburban Australian. To effect it, elements associated with the farm in particular are abstracted, and together with consonant other myths are attached to something more achievable – the backyard. The myth of Australia as the land of democratized home-ownership has had a long purchase and certainly home-ownership was widespread in Australia long before the shifts in the UK. This combined with the idea of the capable self-sufficient bushman able to turn his hand to any necessary task, to produce a vision of the home and its surrounds as a DIY site where one exercises and keeps up the skills and techniques needed for the true calling of an Australian – being out bush. One may no longer be off ploughing the ten-acre paddock, but at least one can still put up a pergola or protect the mango tree from birds. The female version of the myth has the woman, also widely capable, maintaining the home and its surrounds in the absence of the male and so in its contemporary version it is quite capable of a unisex articulation.

Situating *Burke's Backyard* among other Australian programmes

In placing *Burke's Backyard* as the quintessential Australian programme, it is important to start by noting two other programmes – one which relates to it closely and one which is emphatically other. *The Bushtucker Man* was a popular ABC programme which was exported to many other markets but offered a totally different kind of experience from *Burke's Backyard*. It was concerned not only with the actual bush and surviving in it, substantially by calling on aboriginal knowledge, but also with respecting it and leaving it unaltered. Although it continually used direct address to inform the audience of ways to find food in the outback and ways to cook it, it did not do so in the expectation that viewers would have occasion to call on the knowledge. The eponymous presenter, Les Hiddens, had honed his initial knowledge, gained in childhood, further as an officer in the Australian army, specializing in training soldiers in survival skills, and it was these rather than camping tips that formed the basis for the information being passed on. This was not domestic knowledge, even though it must be seen to have played a significant part in the growth of the bush foods industry and the incorporation of bush flavours into the higher echelons of Australian cuisine. Australia did not, as a consequence of his programme, become a nation of people gathering foodstuffs from the wild; instead the lemon myrtle and the bush tomatoes now eaten more widely are bought in supermarkets and delicatessens.

The programme which does relate to *Burke's Backyard* is a radio one, *Australia All Over*, a Sunday morning ABC request and talk programme of music and reminiscence about bush life. Bullamakanka, the bush band who sing the *Burke's Backyard* theme song, are frequently requested performers on the radio show and the original or the non-commercial version of the TV show theme, called simply 'My Backyard', is regularly heard on the radio show. Although the listening base is heavily urban, the content is overwhelmingly rural. The majority of callers assert a country town location and the minority urban callers need to establish their rural credentials almost immediately. They customarily do so with reference to the past in which, if they did not themselves live in the country, at least they frequently visited a relative who did. There is no space here for acknowledging the present as valuable or enjoyable. 'Authenticity' is spoken of frequently and a nostalgic mode dominates. Burke draws on this sentiment and the idiom in which it is expressed within his more decisively urban programme.

In addition to these two poles where the bush has a degree of actual presence through people who continue to live in it, there are other programmes which place *Burke's Backyard* in the contemporary world of lifestyle television and emphasize its place in the dominant discourse of the transformative power of television. They effect a further lateral harmonization even though the programme does not require 'indigenizing' since it is not a formatted one. Harmonization is thoroughly sustained by links to other Channel 9 shows, especially the spin-off *Backyard Blitz,* whose presenter, Jamie Durie, intermittently appears on the older programme and regularly features in the *Burke's Backyard* magazine. Durie's programme, begun in 2000, has taken the makeovers once common on the older show and expanded them into the sole content of the descendant show. Occasionally, all the Channel 9 home and garden shows will combine for a special programme like the annual *Renovation Rescue* when the network moves into sustained fairy godmother mode and transforms the domestic situation of some deserving family. A recent family had featured in *RPA*, a real-life hospital series also on 9 (and similar to ITV's *Jimmy's*), where, despite the hospital's efforts, the father had died. After a short interval, personnel from eight of the network's programmes (including *Getaway*, the holiday show which removed the family while the surprise was being produced) refurbished the house, garden, computer facilities, the family finances and took care of its pets in a two-hour spectacular.

History

Burke's Backyard was the first undisputed lifestyle programme on Australian television, starting in 1987. That it has been running since that time is a rarity for Australia where few programmes last more than four or five series. Presented by the horticulturalist and author Don Burke, the programme was developed from his radio show and newspaper column, initially as a late-night, low-budget television programme, but very soon after its ratings figures were observed, it became an hour-long, Friday night, prime-time show repeated on Sunday afternoons. Unlike the situation in the UK, repeats during the first transmission of a series are very unusual on Australian television and signal a programme which is in some way specifically important to the network's profile. (The other major example is SBS's *The Movie Show*, also an extremely long-running, flagship show.) In the feature articles which followed its establishment as a fixture on the Australian television scene, Burke was insistent about his determination to make a television programme about the Australian backyard and about his ideal of the backyard as a place he remembered from his childhood in the 1950s being a 'mecca for kids ... it was a messy place with a Hills hoist, dad's vegie patch, swings and holes dug by enthusiastic kids with lots of natural bush' (Weaver, 1990: 92).

From the beginning it was built around the presenter and his idea of what a backyard and a television show about them should be. The celebration programme for the tenth anniversary began by juxtaposing the past and the present as the Burke of 1987 introduced the first programme saying it was 'created for the ordinary Australian family a bit like mine, one which lives in their backyard. We will look at gardening, but at much, much more ...'. This was followed by the 1997 Burke commenting how 'we'd sort of dreamt up the idea of doing a lifestyle television program but had no real idea of how to do it, because it hadn't been done anywhere in the world to that stage'. From the beginning, the keynotes have been the life of the Australian and how it was embodied in the figure of the host, but only after it had been running for a while was it possible to enunciate the focus as being on 'lifestyle'.

The appeal of the programme can be seen in another piece of tenth-anniversary programme information, this time from what Deborah Malor calls the 'fact tag' flashed on screen at the end of a segment (1991: 61); in the first ten years on air, *Burke's Backyard* distributed more than two million fact sheets. After the anniversary had passed, a print magazine version of *Burke's Backyard* appeared and less than a year later its circulation was over 100,000 a month, putting it ahead of such long-term alternatives as *Gardening Australia* and *Australian Home Beautiful*. The magazine was published by ACP, making it, like Channel 9, a Packer property. As well as calling on the same cast of experts that the programme does, the magazine provides behind-the-scenes glimpses of the making of the show and extends the range of material covered. Together with reciprocal referencing, this ensures that both versions have something distinctive to offer.

Content
_____

The programme focuses on the backyard as a distinctive Australian space which can be all manner of things as long as it is located off-stage with regard to the house (behind, beside, on top of, just not in front). This brings together various-sized plots of land from terrace gardens, through suburban blocks to hobby farms. It allows the combination of gardening segments with exterior building tasks and, aided by the great range of climates in the country, can consider plants from tiny alpines to tropical trees. Burke has a passion for native plants and his status as an authority on the family Grevilliae is frequently referred to.

A standard programme will contain a visit to the home of an ordinary family to observe something special about their backyard, which may be a problem they have written asking for help with, or an unusual feature they want to show off (for example, there was a visit to a couple who had covered just about every part of their house and garden in shells). There will also be a call on the week's celebrity gardener who may be, but more often is not, the subject of a garden makeover. These visits, both the ordinary and the celebrity, are always conducted by Burke himself; he is the central personality and to be visited by someone other than him would be to be short-changed. Indeed, most of the segments involve him, even though there are several regular reporters. For the last four or so years the linking segments and the close have come from Burke's own backyard where, accompanied by his dog, he addresses the camera from a squatting position, atypical for television presenters but sanctioned here by its traditional Bush connotations of being standard for men of the outback when they are not riding horses. An average show has up to ten individual segments, producing a regular eight fact sheets, and only two or three of the items will come from the reporters. Other regular items look at the particular plant being featured, some kind of household hint (from one of the reporters), a garden pest, some kitchen hint or recipe (another item for a reporter), a visit to a recently completed special garden, a small building project in the backyard, something about garden produce and two items about animals.

It is these animal segments above all that make the programme more than a straightforward gardening show. One of these is the long-running 'road test' segment dealing with the suitability of particular pets for various situations; the other looks at native fauna of some kind. If it is an animal, bird or reptile, Burke will often be the reporter now that the previous reporter, veterinarian Harry Cooper, has moved on to his own show, *Harry's Practice*, but if it is an insect or spider then regular reporter Densey Clyne – a rather formal, middle-aged female naturalist – invariably presents it. Using a female for the 'creepy crawlies' more readily domesticates them and Clyne regularly points out their usefulness as garden inhabitants. Clyne, Cooper and a number of less regularly appearing personnel are allowed to occupy the position of 'experts', but as Alan McKee points out, it is part of the way the programme structures the ordinariness of its viewers that expertise is widely spread. Everyone is allowed an area of expertise, most especially evident in the animal road tests, from which they can pronounce on a subject under discussion (2001: 267–9). This demotic expertise is allowable when solicited by presenter or reporters, but in other regards ordinary people are really not in a much better position than those in *Antiques Roadshow*. The owner of a pet with a problem could not challenge the suggestions of the resident vet, nor could someone seeking Burke's advice demur when it was given.

Characteristics

Although the programme is often found in the suburbs, the touchstone is the Bush, which can be evoked in conversation about the past, in reference to native plants or in the incorporation into backyard settings of bush memorabilia. It all helps the programme to maintain its place with the holiday and the fishing programmes' 'mythologising of Australia, its landscape and people' which operates simultaneously with domesticating it, as Sue Turnbull notes (1993: 19). One of the most telling of its many makeovers, in the time before most of them moved to *Backyard Blitz*, was its transformation of the inner-Sydney terrace belonging to a soap actress into a 'real old country backyard' complete with bits of farm implements and a simple clothes line with traditional clothes prop. Rural detritus and the signs of poverty were transformed into markers of a kitsch distinction.

Occasionally, the programme ventures offshore, yet still the quintessentially Australian figure of Don Burke explores the exotic, knowledgeable about the botany but awestruck by the decidedly non-backyard surrounds. He maintains his Australianness in such improbable locations as the gardens of Versailles, not only by his familiar appearance but also through his marked use of Australian locutions. The programme is always introduced with a now unremarkable 'G'day', but closed with the much rarer, rural departing salutation 'Hooroo'. Burke is the lynch-pin of the show (and indeed the owner of the production company), the man through whom the Bush is articulated for the city in a thoroughly suburban way. Archetypally the ordinary bloke, a little on the short side ('nuggety' in the programme's vernacular), able to turn his hand to most things and at ease with all types of people, Burke is one of the most skilled exponents of televisual sincerity that Australia has produced. His ability to convey both sincerity and trustworthiness is key to his place as the person who has been the longest-lasting of those persuading viewers about the desirability of this week's lifestyle suggestions.

At core a gardening programme, *Burke's Backyard* carries its distinctiveness and difference in its title; not a garden and certainly not a front garden, but a backyard. The casualness of the space, the diversity of activities it can be used for and the way the name disguises its size are key. A backyard can be anything that lies behind the house, from the small piece of ground behind an inner-city terrace to a couple of acres/hectares with livestock, but ideally the term evokes certain fundamentals – a shed, an animal or bird and its housing, a washing-line and both edible and decorative plants. The theme song lists the desiderata explicitly: 'Flowers down the fence and vegies down the back. A dog or two and a barbecue.' Bullamankanka, the group who perform the song, are of course a bush band. This form of music and the dancing that accompanies it (a revival of the more rustic types of ballroom dancing together with set-pattern country dancing derived both from British and American forms) was at the peak of its popularity in the 1980s when *Burke's Backyard* first became established.

Burke's Backyard is a very clever mix of nostalgia and the contemporary. It operates on the principal of Australia being a classless society, treating pensioner and wealthy gardeners both as interesting and able to illustrate valuable lessons for viewers. The dominance of egalitarianism can be seen at its most bizarre in the regular celebrity spots. Given that celebrities tend to be wealthier than most viewers, the programme needs to negotiate the problem of wealth and inequity very carefully. One such item, on the businessman Sir James Hardie, asked about his yachts but focused more on his installation of a small watering system for his rooftop garden (despite the undeniable presence of a normative definition of the backyard, in actuality 'backyard' is interpreted very liberally).

Celebrity gardeners really do have to try to be ordinary and to say that they have a personal engagement with their garden; that, for example, they care for the lawn themselves or that they used professionals for the design but that was all. Only people with professional associations with gardening themselves can shamelessly display acres of water garden unable to be maintained without continual assistance.

While the programme is generally direct in its approach and only moves into the humorous when there are misadventures of the physical kind, as in one notorious encounter with an amorous lyrebird, there are still times when the viewer can be left uncertain about whether an item is serious. These usually operate around matters of taste with the application of the term 'kitsch' left open, so presumably the polysemy is intentional. The shell house visit was certainly one, but another was a visit to the home of a celebrity sporting couple, Warwick and Joanne Capper, which in the absence of any signs of an interest in gardening apart from a couple of pot plants by the pool, moved inside the house where the camera lingered on a large nude portrait of the couple placed above their bed. Ordinary conversation about the programme is frequently about the peculiarities revealed in the celebrity visits and the Capper one is reasonably famous.

The insistence with which the programme presents animals as an inevitable component of backyard life and the way it considers not just pets but also wild animals, reptiles and insects which are not being deemed pests to be destroyed, are keys to its distinctiveness and its link to the Bush. An item looking at the blue-tongued lizard was typical. These quite large reptiles are frequent visitors to suburban gardens and the accompanying fact sheet assumes this locale in its hints about being careful not to run over a basking lizard with a lawnmower or car, but the item was filmed in a fully rural locale. From all the various visits made to other people's gardens, those situated in rural or semi-rural areas are most privileged and more time is spent on them. Often second and even third visits will be made to see how plantings, or even reafforestation, has developed.

These rural visits are often occasions for an explicit address to the nation since they are more able to be the sites for conservation messages which stress the selflessness of those engaging in 'proper' plantings (of native plants) or of 'sensible' water use practices, since they are contributing to the improvement of the national estate. But it is also possible for this kind of discourse to be activated in cities. There is a continual implicit argument that tending one's backyard in ways that increase the presence of plants enriches more than just the owners of that plot. This becomes explicit when Burke shifts out of the backyard into public areas approving both private care for nature strips (the public patches of greenery separating footpath from road) and local authority activity in parks and related areas. An item on a spectacular display of azaleas on a roadside in Sydney not only actively encouraged people to drive by the site but also named the now dead men who many years previously had chosen the variety and planted the shrubs, saying it had been 'a great legacy to leave people in Australia'. The similarity in this articulation to those quoted from *Antiques Roadshow* underlines the banal nationalism each show expresses on a regular basis. Alan McKee also notes the frequency with which Australian national identity is evoked and called into being by the programme (2001: 258–9).

Reference to the work of landscape gardeners in the backyard itself, though, is rather problematic for *Burke's Backyard*. In the article on the programme from its early heyday quoted earlier, landscaping was spoken of as the great evil that had deprived the children of generations after Burke of their backyard heritage. Burke himself, when talking of his own activities in redesigning backyards, rarely refers to the activity as involving landscaping. Yet the spin-off programme, *Backyard Blitz*, is unashamed about its landscaping mission, and when Burke is involved on cross-promotion for the show he, too, enters that space. On a live special programme at the Melbourne International Flower and Garden Show, much of the time was taken up by Burke investigating a range of highly artificial gardens created by landscapers or garden designers where plants seemed very much sidelined by sculptural elements. At moments like these, as in his annual visits to famous gardens in other countries, the backyard fades from view and the programme becomes just another gardening show and one without the sometimes fierce allegiance to native plants that is another awkward element. Ideologically, it is obvious that native plants are preferred and integral to the conservation message that the programmes espouse whenever possible. Yet the practices of the audience, as gauged by requests for fact sheets and requests for advice (both of which enable the audience for *Burke's Backyard* to be more 'known' than is customary for television programmes), make Burke, as producer, aware that non-native plants are essential components of the Australian backyard and his programme.

The contradictions of self-reliance and conservation in the suburban backyard are intensified with the realization that Burke can only mention a plant by variety if sufficient stock exists across relevant parts of Australia to deal with the demand. The programme is a huge, carefully synchronized, commercial operation with spin-off books, a monthly magazine, a range of garden products able to be ordered on its website and spin-off television programmes. In all this it is typical of a highly successful contemporary television programme, yet its address is much more to the 'actual' ordinary Australian than many other programmes. It is possible for much that Burke advocates to be actually done by viewers and the (free) fact sheets are very detailed, arguably even more helpful than the magazine.

The focus on the suburban backyard as the place from which to mount a campaign about conservation and heritage and a significant multimedia industry reveals a knowledge of the Australian psyche and the power of the ordinary. McKenzie Wark, commenting on the programme, has noted that 'what was curious was the way *Burke's Backyard* offered an image of a public life composed of private places and passions. Burke appeared as the public figure as gardener, as someone who shares a suburban dream of tending one's own plot, controlling and managing a stable world behind the fence' (1999: 152).

Burke has managed to maintain this public image of the ordinary man unfazed by larger events and sustained by ties to a country background. In a television industry marked by the brevity of most of its television programme runs, it must be because the resonances of this position run deep. The mix of conservation, an ideology predominantly of the Left, and heritage, predominantly of the Right, is not incidental here. Behind the fence in the private space of personally owned land with its illusory links to the mythic past, there is no problem with holding these views in balance. It may be impossible to use the word 'cosy' to talk of the *Burke's Backyard* view of the nation, but in the favourite term of John Howard, the current Australian Prime Minister, it is certainly 'comfortable'.

These programmes demonstrate that there remain places within the contemporary television schedule for shows that are resolutely national in their address. I have chosen very established, prime-time examples but there are many more in each country scattered throughout the schedule, both long form and short form. *Antiques Roadshow* and *Burke's Backyard* both speak to a romantic, old-fashioned view of their respective countries, one that has roots in past glories and is most powerful with remarkably similar sections of the population. The Australian show is certainly less staid than the British and can speak only of a much more recent past, but their tasks of suturing the national into the televisual through a single commodified image – the antique or the backyard – is shared. Together with local versions of international formats and the shape of the schedule, which both speaks to and creates a distinctive pattern into which to insert the fully imported shows, they place limits on the extent to which globalization can determine the nation's television viewing. Because imported television is far more likely in both countries to be drama, ordinary television (in association with sport and news programmes) plays a substantial role in the production of an assertively national television system.

CONCLUSION

Looking at the programmes of ordinary television has shown that there are continuities across what both the industry and the academy regard as disparate programme types. I have not argued that the popular and industrial distinctions between such types as game shows and lifestyle programmes are unnecessary or misleading, but I do believe it is valuable to see these non-fiction television programmes, which are generally disregarded as too trivial to be worth critical investigation, as a reasonably cohesive field. Doing so enables us to deepen our understanding of the social, cultural and even the political operation of what continues to be the most significant of contemporary mass-media – television.

The rise of entertainment as the overwhelmingly dominant purpose of television, especially at the expense of education, can most clearly be seen in the shifts in these programmes. The related aspect of the tabloidization of news and current affairs has not been explored here but can be better understood when placed in conjunction with the other shifts in non-fiction television, including the changes in much of what can be considered documentary. The demise of light entertainment as a recognizable category has not meant the disappearance of the programmes it named (nor indeed of a kind of industrial contempt for their quality), rather there has been an expansion and something of a re-articulation of the domain.

The key characteristics of ordinary television were identified as being its mundanity, a style which attempts to reduce the gap between viewer and viewed and the incorporation of ordinary people into the programmes themselves. It is the latter which may be regarded as the most significant, even though there are some pieces of ordinary television which do not do this to any major extent. One of the terms used during the 1980s when the changes in programming were becoming sufficiently noticeable that new names were required, was 'people programmes'. It did not catch on as 'infotainment' did, but it served to identify one of the changes – far more people had started to appear on television and the majority of the new numbers were drawn from the ranks of viewers, not professionals. It also indicated an increase in the mundanity of the concerns of the shows; they were 'people programmes' also, in that they took the ordinary, uneventful concerns and everyday practices of the people viewing as their subject matter.

But not everything was about the viewers' lives. Another theme most evident on ordinary television is that of the importance of the medium itself. In addition to programmes celebrating the medium, like clip-shows, anniversary specials and game shows where the subject is television, many other programmes promote the power of television to transform the lives of its viewers, be it through makeovers or more overtly charitable interventions. Even in allowing ordinary people to appear on the medium as contestants, to watch productions as members of a studio audience or to help determine outcomes through voting on an issue under discussion, or in some competition, television presents itself as a beneficent presence in the lives of its viewers. It presents the gift of its attention as rendered devoid of self-interest, but ordinary television has an omnivorous need for the bodies of its viewers, not just in front of the sets in their own domestic spaces, but also in the studios participating in the programmes.

If television is understood as comprised principally of drama, news, current affairs and sport – as well might be the case given both the tendency of television studies and the industrially linked coverage which pays most attention to programmes that require the greatest monetary investment – then it is possible to regard it as a medium linked strongly, but only indirectly, to the lives of its viewers. According to this conception, television comments on their lives and on issues held to be important to them; it (mis)represents them and it caters to their fantasies, but it does so at one remove. Viewers may make a psychic investment in television but they do not have a physical involvement. Once the extent to which it does entangle itself with their actual activities is admitted, arguments about the separation of what is televised and those who view it need to be modulated. The calculations of Chapter 2 indicate that something like a quarter of a million ordinary people a year are needed by ordinary television programmes on British television, largely as studio audiences. This calculation pays no account of those who vote or call in with comments to such programmes as require this. I am not pretending that there has been a move to public access to television production in the way that was hoped for as a democratizing practice during the 1970s, nor that those who do participate have any real power over the programming. My argument is a smaller one; that the separation of production and reception of television is not as absolute, nor the processes of production so mystifying, as may once have been the case.

As the case of Gilbert Harding, discussed in Chapter 3 made clear, the development of television celebrity was not just a promotional ploy foisted on an unaware public, it was a two-way activity, a manifestation of the viewing public's desire to bridge the gap between what they watched as images and the reality of its production. There has been no diminution of this desire. For many years programme promotion was the principal way in which it was exploited, although studio audiences have been with television almost from the beginning. It is the great growth in the number of television programmes required and, in particular, of ordinary television programmes as a proportion of that number, that has led to the ready availability of a direct experience of being present during production, if not actually being on television. This increased presence of ordinary people in programme material contributed to the stylistic change whereby a formal demeanour on the screen became rare – even news programmes are now more casual – and the demotic came to dominate output.

The incorporation of viewers into the programmes and the use of a casual address to the audience were only part of the way in which ordinary television presents itself as ordinary – or at least close to it. Located overwhelmingly in studios dressed as living-rooms or in the actual domestic spaces of its specially chosen viewers, speaking of their day-to-day concerns and using presenters who position themselves as speaking on behalf of their viewers, this is a television which insists there is nothing special about itself (while engaged in a process of disavowal around the matter of celebrity, whereby a presenter is only a celebrity off the set of his or her own show). Sociability is the keynote of exchanges between those who appear on television, and sociability requires that speech be of no particular moment and (appears to be) between equals. It acts to keep both awe and (hopefully) condescension at bay.

The growth of reality television, especially of reality game shows, has a special place in this development. One of the major changes of television during the 1990s, these programmes did not arrive out of the blue, being foreshadowed, especially in the UK, by a range of programmes daring contestants to perform variously dangerous or humiliating stunts and by instances where television cameras left the studios to invade the homes and lives of viewers (or in the case of the family that moved into *The Big Breakfast* house, transplant the lives of selected viewers into a studio/home). John Dovey, examining a smaller grouping of programmes which overlaps substantially with mine, talks about the rise of first-person media as the defining difference of the new factual television, and this too acknowledges the increased presence of viewers as television subjects. His requirement for the appearance of unmediated or minimally mediated access to the individuals concerned means that his focus is a different one, but he also registers an equivocal change whereby a greater presence of the personal is made available, but only subject to particular conditions which include a focus on the individual self and quick-fix solutions (2000: 117–21).

Looking at a wider grouping of programmes, their preoccupation with a small range of topics and the discourses that pervade the grouping becomes apparent. Consumption, family, health and sexuality are paramount and interlinked. Ordinary television operates, in Nikolas Rose's term, as a 'consumption technology' (1999: 86) showing both the commodities and the ways they can be incorporated into fulfilling, even ethical, lives. The importance of the term 'lifestyle' to ordinary television is far greater than its naming of one type of its programmes. A person's lifestyle is a concrete expression of self-identity, not a trivial addition, and the components of that lifestyle are substantially what ordinary television is concerned with. Tastes, practices and possessions are all seen to reveal the self, and television programmes provide guidance in what these mean and how they may be modified. The key aspect which makes this able to be a continuing activity is the phenomenon of fashionability. The meanings attached to commodities and to many practices change over time as they are deemed dated and in need of replacement or refreshing. Ordinary television programmes provide advice on this, most especially in the many makeover programmes which are far more likely to be premised on the look of a room, a person or a garden being dated, than their being unusable or offensive. Talk shows and reality game shows may address changes in behavioural practices in a similar way through opening up topics for discussion on the programmes and among audiences.

Yet this is not to suggest that television is engaged in a selfless activity of helping its audience make sense of their place in the world. It may provide assistance in this regard, but there is nothing selfless about the medium. The shift to placing commodities increasingly at the centre of the programmes themselves rather than relying on their being the concern of advertisements which interrupt programmes, follows the decline in audiences' attention to advertisements following the introduction of devices like remote controls, video recorders, and personal television services such as Tivo, all of which enable viewers to avoid commercial breaks. The industry needs to retain advertisers and to do that it needs to retain viewers. Lifestyle advice, commodity promotion and the importance of television itself are brought together in the most insistent ordinary televisual discourse of all: the role of television in the transformation of the self. Makeover programmes, talk shows and game shows – reality or not – which have prizes sufficiently substantial to be able to promise to change the lives of the recipients (or which offer fame as an acceptable alternative path to the same end) are all central to this. Television not only shows people how to manage their lifestyle to reflect the identity they would like to present; it also intervenes in its production for numbers of actual viewers. Here the greater involvement of ordinary people in the programmes themselves has an added attraction. Ordinary television becomes a fairy godmother able to make the wishes of (a few of its) viewers come true. That the logic of all this applies only to commercial broadcasters has not led to a different situation pertaining to public ones. Declining government support for an alternative system, reliance on the same methods of measuring audiences and outsourcing of programme production to the same companies that produce for commercial systems all mean that the differences between the two systems are negligible.

The other side of the dominant vision of television – helping viewers to actualize their optimum identities through consuming fashionable commodities – lies in the discourses ordinary television does not deem important – education, work, race and class. These all tell a different story, one in which identity is not produced solely by consuming commodities; one where other factors are influential. An odd addition to this collection is economic discourse. It is not that economic matters are unimportant or absent from ordinary television, far from it, nor that they are irrelevant to identity formation, but the extent to which they pervade the schedule is disguised under the stress on lifestyle and television's role in helping its transformation. Yet all of these discourses are still to be found, if somewhat submerged, on ordinary television. Even education, most inimical to the primacy of entertainment and a vision of personal transformation based in commodities and fashionability, is present, especially in programmes linked to history and science. One looking back and the other often conceived as looking forward, they can escape the imperative to work on the self (though they certainly need not, as cosmetic surgery and house restoration segments in lifestyle programmes attest).

The sociability that is so dominant a mode in the interchanges of ordinary television is at odds with a growing presence of selfishness as a characteristic of the design of the newer game shows. Selfishness is always a potential quality when the focus is as much on the self as it is in contemporary television, but this is kept disguised in most of the programmes by the relentless promotion of the ways in which television helps its viewers. It is no coincidence that it is game shows that reveal the greater, but still equivocal, acceptability of selfishness. Competition is of the essence of game shows, and when the prizes are singular, rather than dispersed among contestants, and are also large enough to substantially change the life of the winner, then the disguise, if attempted, is inadequate. There may be a rhetoric of a 'team', as there is in *Survivor* or *The Weakest Link*, but it is rendered meaningless by a game that produces an individual winner. The equivocal nature of the endorsement of selfishness can be seen away from the rules of the games – when some players in *Big Brother*, for example, bond into co-operative groups that both convey conviction and invite viewers to assess the sincerity of participants.

Because ordinary television ties itself to the mundane and ordinary lives of its viewers to the extent of regularly incorporating them into the programmes themselves, it is less amenable than drama programmes to being imported and exported. Yet even though the programmes are cheaper to produce than drama, there is still an industrial imperative to maximize profit and minimize risk. The selling of formats of successful programmes (and also of ones less successful) is the solution, and all manner of shows are made in versions tailored to fit local situations with greater and lesser variations from the originals. *Who Wants to be a Millionaire?* comes in 40 or so versions individualized to take account of the particular country or area, but this individualization is done through the people appearing and some localized questions; the rest of the formula varies little. This is an example of a tightly followed format and many are a little looser, but even a minor variation of presenter can act to render a programme national through the resonances brought to the show by the televisual history of the people associated with it. This can act as a lateral harmonization of the schedule, inflecting programmes through distinct linkages with others, giving them 'back stories' even before contestants with local stories and accents, or locales with their own specifics, are involved. Some programmes, though, have a much greater tie to the national. As *Antiques Roadshow* and *Burke's Backyard* demonstrate, it is possible for television programmes to speak both of and to the national in a way that gives them a much more substantial and lasting place in the national imaginary.

Ordinary television comprises a substantial part of the schedule and it is not a part that is likely to diminish given the cheapness of its production and the ratings it has managed to sustain. I have examined it here almost entirely through the programmes broadcast on free-to-air networks, but the inclusion of pay services is unlikely to lead to a different situation given that Lifestyle Television is a standard name for at least one pay channel per provider. Many, if not most, of the programmes discussed here, although originating on free-to-air, have a second (and third) life on pay. The strictures on exported programmes not attracting a large enough audience to be worthwhile screening in unlocalized forms do not apply to the number of viewers attracted by individual pay programmes. Even so, ordinary television programmes are also among those most likely to be made solely for non-premium channel pay screening.

Ordinary television appeals to its audience not only by showing them themselves and their own mundane domestic activities, but also by asserting that there is a better, more exciting ordinary to be had by simple methods, and showing how this is to be achieved. As a matter of course, it overstates the ease, the accessibility and longevity of the transformations, healings and achievements it vaunts, but it does value change, it does show and often value difference and it is far more amenable to experimentation and to interventions by its viewing public than any amount of expensive scripted drama or even more expensive televised sport.

References

Allen, Robert C. (1992) 'Audience-oriented criticism and television', in Robert C. Allen (ed.) *Channels of Discourse, Reassembled: Television and contemporary criticism*. London: Routledge. pp. 101–37.

Allen, Robert C. (ed.) (1992) *Channels of Discourse, Reassembled: Television and contemporary criticism*. London: Routledge.

Anderson, Benedict (1991) *Imagined Communities: Reflections on the origin and spread of nationalism*. London: Verso.

Appadurai, Arjun (1986) 'Introduction: commodities and the politics of value', in Arjun Appadurai (ed.) *The Social Life of Things: Commodities in cultural perspective*. Cambridge: Cambridge University Press. pp. 3–63.

Appadurai, Arjun (ed.) (1986) *The Social Life of Things: Commodities in cultural perspective*. Cambridge: Cambridge University Press.

Appadurai, Arjun (1996) *Modernity at Large: Cultural dimensions of globalization*. Minneapolis and London: University of Minnesota Press.

Bazalgette, Cary (1986) 'All in fun: Su Pollard on *Disney Time*', in Len Masterman (ed.) *Television Mythologies: Stars, shows and signs*. London: Comedia/MK Media Press. pp. 29–33.

Bell, Philip and Theo van Leeuwen (1994) *The Media Interview: Confession, contest, conversation*. Sydney: University of NSW Press.

Bennett, Tony, Susan Boyd-Bowman, Colin Mercer and Janet Woollacott (eds) (1981) *Popular Television and Film*. London: BFI.

Bennett, Tony, Mike Emmison and John Frow (1999) *Accounting for Tastes: Australian everyday cultures*. Melbourne: Cambridge University Press.

Bethell, Andrew (1999) 'A job, some stars and a big row', *Sight and Sound*, Media Watch 99 Supplement, 9(3): 14–15.

Billig, Michael (1995) *Banal Nationalisms*. London, and Thousand Oaks, CA and New Delhi: Sage.

Boddy, William (2001) '*Who Wants to be a Millionaire?*', in G. Creeber (ed.) *The Television Genre Book*. London: BFI. p. 81.

Bonner, Frances (1992) 'Confession time: women and game shows', in Frances Bonner, Lizbeth Goodman, Richard Allen, Linda Janes and Catherine King (eds) *Imagining Women: Cultural representations and gender*. Cambridge: Polity. pp. 237–46.

Bonner, Frances, Lizbeth Goodman, Richard Allen, Linda James and Catherine King (eds) (1992) *Imagining Women: Cultural representations and gender*. Cambridge: Polity.

Bonner, Frances (1994) 'Representations of the female cook', in K. Ferres (ed.) *Coastscripts: Gender representations in the arts*. Nathan, Qld.: Griffith University. pp. 63–72.

Bonner, Frances (2000) 'No choice but to choose: lifestyle programmes on Australian television', in Graeme Turner and Stuart Cunningham (eds) *The Australian Television Book*. Sydney: Allen & Unwin. pp. 103–16.

Bonner, Frances and Paul du Gay (1992a) 'Representing the enterprising self: *thirtysomething* and contemporary consumer culture', *Theory, Culture and Society,* 9(2): 67–92.

Bonner, Frances and Paul du Gay (1992b) '*thirtysomething* and contemporary consumer culture: distinctiveness and distinction', in Roger Burrows and Catherine Marsh (eds) *Consumption and Class: Divisions and change.* London: Macmillan. pp. 166–83.

Boorstin, Daniel J. (1992) *The Image: A guide to pseudo-events in America* (25th anniversary edition). New York: Vintage Books.

Bourdieu, Pierre (1989) *Distinction: A social critique of the judgement of taste.* London: Routledge.

Brown, Mary Ellen (ed.) (1990) *Television and Women's Culture: The politics of the popular.* Sydney: Currency Press.

Brunsdon, Charlotte and David Morley (1978) *Everyday Television 'Nationwide'.* London: British Film Institute.

Brunt, Rosalind (1986) 'What's My Line? in Len Masterman (ed.) *Television Mythologies: Stars, shows and signs*: London: Comedia/MK Media Press. pp. 21–8.

Budd, Mike, Steve Craig and Clay Steinman (1999) *Consuming Environments: Television and commercial culture.* New Brunswick, NJ and London: Rutgers University Press.

Buscombe, Edward (ed.) (2000) *British Television: A reader.* Oxford: Clarendon Press.

Buxton, Rodney A. (1991) 'The late-night talk show: humour in fringe television', in Leah R. Vande Berg and Lawrence A. Wenner (eds) *Television Criticism: Approaches and applications.* New York and London: Longmans.

Cavell, Stanley (1996) 'The ordinary as the uneventful', in Stephen Mulhall (ed.) *The Cavell Reader.* Cambridge, MA. and Oxford: Blackwells. pp. 253–9.

Certeau, Michel de (1984) *The Practice of Everyday Life.* Berkeley and Los Angeles: University of California Press.

Chao, Phebe (1998) 'Gendered cooking: TV cook shows', *Jump Cut,* (42): 19–27.

Cohen, Stanley and Laurie Taylor (1978) *Escape Attempts: The theory and practice of resistance to everyday life.* Harmondsworth: Penguin.

Cooper-Chen, Anne (1994) *Games in the Global Village: A 50-nation study of entertainment television.* Bowling Green, OH: Bowling Green State University Popular Press.

Corner, John (1999) *Critical Ideas in Television Studies.* Oxford: Clarendon Press.

Corner, John (2000a) 'Documentary in a post-documentary culture? A note on forms and their function' Changing Media – Changing Europe, Programme Team One (Citizenship and Consumerism), Working Paper No. 1. European Science Foundation, http://www.lboro.ac.uk/research/changing.media/publications.htm.

Corner, John (2000b) 'What can we say about documentary?', *Media Culture & Society* 22(5): 681–8.

Coward, Rosalind (1989) *The Whole Truth.* London: Faber and Faber.

Creeber, Glen (ed.) (2001) *The Television Genres Book.* London: BFI.

Cunningham, Stuart and Elizabeth Jacka (1996) *Australian Television and International Mediascapes.* Cambridge: Cambridge University Press.

Cunningham, Stuart and Toby Miller (1994) *Contemporary Australian Television.* Sydney: University of NSW Press.

Dahlgren, Peter (1995) *Television and the Public Sphere: Citizenship, democracy and the media.* London: Sage.

Dale, David (2001) 'What did you finish watching last night?', *The Age,* Melbourne, 28 April, p. 32.

Danielsen, Shane (2000) 'Backyard blitzkrieg', *The Australian* Media Supplement, 27 April–3 May: 5.

Davison, Graeme (1982) 'Sydney and the Bush: an urban context for the Australian legend', in John Carroll (ed.) *Intruders in the Bush: The Australian quest for identity.* Oxford: Oxford University Press. pp. 109–30.

Dayan, Daniel and Elihu Katz (1992) *Media Events: The live broadcasting of history.* Cambridge, MA: Harvard University Press.

Dodd, Andrew (2001) 'Wounded by surprise sting', *The Australian* Media Supplement, 20 August–5 September: 8.

Dovey, John (2000) *Freakshow: First person media and factual television.* London: Pluto Press.

Drotner, Kristen (1994) 'Ethnographic enigmas: "the everyday" in recent media studies', *Cultural Studies*, 8(2): 341–57.

Dummett, Matt (1997/98) 'Coming up next … see if you can make a difference', *Arena Magazine*, 32: 39–40.

Dyer, Richard (1973) *Light Entertainment.* London: British Film Institute.

Ellicot, John (2001) 'Scratchie winners to go wild for bonanza', *The Australian*, 22 February: 4.

Ellis, John (1992) *Visible Fictions: Cinema, television, video.* London: Routledge.

Ellis, John (1999) 'Television as working-through', in Jostein Gripsrud (ed.) *Television and Common Knowledge.* London and New York: Routledge (Comedia). pp. 55–70.

Ellis, John (2000) *Seeing Things: Television in the age of uncertainty.* London and New York: I. B. Tauris.

Fairclough, Norman (1995) *Media Discourse.* London: Edward Arnold.

Featherstone, Mike (1991) *Consumer Culture and Postmodernism.* London: Sage.

Ferguson, Marjorie (1992) 'The mythology about globalization', *European Journal of Communication*, 7: 69–93.

Ferres, Kay (ed.) (1994) *Coastscripts: Gender representations in the arts.* Nathan, Qld: Griffith University.

Fiske, John (1987) *Television Culture.* London and New York: Methuen.

Fiske, John (1990) 'Women and quiz shows: consumerism, patriarchy and resisting pleasures', in Mary Ellen Brown (ed.) *Television and Women's Culture: The politics of the popular.* Sydney: Currency Press. pp. 134–43.

Fiske, John and John Hartley (1978) *Reading Television.* London: Methuen.

Fleming, Dan (ed.) (2000) *Formations: A 21st century media studies textbook.* Manchester: Manchester University Press.

Foucault, Michel (1980) *The History of Sexuality.* New York: Vintage Books.

Frow, John (1995) *Cultural Studies and Cultural Value.* Oxford: Clarendon Press.

Gardner, Carl and Robert Young (1981) 'Science on TV: a critique', in Susan Boyd-Bowman, Tony Bennett, Colin Mercer and Janet Woollacott (eds), *Popular Television and Film.* London: BFI. pp. 171–93.

Geraghty, Christine and David Lusted (eds) (1998) *The Television Studies Book.* London: Arnold.

Giddens, Anthony (1991) *Modernity and Self-Identity: Self and society in the late modern age.* Stanford, CA: Stanford University Press.

Goodwin, Andrew and Garry Whannel (eds) (1990). *Understanding Television.* London and New York: Routledge.

Graetz, Brian and I. McAllister (1994) *Dimensions of Australian Society.* Melbourne: Macmillan.

Grindstaff, Laura (1997) 'Producing trash, class, and the money shot: a behind-the-scenes account of daytime TV talk shows', in James Lull and Stephen Hinerman (eds) *Media*

Scandals: Morality and desire in the popular culture marketplace. Cambridge: Polity. pp. 164–202.

Gripsrud, Jostein (1998) 'Television, broadcasting, flow: key metaphors in TV theory', in Geraghty, Christine and David Lusted (eds), *The Television Studies Book.* London, Arnold. pp. 17–32.

Gripsrud, Jostein (ed.) (1999) *Television and Common Knowledge.* London and New York: Routledge (Comedia).

Grodin, Debra and Thomas R. Lindlof (1996) *Constructing the Self in a Mediated World.* Thousand Oaks, CA London and New Delhi: Sage.

Gutch, Robin (1986) 'That's life', in Len Masterman (ed.) *Television Mythologies: Stars, shows and signs.* London: Comedia/MK Media Press. pp. 10–15.

Hall, Stuart (1997a) 'The local and the global: globalization and ethnicity', in Anthony D. King (ed.) *Culture, Globalization and the World-system: Contemporary conditions for the representation of identity.* Minneapolis: University of Minnesota Press. pp. 19–39.

Hall, Stuart (1997b) 'Old and new identities, old and new ethnicities', in Anthony D. King (ed.) *Culture, Globalization and the World-system: Contemporary conditions for the representation of identity.* Minneapolis: University of Minnesota Press. pp. 41–68.

Hardey, Michael (1998) *The Social Context of Health.* Buckingham and Philadelphia: Open University Press.

Hartley, John (1991) 'Showpiece: the personalisation of television', in Denise Corrigan and David Watson (eds) *TV Times: 35 Years of Watching Television in Australia.* Sydney: Museum of Contemporary Art. pp. 28–34.

Hartley, John (1992) *Tele-ology: Studies in television.* London and New York: Routledge.

Hartley, John (1999) *Uses of Television.* London and New York: Routledge.

Hartley, John (2001) 'Daytime TV' in Glen Creeber (ed.) *The Television Genres Book.* London: BFI. pp. 92–3.

Haslam, Cheryl and Alan Bryman (eds) (1994) *Social Scientists Meet the Media.* London and New York: Routledge.

Hawes, William (1991) *Television Performing: News and information.* Boston and London: Focal Press.

Heath, Stephen (1990) 'Representing television', in Patricia Mellencamp (ed.) *Logics of Television: Essays in cultural criticism.* London: BFI Publishing. pp. 267–302.

Hill, Annette (2000) 'Crime and crisis: British reality TV in action', in Edward Buscombe (ed.) *British Television: A reader.* Oxford: Oxford University Press. pp. 218–34.

Hill, Annette (2001) 'Believe it or not: television audiences and factual entertainment', paper presented at the Consol(e)ing Passions Conference, Bristol 5–8 July.

Hoggart, Richard (1958) *The uses of Literacy: Aspects of working-class life with special reference to publications and entertainment.* Harmondsworth: Penguin.

Holland, Patricia (2000) *The Television Handbook.* London and New York: Routledge.

Idato, Michael (2000) 'Surviving down under', *Sydney Morning Herald* Guide, 9–15 October: 2.

Joyrich, Lynne (1993) 'Elvisophilia: knowledge, pleasure and the cult of Elvis', *Differences,* 5(1): 73–91.

Kaplan, Alice and Kristin Ross (1987) 'Introduction', *Yale French Studies,* 73: 1–4.

Kaplan, E. Ann (ed.) (1983) *Regarding Television: Critical approaches – an anthology.* Frederick, MD: University Publishers of America Inc.

Kingston, Peter (1999) 'Prime time for reading', *Guardian* Education Supplement, 16 March: 13.

Kopytoff, Igor (1986) 'The cultural biography of things: commoditization as process', in Arjun Appadurai (ed.) *The Social Life of Things: Commodities in cultural perspective.* Cambridge: Cambridge University Press. pp. 64–91.

Kozloff, Sarah (1992) 'Narrative theory and television', in Robert C. Allen (ed.) *Channels of Discourse, Reassembled: Television and contemporary criticism.* London: Routledge. pp. 67–101.

Langer, John (1981) 'Television's personality system', *Media, Culture & Society,* 4: 351–65.

Langer, John (1996) 'A calculus of celebrity: where would news fit into the equation?', *Metro Education,* 8: 3–9.

Langer, John (1998) *Tabloid Television: Popular journalism and the 'other news'.* London and New York: Routledge.

Lefebvre, Henri (1987) 'The everyday and everydayness', *Yale French Studies,* 73: 7–11.

Levitas, Ruth (1990) *The Concept of Utopia.* Syracuse, NY: Syracuse University Press.

Lewis, Bill (1986) 'TV games: people as performers', in Len Masterman (ed.) *Television Mythologies: Stars, shows and signs.* London: Comedia/MK Media Press. pp. 42–5.

Liebes, Tamar (1998) 'Television's disaster marathons: a danger for democratic processes?', in Tamar Liebes and James Curran (eds) *Media, Ritual and Identity.* London: Routledge. pp. 71–84.

Liebes, Tamar and James Curran (eds) (1998) *Media, Ritual and Identity.* London: Routledge.

Livingstone, Sonia and Peter Lunt (1994) *Talk on Television: Audience participation and public debate.* London and New York: Routledge.

Lull, James and Stephen Hinerman (eds) (1997) *Media Scandals: Morality and desire in the popular culture marketplace.* Cambridge: Polity.

Lury, Karen (1995/96) 'Television performance: being, acting and "corpsing"', *New Formations,* 27: 114–27.

Lusted, David (1986) 'The glut of the personality', in Len Masterman (ed.) *Television Mythologies: Stars, shows and signs.* London: Comedia/MK Media Press. pp. 73–81.

Lusted, David (1998) 'The popular culture debate and light entertainment on television', in Christine Geraghty and David Lusted (eds), *The Television Studies Book.* London: Arnold. pp. 175–90.

McKee, Alan (1997) ' "The Aboriginal version of Ken Done ...": Banal Aboriginal identities in Australia', *Cultural Studies,* 11(2): 191–206.

McKee, Alan (2001) *Australian Television: A genealogy of great moments.* Melbourne: Oxford University Press.

Malor, Deborah (1991) 'From the sublime to the ridiculous: Edmund Burke's bucolia – Don Burke's backyard', *Not My Department,* 1: 57–70.

Masciarotte, Gloria-Jean (1991) 'C'mon girl: Oprah Winfrey and the discourse of feminine talk', *Genders,* 11: 81–110.

Masterman, Len (ed.) (1986) *Television Mythologies: Stars, shows and signs.* London: Comedia/MK Media Press.

Meade, Amanda (1999) 'Funny business', *Weekend Australian,* 22–3 May: 19.

Medhurst, Andy (1999) 'Day for night', *Sight and Sound,* 9(6): 26–7.

Medhurst, Andy (2000) 'Every wart and pustule: Gilbert Harding and television stardom', in Edward Buscombe (ed.) *British Television: A reader.* Oxford: Clarendon Press. pp. 248–64.

Meinhof, Ulrike H. and Jonathan Smith (eds) (2000) *Intertextuality and the Media: From genre to everyday life.* Manchester and New York: Manchester University Press.

Mellencamp, Patricia (ed.) (1990) *Logics of Television: Essays in cultural criticism.* London: BFI.

Mellencamp, Patricia (1992) *High Anxiety: Catastrophe, scandal, age, and comedy.* Bloomington and Indianapolis: Indiana University Press.

Mikos, Lothar and Hans J. Wulff (2000) 'Intertextuality and situative contexts in game shows: the case of *Wheel of Fortune*', in Ulrike H. Meinhof, and Jonathan Smith (eds), *Intertextuality and the Media: From genre to everyday life.* Manchester and New York: Manchester University Press. pp. 98–114.

Miller, Toby (2001) 'The populist debate', in Glen Creeber (ed.) *The Television Genres Book.* London: BFI. pp. 76–9.

Moncrieff, Sean (1988) 'That's infotainment', *Broadcast*, 21 December: 18–19.

Moran, Albert (1998) *Copycat TV: Globalisation, program formats and cultural identity.* Luton: University of Luton Press.

Morley, David and Kevin Robins (1995) *Spaces of Identity: Global media, electronic landscapes and cultural boundaries.* London and New York: Routledge.

Moseley, Rachel (2000) 'Makeover takeover on British television', *Screen*, 41(3): 299–314.

Mulhall, Stephen (ed.) (1996) *The Cavell Reader.* Cambridge, MA and Oxford: Blackwells.

Murdock, Graham (1994) 'Tales of expertise and experience: sociological reasoning and popular representation', in Cheryl Haslam and Alan Bryman (eds), *Social Scientists Meet the Media.* London and New York: Routledge. pp. 108–22.

Murrell, Rachel Kerys (1987) 'Telling it like it isn't: representations of science in tomorrow's world', *Theory, Culture and Society*, 4(1): 89–106.

Neale, Steve (1990) 'Questions of genre', *Screen*, 31(1): 45–66.

Neale, Steve (2001) 'Genre and television', in Glen Creeber (ed.) *The Television Genres Book.* London: BFI, pp. 3–4.

Nichols, Bill (1991) *Representing Reality: Issues and concepts in documentary.* Bloomington and Indianapolis: Indiana University Press.

Nicholson, Catherine (1991) 'Good evening and welcome to *Graham Kennedy's Funniest Home Video Show* where you might see your next door neighbour, you might see a workmate, you might even see yourself …', *Continuum*, 4(2): 36–41.

Nixon, Sherrill (2001) 'TV's helping hand in do-it-yourself accidents', *Sydney Morning Herald*, 9 January: 1.

Priest, Patrica J. (1996) '"Gilt by association": talk show participants' televisually enhanced status and self-esteem', in Debra Grodin and Thomas R. Lindhof (eds) *Constructing the Self in a Mediated World.* Thousand Oaks, CA, London and New Delhi: Sage. pp. 68–83.

Riley, Chris (1992) 'Facts of life', *Broadcast*, 31 January: 18.

Robertson, Roland (1995) 'Glocalization: time-space and homogeneity-heterogeneity', in Mike Featherstone, Scott Lash and Roland Robertson (eds) *Global Modernities.* London: Sage.

Rose, Brian G. (ed.) (1985) *TV Genres: A handbook and reference guide.* Westport, CT and London: Greenwood Press.

Rose, Nikolas (1999) *Powers of Freedom: Reframing political thought.* Cambridge: Cambridge University Press.

Safire, William (1981) 'On language: see you later allegator', *New York Times*, section 6, 13 September: 16.

Scannell, Paddy (ed.) (1991) *Broadcast Talk.* London: Sage.

Scannell, Paddy (1996) *Radio, Television and Modern Life*. Oxford: Blackwell.

Shattuc, Jane M. (1997) *The Talking Cure: TV talk shows and women*. New York and London: Routledge.

Silverstone, Roger (1985) *Framing Science: The making of a television documentary*. London: BFI.

Silverstone, Roger (1994) *Television and Everyday Life*. London and New York: Routledge.

Simpson, Philip (1986) 'One man and his dog show', in Len Masterman (ed.) *Television Mythologies: Stars, shows and signs*. London: Comedia/MK Media Press. pp. 16–20.

Stam, Robert (1983) 'Television news and its spectators', in E. Ann Kaplan (ed.) *Regarding Television: Critical approaches – an anthology*. Frederick, MD: University Publishers of America Inc. pp. 23–43.

Stapledon, Ross (1993) 'The mouth from the south'. *The Australian Magazine* July 24–25 pp. 28–34.

Strange, Niki (1998) 'Perform, educate, entertain: ingredients of the cooking programme genre', in Christine Geraghty and David Lusted (eds) *The Television Studies Book*. London: Arnold. pp. 301–12.

Strinati, Dominic and Stephen Wagg (eds) (1992) *Come on Down?: Popular media culture in post-war Britain*. London and New York: Routledge.

Tolson, Andrew (1985) 'Anecdotal television', *Screen*, 26(2): 18–27.

Tolson, Andrew (1991) 'Televised chat and the synthetic personality', in Paddy Scannell (ed.) *Broadcast Talk*. London: Sage. pp. 178–200.

Tulloch, John (1976) 'Gradgrind's heirs: the quiz and the presentation of knowledge by British television', *Screen Education*, 19: 3–12.

Tulloch, John and Graeme Turner (eds) (1989) *Australian Television: Programs, pleasures and politics*. Sydney: Allen & Unwin.

Tunstall, Jeremy (1993) *Television Producers*. London and New York: Routledge.

Turnbull, Sue (1993) 'The great Australian theme park', *Melbourne Report*, 8(6): 17–19.

Turner, Graeme (1989) 'Transgressive TV: from *In Melbourne Tonight* to *Perfect Match*', in Tulloch, John and Graeme Turner (eds) *Australian Television: Programs, pleasures and politics*. Sydney: Allen & Unwin. pp. 25–38.

Turner, Graeme (1993) *National Fictions*. St Leonards, NSW: Allen and Unwin.

Turner, Graeme (1994) *Making It National: Nationalism and Australian popular culture*. Sydney: Allen & Unwin.

Turner, Graeme (1999) 'Tabloidization, journalism and the possibility of critique', *International Journal of Cultural Studies*, 2(1): 59–76.

Turner, Graeme (2001a) 'The uses and limitations of genre', in Glen Creeber (ed.) *The Television Genres Book*. London: BFI. pp. 4–5.

Turner, Graeme (2001b) 'Genres, format and "live" television', in Glen Creeber (ed.) *The Television Genres Book*. London: BFI. pp. 6–7.

Turner, Graeme, Frances Bonner and P. David Marshall (2000) *Fame Games: The production of celebrity in Australia*. Cambridge: Cambridge University Press.

Turner, Graeme and Stuart Cunningham (eds) (2000) *The Australian Television Book*. Sydney: Allen & Unwin.

Vande Berg, Leah R. and Lawrence A. Wenner (eds) (1991) *Television Criticism: Approaches and applications*. New York and London: Longmans.

Wagg, Stephen (1992) '"One I made earlier": media, popular culture and the politics of childhood', in Dominic Strinati and Stephen Wagg (eds) *Come on Down? Popular media culture in post-war Britain*. London and New York: Routledge. pp. 150–78.

Wark, Mckenzie (1999) *Celebrities, Culture and Cyberspace: The light on the hill in a postmodern world.* Annandale, NSW: Pluto Press.

Wayne, Mike (2000) 'Who wants to be a millionaire? Contextual analysis and the endgame of public service television', in Dan Fleming (ed.) *Formations: A 21st century media studies textbook.* Manchester: Manchester University Press. pp. 196–216.

Weaver, Amanda (1990) 'Fearless frontman in the backyard', *The Bulletin*, 18 December, 112: 90–3.

Wernick, Andrew (1991) *Promotional Culture: Advertising, ideology and symbolic expressions.* London: Sage.

Whannel, Garry (1990) 'Winner takes all: competition', in Andrew Goodwin and Garry Whannel, *Understanding Television*. London and New York: Routledge. pp. 103–14.

Williams, Anna (1993) 'Domesticity and the aetiology of crime in *America's Most Wanted*', *Camera Obscura*, 31: 97–120.

Williams, Raymond (1974) *Television: Technology and cultural form.* London: Fontana/Collins.

Williams, Raymond (1989) *Raymond Williams on Television: Selected writings* (ed. Alan O'Connor). London: Routledge.

Wilson, Elizabeth (1986) 'All in the family: Russell Grant on breakfast television', in Len Masterman (ed.) *Television Mythologies: Stars, shows and signs.* London: Comedia/ MK Media Press. pp. 7–9.

Woolf, Marie (1999) 'Blair picks Vorderman to head maths campaign', *The Independent on Sunday*, 14 March: 5.

Index

Printed in the United Kingdom
by Lightning Source UK Ltd.
112150UKS00001B/171